From Lindos With Love

Josephine Kelly

"From Lindos With Love"
Copyright © 2012 by Josephine Kelly

First published 2012 by Lulu.com

All rights reserved. No part of this publication may be reproduced, stored in a retrieval system or transmitted in any form or by any means without the prior written permission of the author, nor be otherwise circulated in any form of binding or cover other than that in which it is published and without a similar condition being imposed on the subsequent purchaser.

Body copy typeset in Palatino 9pt

Further copies of this book may be purchased from:
www.lulu.com
& Amazon (both in book form and Kindle format)

1st edition • June 2012

Front & back cover photography & design
© John Manuel:
http://ramblingsfromrhodes.blogspot.com

ISBN: 978-1-4716-1692-1

Lyrics from "Oh What a Beautiful Mornin'" from the musical Oklahoma! written by Richard Rodgers and Oscar Hammerstein II

"Shrimp Boats Song"
written by Paul Mason Howard and Paul Weston

"Star Trekkin'" lyrics written by Lister/John O'Connor,
recorded by The Firm

"Stranger in Paradise" sung by Tony Bennett.
Taken from the musical Kismet by Robert Wright
and George Forrest

Josephine Kelly was born in London in 1938. She attended Dalston County Grammar, but left school at fifteen to follow her dream of working on a farm. In Bedford she met her first husband Patrick O'Leary and married before her eighteenth birthday. They moved to Northampton and, when the youngest of her four children started school, she gained a Certificate in Education as a mature student with Leicester University and subsequently taught at St. Pauls V.C. school in Semilong. She has also taught floristry, chinese painting and was a tutor and walking leader for H.F. Holidays. Before retirement she spent several years in Wiltshire and Berkshire, pursuing a new career as a housing officer for the elderly.

Josephine's primary interest now is travel, particularly when it involves visiting her family, and spends much of the year in Greece, with her daughter on the Greek island of Rhodes.

This is her first full length novel.

Yesterday is history.
Tomorrow is a mystery.
Today is a gift, called the present.

From Lindos With Love

PROLOGUE

They will steal almost anything in Lindos. Your heart many times over, and your mind may never be entirely your own again. Even a few years of your life can get taken, and you will look back and wonder where they went. But never, ever, will anyone steal your material possessions. So Tanya closed her laptop, satisfied with her layout for the new leaflets, and placed it at the end of Giorgos bar. She knew it would be there later when she returned from her walk, no problem.

For Tanya this time of early spring was the best part of living on Rhodes. Quiet empty streets, the hillsides full of flowers and even the donkeys were relaxing in the fields. And now there was the frantic white washing of the village ready for the glorious celebrations at Easter and a new tourist season will begin.

'*Kalimera*, Tanya, *ti kaneis*, good morning, how are you?'

'*Kala, poli kala,*' she replied.

Certainly it had been a wet, chilly winter. After three

years in Lindos she was accustomed to frequent power cuts, phone lines going down when lightning strikes and the narrow streets becoming torrents of rushing water in a storm. But with barbeques in the streets at weekends, 'name day' celebrations, and a Bethlehem stable built in the donkey station at Christmas, the colder days had soon passed.

Tanya walked up from Giorgos Bar to the main street and turned right past the empty, shuttered shops. Kostas, the corner shop by the church was open and she went in to get a couple of bars of Kit Kat, her favourite munch.

'Hi Sandra, are you counting the days?' she asked her, knowing Sandra was expecting her daughter back from Oxford University for the Easter break.

'I am but I know I will not see much of her when she is here. I expect she will be off out and about with her friends, or visiting her grandparents,' was the reply.

But nothing hid the shine in her eyes whenever asked about her daughter who was studying in England.

Past the church and into the square, Tanya glanced up to the balcony of Steps Bar. No sign of life there yet, but Steve had only just returned from England and would need a day or so to get sorted before he opened up. Tanya turned right and started on the long walk down to the beach. The road she had chosen led to the far end of the big beach. She waved to her friends, Rosanna and Nikos, at Palestra.

'Why are you not having coffee today? Come and sit for a while?' Rosanna called to her.

'*Signomi*, sorry, thanks, but not today. Another day would be good,' Tanya replied, and headed off along the big beach and across the path in the rocks. She did not stop there but went past Giorgos Two and took the little alley behind Jack's Supermarket and Skala Restaurant and away out onto the rocky field above. She found her favourite flat-topped stone to perch on and sat looking out to sea. Tanya considered this to be one of the best sites in the village for just sitting and thinking. She had tried bringing a book with her but it never got opened. The beauty of the expansive view was always so compelling, she just had to sit and take it all in.

Tanya first came to Rhodes, to Lindos, three years ago when, Ed, her partner, was ill. It had been wonderful that winter, deserted beaches to walk along, people in the village to stop and chat to, with the warm winter sun on their faces whilst wrapped up against the sharp wind in colourful fleeces. It was a wonderful time, where they hid from the reality of his illness and talked of other things. Then they had returned to England to be near his family and when it was over, and still in a daze at the finality of it all, she came back to stay with her aunt.

Her mind drifted onto practical matters and she wondered how she would manage this season.

The first thing was the May "card and craft" week. June, her aunt, had taken on the lease for a Captain's

House in Lindos some years ago and had run craft holidays. Only one week in May and September, enough to give her an interesting hobby. Now June had met up with an old friend in England and had decided not to come back to Greece this summer. Tanya had been asked to pick up the reins. Thankfully there would be no craft weeks to plan and think about in the middle of the summer when the bar she worked in was very busy - she would not want to let Steve down.

Tanya enjoyed the bar work. She also enjoyed helping with weddings at St. Paul's Bay, but she could not say she felt the same about the craft holidays. The people were always lovely but teaching craft was not really her thing. But despite this she had agreed to keep the ship afloat, little enough to do for her aunt when she thought about the kindness June had shown to her and Ed. The response to the May craft week had been better than ever and she had closed the bookings. As she was going to be the main demonstrator, Tanya had decided a group of ten was enough. She thought that adding the bit of blurb about Lindos to the website had worked well, although she had gone over the wording so many times she could almost say it in her sleep.

A card and craft holiday in beautiful Lindos, Rhodes Island, Greece. The ancient Acropolis rises above a whitewashed village. The fortress, built in medieval times on an ancient fortified site by the Knights of St. John, gives Lindos its unique fairytale landscape, the perfect venue for a relaxing but creative break.

Now she had added it to the new leaflets and would post them out to craft groups and libraries for the September bookings. Tanya had helped her aunt often during the past three years and although out of her comfort zone, she knew that she could cope. And cope well.

But once more she found herself going over her mental checklist. Card making she could handle. She had lots of samples made up and printouts of instructions for people to refer to once they had seen a demonstration. Few people asked about the glass painting, but that did not take long to explain, adding it in with a card demo. Introducing the Chinese was more difficult, but again, there were lots of samples on file. And with the encaustic art, which she loved, you just experimented once you had been shown the basics. The only wedding she had that week was on the Saturday afternoon so everything would tie in well. And except for those two craft weeks she would have plenty of time to herself this summer. All things considered she was managing very well. Quite strange really that here on a cliff top on a Greek island she felt Ed with her. Yet all their old London haunts meant nothing. At the moment she did not want to move on or get over it for fear that she would lose something she could never replace. So this was her new life, without Ed. She was not sure how to make the break with the past, and in her heart she thought, no not yet.

'I expect it will just come to me,' she had told Steve. 'One day I will know that what Ed and I had is over.' She recalled the poem her grandfather had written in her autograph book when she was ten years old.

Yesterday is History, Tomorrow a Mystery, Today is a Gift. That is why we call it the Present.

Yes, thankyou for the present, she thought.

TANYA, STEVE AND MILES

'If things carry on as well as they are now, I will get through the early part of the year without any problems,' Tanya told Steve a few days later.

Steve had Steps Bar and that is where the craft group would be meeting every evening for the pre-dinner drink. It was easy to find, being on the main square, and the atmosphere was just what was needed in the early evening. Happy, comfortable, good music, relaxed. Steps Bar was open at this time of the year simply because Steve preferred to be working. He had recently returned from spending Christmas with his daughter and grandchildren in England and he was at a loose end until the season began.

'If I don't come to the bar I just sit in the house getting on my own nerves,' he told Tanya. 'It makes far more sense to open up and chat to friends as they drop by. Mind you, this time of the year is hardly a commercial proposition as no one has any money, least ways certainly not you lot.' He had raised his voice to include a group of young expats that gathered there, marking time 'til their own bar jobs started after Easter. They knew that, despite his protests, Steve had no objection to his bar being used as a substitute for a Y.M.C.A. lounge.

The love affair Steve had with Greece had begun many years before. He had visited many of the Greek Islands, first as a seventies hippy with a few friends, then later with his young family. But all things change and when he eventually moved to Lindos to open his bar it was as a single man.

The buzzword in any business is location, but Steps' location on the square was not the best despite its prime site. The entrance was often blocked by delivery vans. Locals always thought they could just squeeze into the spot directly in front of the steps that provided his customer access, and certainly the exhortations of the tourist police did not apply to them! After all, they were not tourists! Rather frustrating at times but Steve, always philosophical, shrugged his shoulders and said,

'This is Greece.'

Steve and Tanya had been friends since she had come to Lindos. He had fulfilled his ambition to run a bar on a Greek Island and she had no ambition at all except to rebuild her shattered life. The main thing Steve and Tanya shared, which made their friendship special, was an understanding of pain. The sort of emotional pain they did not need to talk about, pain that only time would release them from. If you were in it you recognized it in another. And being silent in the other's company said it all. Not that it was ever silent in the bar. Steve was a product of the seventies music scene and held a CD collection second to none; his original records still back in England. But even with Tanya he never discussed what had happened in his marriage, always talking with pride about his daughters, but never disclosing anything more personal.

His phone bleeped, Miles, of course.

'*Ella*, here, where else would I be? Yes, Tanya is here with me. I will throw out my clientele and we will meet you at Palestra. See you soon.'

Ten minutes later saw Tanya and Steve striding out down the steep road on their way to meet their friend Miles. There they would sit and enjoy the warm winter sunshine, a cold beer, the empty beach and the magnificent view. At this corner of the big beach the sea lapped against the rocky outcrop that formed one arm of Lindos Bay. The water was calm and as clear as any in the world. At the mouth of the bay were two large rocks, like sentinels, to break the force of the sea on stormy nights, and in the distance, to their right, was the fairytale silhouette of the Acropolis, the white washed village strung out beneath in haphazard fashion. They waved to Stefanos, who had a kiosk by the beach and kept his small boat tied up to the old pier. Stefanos went fishing most days, just as he had done for more than seventy years. He returned their greeting, then turned his attention to unloading his morning catch. A few steps further to Palestra, their favourite winter bar.

'Yia sou. Ti kaneis? How are you?' Greetings exchanged and beers ordered, they sat on blue, rush-seated chairs at a table with a snow white cloth. This was perfection. This was Lindos.

'Now tell me,' Miles paused as he always did mid-sentence, making sure he had the listener's full attention before continuing. 'All ready for the season, Tanya?'

'Ready, yes. Are we going to make any money, who knows? Would you believe we now have a non-paying guest? Tanya replied, mock indignation in her voice.

'Only two weeks a year and we are offering free places. I wonder what we will be offering next?'

Steve took another draught from his glass before replying.

'I know June is a kind lady, but this is a bit on the generous side. There must be more to the story than that?'

'Well, it's a bit of a long story, but there is this elderly lady, a regular in Lindos, who is coming over for her granddaughter's wedding. June met her at a craft show and no way could she take money from her. Maybe she will not turn up for the classes once her relations begin to arrive. Anyway, we have a full quota, so, give a bit back to the gods and all that,' Tanya shrugged her shoulders and smiled at her friends by way of apologising for being a soft touch.

'What fascinates me is the range of backgrounds our group comes from, but I must admit I am looking forward to meeting Margaret as much as meeting any of the others.'

'Yia mas,' said Steve as they raised their second beer.

'And,' Miles paused until he had her full attention, 'are you going to tell us more?'

'Well there is a retired teacher. Teachers are always a problem. They are so used to giving out the information but do not listen when you tell them anything and are then too embarrassed to ask.'

'Ouch!' another pause, 'Rather a generalisation, I think, but no doubt drawn from experience.' His enquiring brown eyes met Tanya's. 'Anyone I might be interested in?'

'I will totally ignore that remark, which I presume was sexist,' Tanya chided her friend. 'There is a St. John's Ambulance man who is not interested in the craft content, but wants to join a group holiday for company in the evenings. He wants to research the history of the Knights of St. John on Rhodes.'

'Wait a moment, if you have one free place and one paying but not joining in, I think that makes it quits,' Steve interjected.

Tanya shrugged, 'In theory yes, but I bet he will need as much input as the rest put together. However, we have a full complement of single young women and a retired wing commander. And that is all the information I intend to divulge.'

'You said the last two bookings, so the other was?' Miles smiled as he asked, expecting yet another verbal slap from Tanya.

'There is an eighteen-year-old girl on her first summer holiday abroad on her own. Would you believe her grandmother rang me to ask for references? Then she rang again to ask if we would keep an eye on her. Unbelievable.'

'But you will,' Steve added as he drained his Amstel and indicated to Nikos that they would like to have another beer.

'Within limits yes, she may need an escort,' Tanya replied. 'Someone I can rely on to keep a look out for her in the bars. I doubt if she will be clubbing, but you never know. It very much depends on the rest of the group. Not that she is in any danger but she may get lost going back to the digs. You know what it is like for people not used to drinking the sort of measures they pour here in Greece.'

'Now that I can manage, escorting an eighteen-year-old back to her apartment, just my sort of assignment,' Miles added with raised eyebrows and the usual smile.

This time he did get a very sharp slap on the wrist. She knew it was too early to talk about Miles contributing his artistic skills to the programme but his session on caricatures always went down well. He was light hearted and very talented, just what was needed as a diversion towards the end of the week when even the most enthusiastic guests were getting tired.

The conversation turned to more pressing matters, the latest ruling about music licenses and the failure of the ice machine in Steps.

'The problem with the ice machine is that it is still under guarantee,' Steve explained. 'So they keep sending someone to fix it, without any lasting success. I relied quite a lot on Peggy and Mike at Sinatra's last year, but now they have moved to Lardos.'

'Bojangles, that is the name of the new place. In keeping with the 'rat pack' theme,' Miles told them. 'I took Mum and Dad there last weekend for Sunday lunch, quite a jolly crowd.'

Which prompted Steve to ask about the wellbeing of Miles' parents.

Their news now brought up to date, they just sat and looked at the sea, the rocks guarding this natural harbour and the small fishing boat bobbing up and down in the light spring breeze. They stayed there until the sun had moved low enough in the sky to turn the white walls of Saint Dimitrios Chapel to slate blue. It was time to go.

At this time of year it turned quite chilly in the early evening. Steps Bar was supposed to be open by five o'clock and 'mine host' was still relaxing at the beach. This would never do.

They settled their account with Nikos and started the steep walk up from the beach, each trying to prove they could walk briskly up the road without stopping for breath, but the lack of conversation in the steepest part told its own story. They took their leave with a kiss on both cheeks and as Tanya strolled back to the house, her thoughts returned to the craft bookings.

Amazing how the small groups of strangers always became so close after only a few days in each other's company. She could not imagine going on a craft holiday herself. Not her thing. But she felt a great responsibility for this group of people who would trust her with their precious holiday week. Yes, quite a responsibility.

MARGARET

'Peg o' my heart, I love you,
Don't let us part I love you,
Dah didi dah dah didi dah,
Dom di dom di dom di dom di.'

One day I will learn the words to that song, Margaret thought as she gave the Hoover a final push around the living room. So she had been promising herself for more than fifty years and where was she going to find the words now? Would anyone remember them after all this time? Margaret had a great repertoire of these old songs and would pull them out of her memory box whenever she was happy and, as that was most of the time, her selection got a regular airing.

'Dum di dum di dum di didi dum.'

Well, *that* presented no problem, she mused to herself, as she hummed the signature tune to a radio detective story. There were no words. The lady in the series was called Steve, but little else had made a lasting impression, apart from the tune that sounded like a train getting faster and speeding through the countryside. Was it 'Royal Scot' or something?

Margaret had less than an hour to catch the train to one of her favourite destinations, the National Exhibition Centre in Birmingham. She liked to leave her small flat neat and tidy, so, with one eye on the clock, she made her bed. Then she dressed in a corduroy skirt and a lightweight jumper, added a hand-painted silk scarf and was almost ready. Her mac was hanging in the hallway. She wore a rain hat but did not take an umbrella and was at the bus stop in good time. With her senior bus pass she could catch a free bus to and from the train station and even use a bus pass on the local trains in the north. She could go nearly into Liverpool, where she got all the material for Tracy's wedding dress, and out to Southport in the summer. Margaret loved Southport. They had the most interesting craft shops and lots of arcades and back turnings to potter about in, and the occasional craft show.

But today Margaret was using her senior rail card to travel to the N.E.C. Knitting and Stitching Craft Show. She had a passion for such shows. She was interested in anything to do with handiwork; embroidery, tapestry, stump work and quilt making, though dressmaking was her main skill. She could shorten or lengthen anything, trousers, a skirt or a pair of curtains. But if you were to ask her why, with all her experience, she still went to shows, she would tell you that there is always something to learn. She didn't retain things like she used to so it didn't matter if she saw a demonstration twice, or even three times over. Margaret bought very little for herself at the shows, just an occasional treat of something she hadn't noticed in the local shops in Wigan or Southport.

She always travelled alone as most of her friends had other priorities for their spare cash. But as Margaret only enjoyed the occasional sherry, or port and lemon and she didn't like bingo. All her pennies left over from the pension when the bills were paid, were enough to pay for her hobby. Well, not quite, if the truth were known. She also had a little side-line. She gave craft demonstrations on some Saturday mornings and talks and slide shows to the W.I. Sometimes she wondered if she should declare it on a tax form, but her daughter had said not to.

'Mother, you forget that although you take sandwiches and a flask with you for the journey, you are entitled to claim for lunch and coffee on the day, so there wouldn't be enough left over for the tax man to worry about.'

So Margaret had given up worrying about it. The W.I. now paid quite a reasonable amount, plus petrol or train fare. If the talk was going to be in the afternoon she spent the morning looking around the nearby shops before going to the venue. Charity shops were best. Invariably she would discover some cotton garment that had a nice small print on it, providing another patch or two for her quilts. Margaret was quite famous for her patchwork quilts. She only made the cot-sized ones now, which made very good gifts for the elderly as well.

Not that she sewed them by hand. She had a sewing machine, quite a good one, and it had paid for itself by the time she had altered a few pairs of curtains.

She preferred to travel alone as many of her dearest friends had gone, either to that big craft fair in the sky, or off to a sheltered housing place near where their family lived. Anyway, there were very few people you could take to a place like the N.E.C. without losing them or wishing to murder them by the end of the day. They would be so nervous that they actually saw nothing, only clung to your sleeve, making you feel like a torturer for bringing them to such a dreadful place. The bonus of travelling alone was that so many people stopped to talk to you. This morning the train journey flew by as the elderly man opposite explained that he was going to Coventry Cathedral for his grandson's ordination. He was changing trains at Birmingham New Street.

The distance between the train and the exhibition centre seemed to get further each year. She'd sang *la la* to the tune of 'Marie's Wedding', but once inside she forgot about her knee and set a plan for going around the stands. Unless you had a plan you would miss something of interest. The demonstrations were a handy place to take a rest and, if you arrived early enough, you could probably find one that you fancied and book in.

On this particular day it was hat making. She did not intend to make hats, but was interested in how you did it and the demonstrator was very good.

Well-rested and educated in the intricacies of blocking, Margaret moved on.

'Where did you get that hat, where did you get that tile?
Isn't it a lovely one and quite the proper style,
I should like to have one, just the same as that,
Where e're I go they shout hello,
where did you get that hat?'

She knew that one; they had sung that at a community hall concert last year. She bought an unusual six-sided picture frame, to hold an embroidered picture which she had just finished, and some more silk paints for the classes she held on Saturday mornings. Margaret knew where she needed to go to get glass buttons for Tracy's dress. She had put pearl buttons on, but decided glass ones would be better. The dress had been finished ages ago, but since then her granddaughter had slimmed down for the wedding. Margaret had nevertheless refused to alter the dress yet, quite firmly saying it would only take a day to do if it needed taking in. The dress, in the style and material that Tracy had chosen, was

Margaret's wedding present to her granddaughter. They had had a lovely day out in Liverpool, John Lewis' had had everything they needed and that was where Margaret had bought her own suit for the occasion.

'I'm not a tailor, I know my limitations. I have a hat that will pick up the lilac in the flowers and beige bag and shoes,' she had assured Tracy.

'Nan, you know it might be very hot on the day, and quite a walk down to the church,' her granddaughter had reminded her.

'That's why I need a summer weight suit, much cooler than polyester. A cotton dress would crease, and I know I can walk anywhere in those beige shoes.'

Tracy might have guessed that her Nan had it all worked out.

Glass buttons safely in her bag, and having bought a last minute cream flower spray that she might add to her own hat, Margaret was ready to call it a day. Then a small stand near an emergency exit, caught her eye:

'A CARD AND CRAFT HOLIDAY IN GREECE,'

it said on the sign above the stand. Margaret checked her watch. She had at least half an hour to get the train so she decided that she could spend ten more minutes having a quick look at the stall.

'I know Lindos very well,' she told June, the lady running the stand, who had been very interested when Margaret had explained how she had been a frequent visitor to Rhodes over many years and would be there for

Tracy's wedding.

'Don't bother to book,' June had insisted, 'just come along and join in. You may find you won't have much time to spare with the wedding and all the relatives there. My niece Tanya will be running the course. I will tell her that you will drop in when you can. You will be most welcome. Even weddings in Lindos can eat up the pennies and I hope we're never in a position where we have to charge Lindos lovers like yourself. I am sure Tanya will be only too pleased to have someone on hand who knows their way around the village and would not mind giving a hand with the coffee cups.'

Margaret made her way to the station platform in good time. Once seated she delved into her bag for her mobile phone to text her daughter, just to say she was on the train and would be grateful for a lift from the station at that time of night. She could not wait to tell her about the craft lessons in Lindos. What an unexpected end to the day, she thought. Imagine meeting someone in Birmingham who knew Tsampikos and Eleni from Giorgos Bar in Lindos. Margaret had been assured of her welcome and more importantly, of being able to repay this kindness by giving a helping hand. How kind of that lady (was her name June?), for saying she would be a great asset, being an experienced crafter and knowing her way around Lindos. She would not tell Judith all that, just say she was going to Greece on the Saturday instead of the Wednesday, to join a craft group. Best not to text about that. The predictive sort was quick to use but sometimes if she was not careful, it did not always say what she intended to say. She decided to wait 'til Judith picked her up in the car. She sent '7:45' to her daughter, and then set the alarm on the mobile in case she dozed off before the train got to Wigan.

> *'The day Thou gavest Lord is ending.*
> *The darkness falls at Thy behest*
> *To Thee our morning prayers ascended*
> *Thy praise shall sanctify our rest.*
> *La de de la de de la de la di de dee la*
> *dee la di dee la dom di dom.'*

Yes, there were some words you never forget.

RUTH

Retirement. Ruth tried to hide her bubbling jubilation. It was not her last day exactly, that would be tomorrow. But it was so near now, so close she felt as though it was a physical thing that she could touch. Something that she could pick up and hold close to her heart, retirement.

The headmaster drew his end of term speech to a close.

'Now it only leaves one more important thing to say. As you all know, Miss Wallis is retiring tomorrow, so today is both a happy and a sad occasion for us. Sad to lose such a valuable and long-serving member of staff but pleased for Miss Wallis as she looks forward to a well-earned rest.' He waited whilst a resounding round of applause rippled through the school hall, then thanked her for her contribution to both the school and the community, as a colleague and a friend.

'Now it is our pleasure to send Miss Wallis off with mementoes of her time at St. John of God.'

On this cue Ruth arose from her chair on the platform and the applause rose with her. How children love to clap their hands, she thought. Mr. Costello asked Mrs. Ryan to step up and present a gift from the parents. It was a lovely tall glass flower vase. The wrapping had been left unsealed so that the children could see the gift. Two children from the top class came forward with a scrapbook the class had put together, using their grasp of technology to copy photos and press cuttings from the school diary.

Her long-time friend and colleague, Lynne presented her with a small package. It contained a Moleskine notebook, a matching passport holder and a cheque. They were her gifts from the staff. Applause came again as she walked to the front of the small platform. Showing appreciation was not difficult, as she did appreciate the kind words and tributes for her thirty years as a teacher. She thanked them, with a slight catch in her voice, clearing her throat, hesitating as she looked around the school hall. She thanked them for their kindness over the years, for the joy of seeing each new group of shiny faces each autumn.

'To you, the parents, without you there would be no school.' Laughter now came from the back of the hall. 'Without you we would not have costumes each year for the town festival pageant, or a lorry to stage it on.' Whistles rang out from a couple of the men to acknowledge the local building firm who supported the school in this annual event.

'But for me it has been the music that has held such a special place in my life at St. John's.' Ruth paused, spreading out her hands to acknowledge the children on the hall floor in front of her. 'What a joy it has been to be their teacher,' she told the adults, 'when they have given such glory to God with their voices. Did not the Pope say, "To sing is to pray twice?"'

Being able to play the piano had given Ruth a unique status in the school from the start. There were many members of staff who could play in those days but most had been rather hesitant to put themselves forward as assembly pianist, they saw it as a chore best avoided. No such hesitation for Ruth. She played as best she could, and if she lost the place, well, she stopped, smiled encouragingly at the children and they kept singing. It was as simple as that. In fact, it became such a feature that all considered it her style of training the children to carry the tune. There were times in the first year or two when she said 'thanks be to God' at the final blessing with more understanding of the phrase than most of her colleagues. Staff members had come and gone over the years. There were the occasional times when a new head teacher would try to introduce some modern fad, the "new broom" and all that but after a year everything reverted to where it had been. New ideas came and went. Ladybird did the job. No child left her class unable to read and no one at any time interfered with her music. In that way the whole school was a sounding board. Ruth had expanded the repertoire with more modern tunes. From Andrew Lloyd Webber's 'Joseph' to the joyful hymns of Graham Kendrick, back to the traditional, like 'All Things Bright and Beautiful' and 'I Love to Hear the Story', so that the past was not lost. Yes, she was most proud of her contribution to the musical education of so many young minds.

'I thánkyou all for the kind words you have said about my years here as a teacher. It has been my joy to spend much of my life here with you, even when Tim O'Leary was in my class!' The hall exploded with laughter and shouts of, 'Good on yer Tim,' as Tim, once the class clown, then the first punk and now a respectable young businessman with two small daughters at the school, raised his clasped fists above his head to accept the honour of being singled out.

'So, to you all, my heartfelt thanks. Thank you, Headmaster.'

The applause lasted for quite a while until Mr. Costello resumed centre stage and told parents and guests about the buffet and where to line up for tea so that everyone could be served. Tim was at the bottom of the steps to assist Ruth from the platform. He did not wait for others but put her arm in his and led her to the back of the hall where his wife was waiting already armed with cups of coffee.

'Was I that bad Miss?' Tim asked with a grin.

'Do you want me to answer that with your children within earshot?' Ruth teased him, calling to mind the six-year-old with the fire extinguisher foam, spraying every coat in the infants' cloakroom. The parents had to have their children's coats cleaned and all had agreed that Tim was a very naughty boy, but no one sued anyone or even thought of it. Strange really, more fun and community spirit existed in those days. Fundraising was a priority if you valued your faith and everyone did value their faith. She thought of all those parish dances and bingo nights. Not that bingo was for her, but it was expected that the staff would put in an appearance at all such events. Now the parish hall was a Community Worship Centre and you could not have a bacon and cabbage night in case you offended some group or other. Not that the young people would come to such an event now anyway. What would 'health and safety' think of a tin bath, filled with unpeeled potatoes, balanced on three rings of a cooker. Who knows?

At last Father Michael was at her side saying how sorry he was to have missed the presentation. Tim and Sally smiled and understood that she was being drawn away. While Father Michael told her of his delay she found herself thinking of Paul Hardy and wondered what had happened to keep him from the afternoon's event. Then, as though by some telepathic signal, Father Paul was standing beside her.

'My dear Ruth, you are looking good. Are they retiring teachers early these days?' Just the normal sort of banter she had grown to expect from him. Father Paul was like a member of the family. It seemed as though they had known each other forever. The day would not have been the same without him, but she knew his own parish needs would have come first.

'Well certainly this is the end of an era, I began to think they must dust you off when they dust the statues these days, you have been here so long,' Paul teased.

'Excuse me, but have you ever seen this good lady stay still long enough to gather dust?' Father Michael was laughing as he sprang to her defence. 'And if you remember so far back that means you are no spring chicken yourself.'

'True, true, but there was a time when I was young and reasonably fit. Those were the days my friend,' said Paul, thinking back over the years.

'Not without their moments of hilarity,' Ruth reminded him. 'I remember being unable to find the path down off the Malvern Hills when out walking with you many years ago.'

'Not sure I should be party to this conversation,' joked Father Michael, taking the opportunity to move off to talk to the headmaster and leave the friends to chat.

'Do you remember how we laughed at the thought of

the newspaper headlines if we had been stranded up there all night?' Paul recalled. 'Did we stop at Stratford Upon Avon or somewhere to eat on the way back?'

'Yes, not like you to remember those sort of things, definitely a sign of approaching old age,' Ruth replied, laughing as she recalled the meal they had enjoyed looking out over the Avon, before the drive home. Not the same today, she thought, when most priests have three parishes to run and even their day off is no longer taken for granted. There was no stand-in for Father Michael this afternoon and she knew that Paul would be the same, lucky to get a break for an hour or two. They made their way to the tea queue but were noticed and shown to their seats, their tea and cakes brought to them on a tray. They continued to chat on about everyday issues, particularly how Father Paul still managed to keep his youth work going, even taking a group camping in France as he had done for so many years.

Finally it was time for him to go. 'Now I must leave before the rush gets onto the motorway. Keep in touch and let me know what interesting things you are doing with all this free time. And always remember if ever you need anything, anytime, ring or email me, promise me that.'

'I promise,' she replied. 'Safe journey home.' And Paul was off. For the first time that day tears were near to spilling over. She made for the staff cloakroom to give herself a moment of privacy. Yes, when she thought about it, and Ruth had certainly done that in the past few months, she had chosen the best of times to be a teacher. Long lazy days of the summer holidays, days spent with her brother in the cottage near Carcassonne, half terms spent walking in the Highlands and in later years each lovely Christmas at The Old Barn on the Yorkshire moors. And little children, happy and eager to learn, children she had the chance to borrow as her own. Only Francis, her dear brother, had known about this empty space in her life. Now that he had gone, no one knew what had shaped her existence, not even Paul. It was between God and herself. She could not say any of that here, it would be inappropriate, not the time nor the place. There would never be a time or a place. Not now. She was from an era when knowing the right time and place was important.

The day drew to a close and having accepted a lift home from the Head, with her gifts and cards full of good wishes, she put the key in the lock and let herself once more into the empty house. She opened the fridge door but nothing tempted her as she had eaten more than enough from the buffet that afternoon. She hadn't intended to, but people had kept coming up and saying, 'You must have some of this, Miss.' As she did not know whose mother had made that particular offering and not wishing to offend, she thanked the bearer of yet another gastronomic gift and 'had some of this'. She poured herself a celebratory sherry and sat back in the recliner.

Now just tomorrow to face and she would be free forever. Free to stay in bed in the mornings. She smiled at the thought. She had never stayed in bed in the morning. She doubted she would ever do that through choice, but to have the choice was the thing.

Teaching had been such a happy career for her, not her first choice, but a good one nonetheless. She suited both the discipline of an ordered day and the autonomy to plan her day as she wished. People thought that teaching was a sociable vocation. Few realized that a child, whilst often endearing, was hardly stimulating company in the accepted adult sense. Rather late in her life to consider such things now. Should she have another sherry? No, not the way to start this new part of her life, was it? Alcohol did not worry her. If she was going to turn into a lush she had had plenty of time to practice as she only ever enjoyed one drink.

Over the previous twelve months Ruth had managed to divest herself of most of her charitable enterprises. She was no longer chairwoman of the Legion of Mary; had dropped out of the flower arranging rota and even managed to persuade old Mr. Marks to take over the book stall at the early Mass. Above all else, she had not allowed herself to be signed up for anything. 'But Miss Wallis' Father Michael had protested when she turned down another kind offer to put her in charge of something (she had quite forgotten what). 'What are you going to do with yourself all day?'

Ruth could not remember how she had replied without being rude but she had and he had stopped asking this past few months. Interesting thought. What was she going to do with herself? Apart from a craft holiday in Greece, which for some obscure reason she had booked for May, she neither knew nor cared at the moment. She needed to get tomorrow over with first. Then she would have the rest of her life. It would be a new life, a different life, please God.

'One more day,' she laughed as she sang to the chords of Les Mis. One day more, one day more.

ROB

Card and Craft Holiday, Lindos, Rhodes Island, Greece. A Greek village with Acropolis and Medieval Castle. The perfect venue for a relaxing creative break.

Rob always read everything on the library notice board. Now and again there was something that particularly caught his attention: a talk by an archaeologist, or a seasoned traveller speaking about their exploits with a slide show. The latter always appealed to his wry sense of humour, regardless of the content of the talk. Photography he always found interesting, though any technical details sailed quite happily over his head. Now and again there was an advance notice of a celebrity 'one man show' at the town hall. The public had to book quickly if it was someone like Alan Titchmarsh, and the tickets were quite expensive. That was not a problem for Rob, as he was a St. John's Ambulance man. Sometimes he missed out when too many people wanted to be on duty for the same thing. Rob always allowed his name to be moved down the list. After all, it was difficult to get people to commit to something like St. John's and he would not want a young person dropping out because they missed seeing Swindon play at home. No, Rob had had his share of freebies over the years and in no way was he a greedy man. In fact there was little unkind that you could say about Rob. 'Committed' was the word that came to mind when you considered his St. John's work. 'Good son' to his elderly parents (until they passed on) and 'good neighbour' in a more general way.

He did not go rushing into other people's homes when there was a crisis. He would be called if needed.

Last year, three doors down, the little boy fell in the pond. They got him out in time but they sent for Rob.

'Hospital for a check-up,' he advised the parents. Rob called the ambulance. They had confidence in St. John's and confidence in Rob.

Involvement in the St. John's Ambulance Brigade had been his life since a lad. Only on the rare occasion when he was asked to talk publicly about the service did he stop to think about what they did, he and his colleagues. Just ordinary working blokes and girls, out in all weather, just in case someone was in trouble. Then there was the training of the young people, doing for the next generation what had been done for him. Always hoping they would choose a life of service and have a pride in themselves and the brigade.

Rob lived alone and had done so for nearly ten years now, since his mother had died. Before that he had helped nurse his dad, and now there was just him. He was as content as a man could be. He had enjoyed his years as a driver on the local buses but when the chance came to join the newly formed Kennetcare, the bus service for the elderly and disabled, Rob was first to apply. There was no problem transferring his pension rights, and his St. John's service made him an ideal candidate. He loved the job. He had missed the contact with older people since his parents had died and though only in his mid-forties, he was quite at home in their environment. He knew instinctively when to move forward to help and, just as important, when to allow someone to negotiate the steps of the mini bus alone. He was not a laugh-a-minute sort of guy, not Rob. Polite, helpful, service with a smile, always the same, come rain, come shine. Reliable.

Assessment, if Rob thought about it, was how he managed his life. He never needed to make rash decisions as he always planned ahead. Even with the grocery shopping he knew what he would buy each week. A box of raspberry ripple ice cream in the summer and an occasional bottle of malt whisky in the winter were the only variations. He grew all his own vegetables so there were lettuces and tomatoes in summer and lovely parsnips and carrots for the winter, with some to spare for the regulars at the British Legion Club. All organised and sorted. He once had the notion to get married but he was not too sure if it was for him. By the time he had considered things carefully, the young lady had got engaged to someone else. He knew that some thought he was a bit strange, living on his own. But he knew he wasn't, so it didn't bother him. His dad had said, 'Opinion can only hurt if you value the opinion in the first place.' He was content with his few friends who shared his interest in brigade work, the mates he played skittles with every Thursday and his job. He loved his job.

Today, the leaflet pinned on the library notice board had caught his eye. Rhodes Island, Greece. The island of the Knights of St. John, after Jerusalem and before Malta, he thought, recalling his knowledge of their history. He had considered going there once or twice over the years, but had never got round to it. He had been to Malta. Lovely place if you like old buildings and Rob did. He could not work out any real connection between those knights and the brigade except the name and the emblem, the distinctive St. John's cross. He presumed it was the idea of helping others that formed the connection not a real historical one. In that respect he felt a strange affinity with these knights of old. Though he had not left his homeland to serve, not even been in the army or anything, he took a certain pride when he attended special civic occasions in his uniform. He knew he represented many thousands of others, just like himself and the many millions of hours they gave. Always ready to help if the need arose. He had been to Malta twice with the Wiltshire Area Brigade, but never to Rhodes. Many people did not even know about the years the knights had spent in Greece. Not so much left to commemorate them as in Malta, he had concluded, though the palace walls still stood. He had seen pictures.

Rob took out his notepad and pencil from the inside pocket of his sports jacket and made a note of the number to call. He assumed that the other guests would be mostly elderly ladies, so perhaps it would be a busman's holiday. But that would not bother him. It would be nice to have a group to go to dinner with in the evenings. That is what it said on the flyer, *'You only eat alone if you choose to do so.'* He did get fed up with eating alone all the time, if only because he ate too fast with no conversation and then had indigestion. He was not really interested in the arty bit, but he expected the organisers would be just as pleased to have one less to bother with.

'That's settled,' he said to himself. 'Got yourself a nice holiday lad, if it's not all booked up.' He put his library books in the pannier and cycled home.

CLEAN MONDAY

Tanya, Steve and Miles sat in their usual places in Steps Bar. Steve was at the end of the counter, and his book, as ever, was face down, to be retrieved if there was a quiet moment. From this stool he could easily move behind the bar to serve a customer or go out into the lounge area to collect glasses. Miles sat near him and Tanya on the next stool. If customers came in who wished to sit chatting at the bar Tanya and Miles would move to the sofa where Steve joined them when free to do so. Their conversation had moved to the Greek custom of *'Clean Monday'* and Carnival.

'So,' Miles paused, 'What is your fancy dress going to be this year?'

'Let's say it will be a surprise,' Tanya replied. Tanya was not going to be drawn on this one, mainly because she had not decided if she was wearing fancy dress. Not one for making an exhibition of herself in the normal scheme of things, Tanya was always surprised at her own enthusiasm for Carnival, Greek style. All countries in the Christian world celebrate the start of Lent in some way or another. In Greece the weekend preceding the start of Lent was Carnival. Face painting and cross-dressing, play acting, and fancy dress, informal groups, individuals and organized floats, with dancing in the square sponsored by the village committee. Those of the expat community who had stayed on Rhodes for the winter would be welcome to join in this fun time. The Monday following was called *'Clean Monday'*, when the cooking pans, cleaned of meat, were made ready for the meals of fish which would be served until Easter. Traditionally Lindians would go to Pefkos and picnic on the beach or by the church, their main meal being fish. Some families still did this but for many *'Clean Monday'* became another day of joining friends and family in a restaurant, another reason for a party.

'I fancy,' said Miles, 'being a knight in shining armour.'

Steve gave him a quizzical sideways glance. 'Well you would, and you could carry it off quite well, but it needs planning and you tend to be a rather spontaneous type. I think a toga and a bit of laurel is more your style,' He did not want to be party to some wacky plan that fell by the wayside, especially if the good hearted Tanya had taken time and trouble with making a costume.

'I don't think,' said Miles, 'that it works with too much

planning. It has to be last minute and a bit of a giggle otherwise it loses the spirit of the occasion.'

'And on that note I think we will have another,' Steve left his stool at the end of his bar and to fetch an Amstel from the fridge.

Three young women in their early thirties had entered and sat down on the other bar stools. They looked at Miles, nudged each other and smiled. Was he local talent or an early season holidaymaker like themselves, they wondered?

'Good evening, ladies, and what brings you to Lindos?'

'An aeroplane. Same as yourself,' was the smart reply, which some may have found funny but this was not Miles' style of conversation. He smiled politely and left them to order their drinks from Steve who, as host, was obliged and quite happy to join in their holiday humour, laughing and chatting.

Ensconced on the small settee Miles addressed Tanya once again. 'Tell me more, who else is on your guest list?'

'A wedding stationery maker from the Cotswolds, and a young mum from Edinburgh. Two sisters, mid-thirties I think, can't remember where they live. I know nothing more about them than that. I tend to be to the point when I email, I do not ring to chat like June does.'

'The next few weeks will rush by once you start doing the preparation.'

'You know I always like to have everything covered, then it will all seem smooth and effortless when the classes start, which is as it should be.'

'Just let me know what and when you need from me and I will be there.'

'Thanks, Miles, that is the one thing I will miss if I leave this place, friends you can rely on.'

Tanya gave Miles the customary quick peck on both cheeks and waved 'cheerio' to Steve who was busy with customers. She was looking forward to Easter, which was very late this year. Then, only a few days after that, her craft group would arrive. Yes, if she was honest with herself, she did enjoy the challenge after a winter of self-indulgent sitting around, spent reading and watching her collection of old DVDs, mostly for their third viewing. Even for Tanya there was a limit to how many times you could watch Sex and the City and West Wing. Miles had leant over the balcony and waved to Tanya as she went off home. Tanya loved Miles as if he were her younger brother. Not only a talented artist, but with his dry wit and unflappable charm he was always good company. Since coming to Rhodes, Miles had lived in the next village where his parents had a modern villa. Apart from his company, Shirley and Fred had a willing pair of hands in maintaining an extensive garden and large pool. Miles often drove his mother shopping or his father to the bar for a sociable evening. At the same time he led his own life, sometimes staying in Lindos for a night or two and always working on some new art project. At the moment his passion was mosaics: large tiled collages that could be put into a patio or pool surround. In the summer he carried his sketchpad and pens with him into the bars. There he would find a ready mix of tourists anxious to have their portraits drawn in caricature fashion.

And this year he added the craft group to his commitments. He promised Tanya he would join the group for dinner if she wished him to, as there were invariably more ladies than men. Hardly a chore, as Steve had been quick to point out, but for Tanya entertaining them at dinner was one extra thing she did not have to think about if Miles was there. Should the need arise he would take an evening session and talk about some aspect of his art work, so the guests thought it was an impromptu arrangement - a bit extra they were learning on the course. Ultimately, it meant there was backup if required. Most important, now that she was running the week on her own. As she walked through the narrow streets to her home she thought how fortunate she was to have such good friends.

MELANIE

Mel just loved the big old vicarage. It smelt of old furniture polish, though she was sure it was some time since that particular room had seen any polish, old or new. She liked being in there by herself, in the quiet. Well, it was quiet until the phone rang, but they had an answer-phone now so at least she did not have to take the calls.

She never did know what to say. People assumed that if you answered the vicar's phone you would know all about the dates in his diary and she didn't. She was only there to add the latest information to the newsletter each week and to the magazine each month. It was all on the computer now and as long as she was careful about pushing the right button, it was easy. It was not really a job as such. Certainly she was not paid to do it. They were church people and there was no question of asking for payment for such a small service to the community. Don, the vicar was rarely there as he lived in a small cosy house at the other end of the village with his wife and young family. They did not have time for these small but important jobs. What Mel liked was being able to use the computer. She had missed out at school as computer lessons had not been available for the students until the year after she had left. She had grown in confidence the past few months. The thing was, whilst she enjoyed doing it and enjoyed the peace and quiet of the old vicarage, there was no one to chat to, no laughter. These days, Mel needed a good laugh as much as she needed to use her brain a bit. That's why she looked forward to the job she had at the supermarket three evenings a week. Certainly it was mind numbing, but a good laugh.

Later that night, after she and Keith had finished their tea and she had washed up and tidied the kitchen, Mel set out for her evening job. It only took ten minutes to drive to Waitrose on the new retail park. By nine o'clock she had put the last tin of beans with sausages onto the shelf.

'A penny for them, Mel?' her friend, Ann, offered.

'Oh, nothing in particular, just sort of everything, I suppose. I had to take the dog to the vet again today. Then Carol was in a foul mood as she had done this difficult homework and then forgotten to take it in to school with her this morning,' Mel replied.

Maybe it was the weather, the time of the year, the

time of the month, the time of her life, but everything seemed to be a chore lately. Apart from the chats with her friend, shelf-filling was not quite her cup of tea. One night she dreamt that all the shelves in Waitrose had been chopped up to make garden sheds and that everything was in sacks in the car park. You just drove up and what you wanted was thrown into the boot. The car went through a bar coding check and the cost was deducted from your account as you drove out. But no, when she went in to work on Thursday night the shelves were still there. But they did have a laugh when she told the other girls.

Keith had asked her not to take the job. 'We don't need the money, we have always got by, you at home is how it has always been.' He liked things to stay the same, and in many ways Mel agreed with him. It was not that she wanted to stack shelves, but she needed to do something. She'd had an idea some months before and it seemed to be gathering momentum: wedding stationery. It was all the fashion now to have everything handmade, so that it looked as though you had done it yourself, though everyone knew you had not. She had done some for Ann's daughter as a wedding present and Ann's niece had put an order in straight away. Mel didn't want to charge for it at first until Ann showed her a brochure from a local firm and Mel realised she could do a great job for a smaller price and still make a profit. Without the computer skills she had learnt at the old vicarage none of this would not have been possible. She had told Ann when they met in The Bakery for coffee one morning.

'There are so many things I don't know. I need fresh ideas before I can start to be a real business,' Mel had explained. 'I need to know what is fashionable and what is a good use of resources like any business enterprise. I want some sort of style lessons to get me going in the right direction. Stay friendly, I hope, but be more professional.'

'I have improved, but not enough,' she told herself as she sat placing gold doves on the corner of Order of Service sheets on Tuesday evening.

'Mel, where is my shirt? The one with the blue stripe,' Keith called, as he leaned over the banister on his way between the bedroom and the shower. It did not occur to Keith that, Mel, his wife, might be doing something that was important to her, something she might not want to leave immediately. Naturally she would go upstairs to take a blue shirt off a hanger in the wardrobe and place it on the bed. Why should today be different? Hadn't this been the way of things for almost twenty years? Mel get me this, Mel get me that. And whose fault was it? When they were first married it seemed natural for Mel to do for Keith what her mum had done for her dad, the dinner on the table when he walked in, the house perfectly clean and tidy. Not exactly slippers by the fireside, as Keith preferred to walk around the house in his bare feet. But if slippers had been his thing, then yes, she had to admit, she would have had them waiting.

Keith was still at school when they had first started hanging around together. Before that it had been a gang, not a gang of kids who were up to no good, like they seemed to have in the town, but a gang of teenagers who all went to the youth club. When Keith had left school to be an apprentice at Blakelock Wood Yard things had changed. He'd had money in his pocket and asked Mel to go to the pictures with him. After that they were 'going out' and everybody asked were 'Keith and Mel' coming to the dance? Or were 'Keith and Mel' going on the trip? On Keith's twenty-first they had got engaged and no one had been surprised. They had a buffet in the pub; the same pub they had held the sit down dinner in for their wedding reception a year later.

'Mel, can you get my shirt please? Not this one, the other blue stripe. The one your mum got me for Christmas.'

Mel had finished sticking the peel offs onto the last of her Order of Service sheets. It made such a difference, that little gold dove in the corner. Nothing too much, just something that emphasized the handmade touch. Well, that's what her grateful customers had told her. And the customer is always right, she thought. Well, not always. She had learnt the hard way. Not too much information. She no longer asked if they would like a red rose or a pink angel instead of a gold dove. On more than one occasion the girl had said, 'Yes please,' to all three. But now she had samples of different styles. She kept them in a clear plastic folder. Each double spread was one design and had a name. Her favourite was the Gold Dove. She would change the colour scheme to silver, bronze, red or gold, but not add bits. 'It's not really done,' and a cool stare, solved it all.

She must be doing something right as the orders were increasing. So much so Keith had converted the space under the stairs into a store room for her bits and pieces. One thing about working in a wood yard, these jobs always got done. He only had to hand the measurements in to one of the cutters and the wood was waiting for him to take home at lunch time. But something about Keith had changed this last twelve months.

In the past he had always done things for her with a bright, 'Yes love, no problem.' Now it was, 'What now?' if she asked for anything. Mel had seen too much of his moodiness this past year. Not really her Keith at all. He was such a good guy and she loved him, but, not being appointed manager affected him more than he cared to say. She felt sad that Keith was not getting over the disappointment. Though he said he understood the situation when Mr. Blake had explained why he had been passed over, it did not make it easier to take. 'It's understandable, Mel, after all Colin is family, old Mr. Blake's grandson. What was the old man to do when he was out of university for a year and no job?' Keith had explained to his wife. Mel knew that Keith had worked for years on the promise of that position. He had been offered a managerial post in the new DIY shop on the industrial estate, but he would not leave Mr. Blake without a foreman as old George the manager was off work more often than he was there with his sciatica.

The other problem that was never mentioned was their house. It was a tied cottage and it went with the job. Not that Keith thought for a minute that his boss would turn them out on the street, but if they left the wood yard they would feel obliged to leave and find a new home. It was a lovely house. Originally two farm labourers' cottages that had been knocked into one to make a spacious modern home. Mel and Keith had moved into it just after they were married. Over the years Keith had added built-in cupboards and moved the bathroom to the old kitchen space. Now they had a shower with blue tiles and a new kitchen in the conservatory extension he had built on the back, looking out over the garden. And there were the cherry trees they had planted when the children were born. Where would they find another house like this one? They could not afford to buy and rents were high. No, they would manage as they had always done and maybe the wedding stationery would take off.

Now and again she felt stifled, and if she admitted it to herself, a little bored. She had grown up since those early days, and now with Peter at technical college and Carol hardly ever at home, she needed to be herself, her own person, not Keith's wife or Peter's mum or Carol's taxi service. Mel went upstairs again, put the blue striped shirt back in the wardrobe and took down the new shirt still in its packaging. 'This will need an iron,' she thought as she took out the pins and shook it. She wanted to shout and ask what was wrong with the other one, but thought better of it. It was only the darts match, but Keith felt he must be presentable as Mr. Blake's foreman. Sometimes the old man came in for a pint on darts night with his wife.

'You do us proud, Keith,' she had said at the Christmas do, 'always so smart, a credit to the firm.'

'It's Mel,' he had replied. 'She won't let me out the door any other way.'

Keith glanced at Mel's face as she went down stairs for the iron. She seemed a bit fed up lately. Maybe that few hours she was doing filling shelves at Waitrose was too much. After all there was the house and garden, the dogs and the kids, not that they saw much of either of their children these days. Now she had this craze for doing these wedding things. If the Vicar had not asked her to help with the newsletter she would not have gone computer mad. He knew young Carol got fed up with continually being asked to upload or download or whatever it is you do with these things. Thank God they had Judy at work to deal with all this stuff. Measure twice and cut once was the only computer he needed. Still moaning about the heavy rain and that it was an away match, Keith shut the front door and Mel relaxed.

She would make a coffee and look at the advert from the magazine again. Silly, but she felt almost as though she was telling lies just by not telling Keith about the craft holiday. It was not as though she had booked it or anything like that, she had only cut out the advert and sent off for more information. She could book via an email - she knew how to do that, but Carol would see the reply, and she wasn't ready to discuss it with anyone. Certainly not before, she had told Keith. OK, she was going to tell Keith, not ask him. If she asked his opinion and he said he thought it was a daft idea, how could she then go and book? If she just said she was booking this holiday, he might think her daft, but it would not be a discussion.

What was happening to her? What was happening to them? Was it that nonsense you read about in magazines, about women and the 'change'? Maybe she should talk to the Doctor. But then Keith and Charles were Church Wardens and on the rota for the eleven o'clock service on Sunday. Charles might say something. He would not imagine she had not things talked over with Keith before coming to him.

Mel read the advert again. A card-making and craft holiday on the Greek island of Rhodes. There was a phone number she had not noticed before. She got her credit card ready. She would pay the deposit.

It was some weeks later before Mel told Keith about the planned trip. Partly because she had been too busy with her wedding orders and her three evenings a week filling shelves to find the right time, and it had to be the right time. Also there was a problem at the wood yard. Collin had not credited cheques when he should have done. In fact, he had tried to swindle the accounts. Nothing to do with Keith really but he could not help getting involved. The office staff had come to him for advice. How were they going to tell Mr. Blake? He had tried to discuss it with Mel, but she really did not want to know. She got quite cross. 'You are not the manager, so it is not your concern,' she had told him sharply. Not like his Mel at all, Keith thought to himself. But it did not occur to him to ask if she was alright. Mel was always alright. Then she was on about going off on holiday on her own. Something to do with setting up a business to print the wedding invites. How could he manage without her for a week? Even with food in the freezer, and his shirts ironed, and his socks in the same drawer for the past twenty years, how would he manage?

'Mel is off on some jaunt without me,' Keith had told Charles the next Sunday morning. He knew that was not fair, she had shown him the leaflet and it did say 'non-participating guests were welcome', but supposing he was the only bloke there? Anyway, he could not take a holiday at the moment, and he usually took a week in March and October to dig the allotment over.

The next week seemed to fly by, partly because Mel was trying to make sure the freezer was full and the pantry shelves were stocked, as though she was going to be away for a lifetime rather than a few days. Her packing was rather a last minute affair. But at last the choices were made and the red cotton shorts were discarded in favour of the blue denim. No good pretending she had not put on a few pounds since last summer.

Mel felt a bit anxious as she finished her packing. She was glad that Keith had gone off to the pub for a darts meeting. She did not want him to know how worried she was about going through the airport alone. She had only flown once before, and they were together then, and only to Dublin for a friend's wedding. Now she was going to be on her own, and going to Greece. It was too late now to change her mind. Keith was not sure if he should be going out tonight, but it was only a meeting with the next village to sort out the fixtures list. At least Carol had reminded him it was Mel's birthday while she was away. Carol had bought a card for him, which he slipped into the case. That would surprise her. Then he had rung the Chinese, the one they went to for Peter's twenty-first. Charles had given him the number.

Should he tell her? He was feeling quite pleased with himself really. Old Mrs. Blake had collared him at the darts match last night and said she had heard at the W.I. meeting Mel was off to Greece.

'What a very modern young couple you are, taking separate holidays. It was lovely when hubby used to go off with the Territorial Army years ago, like a second honeymoon.'

That had reminded Keith that he and Mel had not yet had a first one. 'Got to move with the times Mrs. Blake,' he had replied. Thank goodness he had read the brochure as other people had asked him about the course. He would have looked stupid if he had known nothing about it. The men were teasing with a wink and a dig in the ribs.

'Off for a week on a Greek island? Didn't think your Mel was like that Keith old son.'

He did not stay to chat after the meeting. Those that had teased him only a short time ago sent their best wishes to Mel, and said they expected to hear all about it on her return. That was nice. When he got home Mel was in the kitchen and called out to know if he wanted hot chocolate.

'Coffee please and two biscuits,' he replied. When they were seated he blurted out about the Chinese. Not quite how he meant to say it.

Mel brushed the tears from her eyes. 'You silly old thing; thankyou. What a lovely surprise that will be to come back to, with the children as well?'

'No, I have no intention of asking them. I am taking my wife out to celebrate.'

'Celebrate what?' she asked with a laugh in her voice at the very idea.

'Just you and me,' he replied.

Nothing I can say to that, Mel thought, so she blew him a kiss across the table. They finished their drinks and went up to bed. They clung to each other in the dark. At first just gentle hugs, then a kiss goodnight. But they had been together too long not to know when a kiss goodnight was not enough. They made love simply and tenderly. No magic moves and things you read about in magazines, just the love and understanding of people who had been happily married for twenty-two years. All this time planning a week away, now Mel looked forward to coming back.

HEATHER

'Are you sure that's everything now?' Ken asked his daughter as he put her case into the boot, but Heather had already turned back to the door, so he waited while she had a last few words with her mother.

Less than two minutes later, seatbelts fastened, he eased the car out through the gate. At last they were on their way. The weather was good, so Ken looked forward to the drive. A bit crazy, he thought to himself, that in this day and age he had to go to Manchester to get to Rhodes or wherever it was Heather was going for the week. He was not complaining. The way things had been since Heather and Dave had split up meant he'd hardly had the chance to have a chat with his daughter.

Heather. Why had he always had that extra soft spot for his eldest child? Had she known he felt differently about her? Even as a kid, dropping her off to school she always gave him a hug and said, 'Don't worry about me, Dad.' No more, but that was enough. They understood each other. Was it because she looked like him? The wide brown eyes and square jaw. As a bloke such looks had served him well, but did not work the same magic on Heather. No one could ever call her a dainty little thing. Honest and hardworking was the impression given to a stranger, and she was just that.

These last few months he'd wondered if he and Shirley had let her down, particularly in those early days when she had won a scholarship to Broughton High. It had been the highlight of his life, except, of course, for when he married Shirley, and when his daughters were born. Heather never minded him driving her to school in the van, or dropping her off at the school gate in the battered old pick up. No posh car or anything, just an old van. He loved the drive through town with her beside him in her distinctive school uniform. He never forgot that it was Heather who had collected her younger sisters from school, and put their tea on the table, when he started his own business.

Shirley had run the office, and they had relied on Heather to always be there, at home. When he and Shirley had come home on winter evenings, the tea would be cooked and ready to put on the table and her sisters would have their homework done too. Even now, all these years later, Ken often wondered if that had affected her schoolwork, as the early promise did not follow through. Instead of attending university, which they'd hoped for, Heather left school at sixteen.

By then Ken had someone running the office and he could not tell her to leave to make way for his daughter. You did not do that sort of thing, not to a good, reliable employee. Heather soon got a job as a box office assistant at the Assembly Rooms. She worked full time in the summer, with the Festival and part time in the winter, which was great, as she helped her mother around the house on her free days.

It was only natural that she would start dating, and he looked forward to having a bloke in the house to watch the football with, and to go for a pint with on Sunday lunchtime. But Dave was not like that. He took a dram or two but only with his mates from the music world: not in Ken's club. Dave had come to Edinburgh for the festival six years ago, as a saxophone player in the orchestra. That was how he met Heather, at the First Night party. Everybody in the theatre world knows about musicians. It is hardly their fault, as the local girls hang around the stage door. Most know they are not going to be whisked away by a leading man, but the smell of the greasepaint makes anyone connected to that magical world a target for attention. Many of the guys go for a quiet drink in the theatre bar, to chat and unwind, and wait till the punters have gone away. Yes, to give him his due, Dave was like that. Well he seemed to be, but once he was dating Heather he liked to be out dancing and drinking, enjoying the young social life of the city. They went to the cafes and student dives behind the castle in The Cowgate and The Grassmarket in the old town. She had loved it, being part of the scene. On more 'upmarket' nights, when someone in the cast had a birthday to celebrate, they were in George Street, the Opal Lounge or the Why Not. A different city to the one Heather called home, yet only a few minutes' walk away from the village, Dean village, where she grew up.

'I know Dave is not quite your cup of tea, Dad,' she had said to him one evening just before she married. 'Don't worry about us, he is a good lad, and he treats me well and I love him, I really do.'

There was nothing Ken could say then, just as there was nothing he could say now, five years later when Heather and Dave had separated. He looked at her drawn face and was glad of the excuse of having to watch the traffic, so she could not see his heart breaking.

Heather. It was always tomorrow when he planned to make it right with her. After all, if she had not minded the kids when they started, they would never have had McPhee Glazing. Those had been the glory years when everyone wanted double glazing. They had moved house not long after Heather's wedding. 'Something better' his wife had said at the time. Well, it was never better in his eyes as they had left behind good friends in the village. But Shirley had put a lot into the business as well, it was right she should have the home of her dreams. Now, with house prices dropping, no one wanted new glazing, and just when Heather needed their help they had nothing to give. All they could offer her was a holiday making cards or some such rubbish. She said it was what she wanted to do.

'What am I going to do on the beach all day Dad?' she had asked, 'Wait for some Greek bloke to pick me up? Even Shirley Valentine didn't have a two-year-old child in tow. Tom Conti is Scottish anyway, no need to go to Greece to find him.'

'What are you going to do lass when you get back? You know you can come and live at home. Your Mam, she dotes on little Lucy, you know that. You could go back to work in the box office. I met Pete the carpenter last week and he said there was a vacancy, at least until they close for refurbishment. Mam would look after Lucy if you wanted that.' She gave him the usual quiet smile.

'Don't worry about me, Dad, it doesn't help. Dalkeith is lovely, but it will never really be my home, not like the Dean with the small streets and the noise of the river. Dad, you can't make my pain go away.' Heather was silent for a while, and then in a more positive voice she told her dad, 'I don't think I even want Dave back now. I did take him for granted in some ways and I got used to the lifestyle down south. The amount I spent in Marks and Spencer, just on food. Imagine buying potatoes already cooked? Sometimes I would think of Granda' digging up the tats for Sunday lunch. Though we called it dinner then, not lunch.'

They laughed at the thought, and both fell quiet once again. It would be so easy to move in with her parents again, Heather thought. But then it had never really been her home. She was already living in Manchester with Dave when mum and dad had bought the new house. Ken pulled into the service area off the motorway. It was more sensible to stop for a break even though he did not really need a coffee or anything at the moment. It was quite a warm night and not much traffic about. Bit of a ghost town these places he thought, when not full of people. They got a can of coke each and sat in the car with the doors open. A breath of fresh air was all they needed, and they would be on their way again. Heather took a long look at her dad. She could not imagine him walking out on his family as Dave had done to her. Even though, to be honest, she knew her mum could be a bit of a pain at times. No, her dad would not have left her, no matter what had happened between him and his wife. But Dave had not actually left them, he had pushed them out, knowing Ken and Shirley would pick up the pieces.

'I know it has all gone wrong Dad but it was exciting. Manchester was the place for theatre work. The Opera House, the Palace, it was one new musical after the other. Look at the stars I have met, and the shows I have seen. The ballet and the opera, I would never have known if I liked all that because I would never have paid for the tickets.'

'You see, Dad, once I stopped work and then had Lucy, I was not interested in the theatre crowd any more. Just the same old gossip with new names of people I had never met. Also there was the problem of finding a baby sitter I felt I could trust. So I dropped out of the party scene, and David went to the First Night parties alone. As a guest at any other party or club opening he naturally took Stella. I knew this but it did not seem to be a problem. She was front of house manager after all. After a while no one notices you are not there. There are staff changes and if I rang up they would ask who was calling, and then say "Heather who?"'

She went silent... and now David lived with Stella in their house. They would buy Heather out. That's the phrase they used. Not true. It was David that had said that. All this was between her and Dave. It was their marriage that had slipped away. She just agreed to everything that was suggested. Yes, she could buy a flat for herself and Lucy. No, she could not afford the house, even with the maintenance money he would pay every month. Dad had offered to get a lawyer involved, but Dave said it would be a waste of resources. In her numbed state she had agreed. She would do anything just to get away and back up to her own place. But where was her own place, where did she belong now? No answers. Was a week's holiday the answer? Doubtful, but she needed time to think. She needed a space where she would be with people, but not really with them. This week in Greece would do.

Ken gave a sigh of relief, pleased to see they were at the airport in good time. Heather waited for that sick feeling that usually came when she saw planes on the runway of an airport. Nothing happened. She realized she had been apprehensive for weeks, not about the flight, but about the future. She had nothing left in her emotional bank to spend on fear of flying. It was fear of landing and the future.

'Don't worry about me, Dad. Don't spoil the baby if you can help it. I will ring as soon as I land, but I will be there before you get home I expect. No, don't park the car. It's a long drive back and with a bit of luck you'll get off the motorway before the traffic gets too bad. Thanks for everything; love you Dad.'

Ken got this strange feeling that if he said one word she would turn tail and get back into the car. After all it was the first time Heather had left little Lucy. It had been hard work getting her to agree to this holiday. It was little enough to give her. Little enough. A quick hug as he took her case out of the boot. He was not looking forward to the long drive home. Wishing he knew how to mend her broken heart. A week away was not going to do that.

A SPECIAL TREAT

Tanya stopped at the top of St. Stefanos' square to buy two cream cakes. She chose the mille-feuille, a pastry slice with creamy custard filling and slices of kiwi fruit on the top. Definitely her favourite and she knew her friend Sam would enjoy the treat as well. Each month she booked with Sam for a facial treatment, her one real luxury, particularly when she was very busy in the summer. But today it was a leisurely mix of treatments and social chat. And a cream cake and a cup of tea would go down well at the end of the afternoon.

Tanya walked across the square in front of the ancient amphitheatre, then up the lane towards the cliff top. This cluster of houses was a century old, and Sam had recently moved into the end villa, which overlooked the sea. The garden at the side of the house gave a bird's eye view across St. Paul's Bay. You could see Dimitris' kantina on the near side and the tiny St. Paul's church in the distance. There was a strong wind off the sea today. It hit her as soon as she came from the shelter of the other buildings. And, as usual for this time of the year, the sea was grey and rough. Small flower beds of geraniums and oleander bushes flanked the front door.

She had rung Sam just a few minutes earlier to say she was on her way, so the large wooden door with its brass knocker was already ajar. Tanya pushed the door and calling out, *'Yia sou,'* letting herself into the spacious courtyard. Sam came from the lounge and greeted her like a long lost cousin, although they had met in the village for coffee just a few days ago, and chatted most days on the phone. If Prince William had been ten years older he would have found his lady in a Greek village, masquerading as a beauty therapist, and calling herself Sam not Kate. The same lovely eyes, flowing hair, and softly spoken tones. But he isn't and didn't. So while Kate resides in a palace Sam is more than happy with her Lindian house.

'Wow I certainly am impressed, the courtyard is lovely,' Tanya told her friend as she looked around. The courtyard was paved with the black and white pebbles, laid in intricate designs, typical of the older homes in Lindos. The grape vine by the entrance door twisted up and over a high wooden frame. There was a pomegranate tree and pink and white bougainvillea at the far end. The rooms were on either side, both interlinked and opening into the courtyard.

'Are you pleased with the move? I must say it all looks so organised and comfortable already, how did you manage everything so quickly?'

'I will let you into a secret,' said Sam as she opened the door to yet another room. 'All the unpacked boxes are in here, out of the way, until I can find time to sort them. Being well organised is just an illusion,' she laughed.

Tanya was impressed. The ceilings were high with exposed wooden beams and the main lounge had a traditional raised wooden Lindian bed, a space which now housed a comfy sofa and the T.V. The large oak furniture Samantha's brother Matt had brought from England worked really well. It seemed as though it were made to go with the Lindian architecture. Sam was a cat lover and five, well-cared for felines lazed on the patio by the kitchen door. They had free range of the house but were never allowed in her treatment room.

The cakes were put in the fridge for later and Tanya followed Sam as she chatted away about her trip to Rhodes Town the day before. The atmosphere in the treatment room was calm and relaxing. Gentle classical music played on FM radio. White walls, naturally, and the sea visible from the high windows. White towels were piled on a side table. Tanya removed her sandals, skirt and top and made herself comfortable on the massage bed. As usual, Sam regaled her with the latest news from Lindos. Mostly just normal gossip about who was seeing who amongst their young, and not so young, friends. But the main conversation consisted of what her cats had managed to do during the past couple of weeks. From anyone else such chatter might have been invasive but Sam had such a soft pleasing tone that it was quite relaxing. Gentle cleansing preceded the astringent. Once the face pack was in place, Sam left the room and Tanya had ten quiet minutes listening to the gentle music. More pampering, balanced between gentle massage and relaxing and an hour later Tanya was dressed, ready and feeling very good, mentally and physically. They chatted on over the tea and cakes at the end of an enjoyable afternoon.

'This is a lovely house, Sam, with so much potential. What are you going to do with all this space?' Tanya asked.

'Well I need to rent out a studio probably to a worker but they would have to be cat lovers, naturally. What would you suggest?'

'You could turn your bathroom into a sauna, that would be quite a new challenge,' they both laughed at the thought.

'I've been chattering on and haven't asked you how your bookings are going,' said Sam, taking the kiwi slices from the top of her cake.

'Actually, better than ever. One lady is coming for her granddaughter's wedding - marrying a Greek lad so I understand. Have you got the make-up booking for that?'

'Yes I know them, Tassos and Tracy, lovely couple, and I think Jenny is doing her hair. She's closed the gift shop and started hairdressing again. It's called Lindos Hair Studio. The website is lovely. So is the studio.'

'And there are two sisters from Reading, sound a bit rough round the edges, but that usually means that they will be a good laugh, and a wing commander no less - made some Christmas cards last year or something. Then last of all a woman from London, wanted to know about booking a ferry to some Greek islands after the week is over. How do you say 'Google it' politely?'

They burst into a fit of giggling and custard cream was spluttered in a very unladylike manner.

It was already dusk as Tanya left the shelter of Sam's courtyard. Not surprising, then, that she bumped straight into Captain Takis who was making his way home. Greetings were exchanged in the usual manner with a kiss on both cheeks. He was everyone's picture book sea captain, ruddy cheeks, twinkling eyes and a ready smile. His smile and good humour hiding the life shattering tragedy of losing his son, Dimitris, when only a young man. Tanya had great respect for this kindly elderly man, who, whilst born in Lindos, had travelled the world as a merchant seaman. She always found him interesting to talk to as he knew all there was to know about the village past and present. It was his grandfather who built the houses, including the one Samantha now rented, and a couple more nearer the church. The Lindian tradition is that every daughter has her own house on marriage and as his grandfather had six daughters, that had meant a lot of building. The Captain always had a tale to tell, usually about someone who had landed in Lindos years ago like a bit of human jetsam, and drifted off some years later in the same way they had arrived, leaving a mark for good or ill on the village community. On rare occasions he would produce his mouth organ and give a brief recital. But on this chilly evening, with the strong wind coming off the sea, it was a quick hello and a discussion as to whether it might rain or not and they parted company.

A lovely ending to a great afternoon she thought as she made her way home. Whatever the summer might bring with its crowds of visitors, tour guides with their placards and someone always sitting in your favourite seat outside Giorgos, it was worth it all for such days as this.

KIM AND BETH

Kim always went to McDonald's. It had this great safe play space outside. Once the kids had had a bite to eat they could run off and do their own thing. She loved her kids, but in small doses. And, although she would hardly call it the most relaxing of venues, it did everything she needed it to. A play area away from the traffic, and she did not pay stupid prices for food the kids did not want to eat. McDonald's would do.

Kim was waiting for her sister, Beth. They had some serious planning to do if they were to get this latest scheme of the ground. Serious planning. To other people a week away might not be such a big deal, but for the two sisters it had taken on mammoth proportions. It was both a battle of wits and a battle of wills. Kim did not intend to lose on either account.

'Nine hundred pounds on the lottery,' Beth screamed

when Kim had told her. 'Bloody hell our kid, are you sure?' She was sure, she already had the money in the knicker drawer upstairs, and had told no one except Beth.

'Are you doing up the kitchen?' her sister had asked once she had calmed down. 'If so I tell you now, that won't go far.'

'Not 'effin' likely,' Kim hastily replied. 'No, this money is for us, girl, for an old fashioned holiday.'

Beth frowned, it did not sound like Kim. She did nothing old fashioned, not even marrying her kids' father when he suggested it.

'You mean get a caravan in Kessingland? You would get at least two weeks and in the summer holiday. Or why not three weeks and have two with Gerry and the kids and I would come down for the third week. It would be a great laugh.'

'You think I would be that daft and squander it on a van in wet and windy England? I mean "old fashioned" in the sense that it's what we used to do, before I got bogged down with kids and you with your dead end, open all hours, job.'

Beth did not think her job was dead end. She worked in the corner shop, and liked it, with no bus fares to find and only down the road, which was great on a wet day. What if Mr. Patel often asked her to stay late? That was the best time to be in the shop. The lads from the building site called in on their way home to their digs. They would finish a pint or two in the Spread Eagle, and only want a packet of fags or tin of corned beef for the sandwiches in the morning. She didn't tell Kim, or even Mr. Patel, but she hung on for a few minutes if they had not appeared by nine o'clock. By the time she had served them with a few slices of ham, shared a laugh and a chat, and then done the till it was often gone ten when she got home. But as she only lived a few doors away it did not matter.

'We can't just sod off,' Kim explained. 'Gerry would smell a rat, and I need to keep him sweet, to get him to look after the kids for the week.'

Kim had no one else to ask. When she went in to have the little one, Beth had taken a few days off work. Mr. Patel was a family man and understood these things. No good expecting their mother to help. She lived in Bristol now, and spent most of her time minding her boyfriend's four kids. Lucky them, thought Kim. She had not spent much time minding her and her sister when they were young. In fact, no one had minded them at all as long as they could remember. It used to matter to Kim years ago, but now, when she heard people talk about looking after their old ones she thought how lucky her and Beth were. As their mother had not spent much time looking after them then, she felt no obligation to concern herself about her mother, now or in the future. She sent a card at Christmas, just because it was Christmas and that was it. Did not matter as her and Beth had got on all right.

Kim saw Beth making her way through the glass door, and thought how great she looked. You would never guess that she was thirty-nine. Hair in a ponytail, with a sparkly thing at the back; she always wore it that way for work, and it looked both smart and girly. Kim could not wait to tell her the plan. Beth waved and made signs to ask if she wanted a refill as she got her own coffee and cheeseburger.

'Well, what's cooking kid? Have you sorted the great getaway yet?'

Kim was a little peeved that Beth did not take it more seriously. After all, her sister could get up and go whenever she wanted. Mr. Patel had been to India for six weeks to his cousin's wedding and he had suggested that Beth take some time off when he got back, on full pay, to show he appreciated her running things while he was away. She had run things, but he had sent his friend from the paper shop in each day to cash up the takings. It was to protect her he said. He did not want her mugged on the way to the bank.

'Right, it's like this -' Kim started to explain. 'I will tell Gerry that you have won the money. He knows we owe you, big time, both for looking after Billy when Katie was born, and more importantly in his eyes, helping us out with the rent when he was off work.'

'But you paid me back as soon as your benefits came through, every last copper. Though I said I didn't need it all at the time.'

'Yes, but you know what Gerry is like, he rates things like that. I will tell him you have won a few quid and you want to go on a holiday. You can't go on your own, and it would not be a holiday if we took the kids. Now, he knows some of the things we did years ago in Faliraki. He would never fall for us having a week there, but I saw this craft holiday advertised in a magazine, and it's on Rhodes. Lindos is not that far from Faliraki. Well that's even if we were going back to our own hotel every night. And who says we will be?'

'Kim, you wouldn't? You couldn't do that to Gerry?'

'You don't sleep with him every bleeding night! Anything more than sleep is down to the once a week, and not even then if West Ham lose and he has got the hump about that.'

This made Beth laugh. She could not remember when she last spent the night with anyone, it was so long ago. There had been chances, but not with anyone she really fancied. But she and Kim had always had different ideas about that. Kim said you didn't know if you really fancied them till you did stay the night. No, she could not change her ways, not even on a week's holiday.

Kim did not feel as brave as she pretended to be. She was having second thoughts about picking up a bloke, but she was not going to say as much to her sister. To tell the truth she did not even think about anyone except Gerry. Never. But how was Beth going to get laid if she never left that soddin' shop? She had to keep talking.

From Lindos With Love

There were many times in the past when Beth had read her mind before she had read it herself. This was not going to be one of them. Kim could do with a break herself and everything she had said about Gerry needing to be almost blackmailed into having a week off work to mind the kids was true. He had talked about re-doing the living room. Now, if he took a week when the kids were at school, even though Katie only went in the mornings, he could get on and do that. It would be like a holiday for him as well, now she thought about it. He said he fancied wallpaper again. She would spend a few bob on that and the paint. They could go together, to buy the stuff, on Saturday.

'Why am I supposed to be interested in a craft holiday all of a sudden?' Beth asked.

'It's not all of a sudden, look at the jumpers and things you do for us all at Christmas, they are fabulous. You could make a living out of your knitting if you were not in Patel's half your life. And they do card making and you would be good at that. And if you stay in that crappy job at least you could sell the cards in the shop.'

Beth suddenly saw it all in a new light. Maybe there was something to this craft lark after all. She did not like Kim telling lies to Gerry, but it was only about the money. She could pay for herself anyway and Kim would have enough left over for Gerry to go on one of these away matches to Germany or somewhere.

'That's settled then, I'll get the kids another milkshake

and we will shove off home.'

'I will call at yours later tonight to look at the website with you, to see what the cost is going to be. Just got time to get back to Patel's, can't be late as he does the cash and carry this afternoon. Bye kids, love you,' Beth called as she blew a kiss in the direction of the climbing frame.

It will be a good laugh anyway, she thought as she hurried back to the shop.

MAX

Max paid the taxi driver and went into the airport through the revolving doors. He smiled as he recalled the old joke, straight through the glass doors. He was always amazed that such childish things never failed to amuse him. 'Silly old fool,' he remarked to himself. That was another thing he had got to stop. He had been so used to Joan saying something vaguely between an endearment and a reprimand that he now said it for her. Well, on that account she would have been right. He was a silly old fool. Is a silly old fool. And who cares. No one cares a jot. Not anymore.

'You can stop that for a start,' he mumbled to no one in particular. 'If you are going to be like that you might as well go home now.' He squared his shoulders and looked around. Check in at desk 5, the sign said, so he made his way round to the desk and stood in the queue. He saw three people wearing the same badges. At least he had the good sense to keep his well hidden in his pocket. No point in announcing to all and sundry that he, Maxim Henderson, Wing Commander Maxim Henderson, retired, was going on a craft holiday. 'Not bloody likely, old chap. Not bloody likely,' he had told himself in the shaving mirror that morning.

So, what had happened to the 'new man' he had read about in the Guardian, and hoped to emulate? Was he a bit of a wimp for not wearing his Card Shark badge that came in the envelope when they confirmed his booking? Was he not 'new man' enough, and as such, prepared to walk around a major London airport with a sign on his jacket? In words of one syllable, no, or was it yes? He meant no, he was not going to wear the badge 'til he got there. Greece. 'A moment of truth here, Maxim,' he had told himself, dabbing his face as he addressed his reflection in the mirror. 'You, son, are the type of guy who books a craft holiday, knowing it might be a bit of a mothers' meeting. Yet, you have not got the balls to wear the badge.'

Joan once described her own involvement in the craft group in the village, 'We are all ladies of a certain age who fill their time making 'billy doos' and sell them for charity.' What the hell was a 'billy doo' anyway? Suppose someone asked if he had one? 'Not anymore,' he would reply, 'not since the wife died.' Sad to say he found that to be the most useful phrase in his vocabulary these days. Particularly when you were asked to one of those confounded cheese and wine things .You only had to say, 'Sorry, old chap, not any more, not since the wife died,' and they gave you a knowing nod and did not mention it again. Shame really, he had always enjoyed any social occasion. Enjoyed being a bit of a flirt, if the truth were known. He could be as charming as he knew how, particularly when in uniform. It dazzled the ladies a bit somehow.

But he could always rely on Joan. Just when he felt he was getting in too deep she would appear at his elbow. Putting her hand on his arm, and nodding her apologies to the woman he was talking to, she would whisper into his ear. It was enough, just enough, to give that clear signal. 'This man is mine and he likes it that way.' And he did. Never once in all their thirty-five years together did he ever want to be anywhere else except with Joan. Why would he? In his eyes, Joan had never changed from that slip of a girl he had met at the Cardington Camp dance all those years ago. It was an assessment camp, and that is what he did, assess people as they came on their six weeks training before their call up posting. It had not taken him long to assess Joan.

The camp was full of young men and every Saturday night there was a dance. To encourage the local girls to attend they ran a free bus from Bedford. This was still the age of the big bands, the R.A.F. had their own full dance orchestra made up of regular service bandsmen, and the sound was like no other. Jive and rock and roll were in the programme but mostly it was good solid ballroom dancing and that's where Corporal Henderson scored points. He was the only boy in the family and with three sisters to goad and encourage him, Max could dance very well. Joan was pretty, with short dark hair, a bit like Audrey Hepburn, he had thought and she wore the latest shirtwaister style that showed off her slim figure. Joan had been to dance classes in her village hall every Tuesday after the Guides meeting. Miss Sylvia, the teacher, had a vast collection of Victor Sylvester records, which she played on an old gramophone. Joan gained a silver medal and she would dance every dance except the tango. She never liked the tango.

Dancing. It had stayed with them throughout their married life, and proved to be such a social cache at the functions they attended as he rose up the service ladder. Once he even danced with the Queen Mother at a regimental ball, not because of his rank but because of his prowess on the floor. But that had changed. Well nothing was quite the same after Jack. Then Joan was ill and then she was gone.

'Snap out of it old man, you're going on holiday,' he told himself.

He stood in the queue and tried not to stare at the people wearing the Card Shark badge. Two young women seemed to be together. Although one was fair and the other quite dark, rather obviously sisters, he thought, as he gave them a more studied appraisal. Nice young things out for a bit of a jolly by the look of it, and why not? The dark one had an ear splitting laugh. It echoed around like a donkey with a sore throat. Max admonished himself for being so unkind. If things had gone differently he could have had a daughter that age, he thought. He could have. But he had not. No family, not after Jack. The lady with the grey hair caught his eye and smiled. She was small and stocky and very business-like. Her luggage was quite expensive-looking and obviously new. The girls checked in first and went off still chattering. So much for a quiet break, he thought, and then chastised himself once again for being a miserable old sod.

There was something about being a forces man that made you toe the line well after you stopped needing to. It clearly said 'stay behind the white line' at the check in desk, so he did. The grey haired lady with the expensive luggage had done the same before her turn to approach the counter. He had noticed that. Now he found himself in a strange dilemma. Her case needed to go onto the rack, and he automatically moved forward to assist.

A young man, an airline employee, put his hand in front of Max. 'Stay back Sir please, give the lady a bit of privacy.'

'I do apologize,' he found himself saying. He wanted to add that he only wanted to help but the lad was already going into a well-used oft repeated script.

'No problem, Sir, easily done. Been to Greece before, Sir?'

'Cyprus, though I was not there as a visitor. I was stationed in Cyprus with the R.A.F.'

He was waiting for the next comment that always followed such a statement. Oh were you? How interesting. When was that? But the young man was already giving his attention elsewhere. The lady with the rather pleasant smile had managed her case easily. She moved away and he took her place at the counter.

'*Kalimera*, window or aisle? Been to Greece before, Sir?'

He hated having two questions thrown at him, but her smile was so lovely that he could not fail to respond. He had always chosen a window seat on any commercial flight, his premise being if he was going into the sea he would like to see where he was when it happened. Now he thought it expedient to sit on the aisles. Easier for him to get to the bathroom.

He had made a good recovery they had told him at the hospital. He was to keep up the exercises, go to the gym, or walk at least a mile each day. None of that had been a problem. It was the tablets that he could not get used to. He tried putting them near the bed, then in the bathroom. Then there was the worst scenario: had he taken them at all that day? He solved this by making a chart showing how many tablets in his possession, set against the date, including the ones in his pockets. The girl in the chemist had offered him a box with the days of the week marked on it. He did not feel ready for that yet. It was when he was rooting around for card to make his chart that he found all the bits and pieces that Joan had used for her craft group. He had enjoyed helping her with her craft projects for years. Particularly that little dolls' house. It was not a real dolls' house, just a strong cardboard box with all the furniture and fittings inside. He had asked one of the electricians to put together a battery lighting set, as a gift for Joan, of course. He had turned it on and off and changed the position of the table lamp to get the best light on the tiny pictures, far more often than she had. Silly old goat. He didn't need Joan to tell him that, but wished she were here now, nagging him about such things. Strange old life, he thought. The way one thing leads on to another. And he was right on that one. If he had not needed card for the chart he would not have started making those Christmas cards. Then he would not have bought that magazine with the advert in it, and he would not be on his way to Greece at this moment.

The lady with the friendly smile was going through to the departure lounge just ahead of him. 'Hello, I'm Miss Wallis. Sorry, Ruth Wallis. Have you been to Greece before?'

ANDREA

For Andrea this was a holiday with a difference. The anticipation had been years in the making, just a childhood dream, a thought to hang on to when there was little else in her young life.

Andrea was in Rhodes with one intent, to find her father. This was a pilgrimage to the land of her conception, if not the land of her birth. So long in the planning, knowing even as a child that it was a journey which may well prove futile, yet a journey that had to be made. For as Andrea grew up she realized she must be a child of that much used phrase, the holiday romance. Little of her life had been as romantic as her parents' brief encounter. Her mother had gone away when she, Andrea, was three. Whenever she had asked her doting grandparents about her mother, they had said, 'We won't talk about that now dear,' so Andrea never knew how her mother had died. All she knew for certain was that to raise the subject upset her beloved Gran and Grampa. So she never did. Just as she knew they'd never had any contact with her father. She knew her father was from Rhodes when she found a small photo in a book. It was dated the year before she was born, and had 'my man' in black ink on the back. The sign in the picture said 'Kleoboulos Tomb' in English and Greek. So she had gone to the encyclopaedia in school and found out where Kleoboulos' tomb was: Lindos, Rhodes Island, Greece. She had not shown the photo to her Gran. It was the only secret she ever kept from her. It was her photo, a bit of her life that no one talked about. Despite the love and care of her maternal grandparents, Andrea harboured a longing to find her father. Longing to find him and learn about her Greek heritage.

Now at last on the plane, she was both excited and nervous. She had flown twice before when Auntie Marian had taken her to Spain with her family, but this was different. She wanted to shout out loud that she was Greek and was going home, but knew she would not. She had no intention of making extravagant gestures but wanted to connect in some way. To tell someone she was not an ordinary tourist.

'My father is Greek,' she found herself confiding to the elderly man sitting next to her in the plane. She hoped he was Greek and that this could be her first proper conversation with a Greek person, even if limited by linguistic differences. He was not. As English as anyone you could meet at home. He had been to Greece before as he had been in the R.A.F. and had been posted to Cyprus. Andrea did not know Cyprus was Greek but she did not say so. Her grandfather had always told her to never volunteer her ignorance. The R.A.F. man had not been to Rhodes before, and therefore not to Lindos, but that was where he was spending his holiday.

The cabin crew came then with the drinks. The nice man passed her a little bottle of white wine and a plastic glass, and insisted on paying, but it was free the stewardess said. He quite quickly fell asleep, and did not wake till their meal was delivered. Andrea thought the meal was quite good considering that a roll and cheese, trifle dessert, fresh fruit salad, knife, fork, milk and sugar, as well as cottage pie, had all been packed into such a small box. After her cup of coffee she fell asleep for a short time and then the seat belt 'ping' went and they were landing. She looked out of the window into the night sky, already changing colour on the horizon, then down to the dark blue sea. Scattered in the sea were small islands and tiny sailing boats dotted about, picked out by the light of the moon. For a moment she thought they might land in the sea, then suddenly the lights of the beach appeared with tall hotel buildings strung along the shoreline. They landed with a bit of a jolt. At last she was in Greece.

From Lindos With Love

When she reached the exit door, she hesitated at the top step, wanting to stay and breathe in the sultry air, Greek air. She wanted this feeling to go into her head and therefore her memory. She almost started to cry but everyone was in a rush to get off so in no time at all she was down the metal steps and into the bus.

Strap hanging in a crowded transfer bus was not really part of her image of arriving, but everyone was laughing and joking, in Greek and English and she was sure she heard some Italian. Soon they were in line to get their passports checked. The R.A.F. man was next to her again and he seemed to know some people in the queue already, the two girls in their thirties and an older rather posh lady.

'This is Andrea, she is also going to Lindos,' he offered on her behalf. 'Kim, Beth and Miss Wallis.'

'No, no, please call me Ruth,' the older lady corrected the man Andrea now knew as Max.'

Once through the formalities they looked for their holiday representative. Tanya stood back from the crowd a little and held aloft a small sign with a picture of a shark. She also wore the bright pink waistcoat they had been told to look for. She already had a small group around her, and her anxious frown changed to a broad smile when she saw the five of them heading in her direction.

'Mr. Thompson, Mr. Henderson, you have independent bookings so please wait just outside the airport doors for a moment whilst I get everyone else ticked off the coach transfer list.'

Andrea was a little reluctant to leave the safety of her new-found friendship. She gave Max a brief wave before following the rest to the coach. Her case safely stowed in the luggage hold by the driver, she clambered on to the transfer bus. A lady patted the empty seat next to her and she gratefully sat down. Somehow she did not want to be alone when she got to Lindos. All her thoughts about coming here were soon to be a reality. For longer than she could remember she had wanted to cry for her mother, and sometimes she did. Not that she could remember her mother, but she cried for the one in her imagination. The one that shone out from photos, the one with the long copper blonde hair and green eyes, just like her.

'I'm going to Lindos as well. My granddaughter is getting married there,' the lady told Andrea.

'The wedding is not 'til Saturday and I do not like to sit on the beach all day, so I have booked into a craft holiday. It will save the family wondering what to do about me. They would not want to leave me sitting in the flat, although I am quite capable of looking after myself.'

Andrea did not say anything about her own intentions, somehow it did not seem the right time or place, however kind the lady was. Instead she told her about Gran and Grandpa, and that they said they would not worry about her travelling to Greece on her own if she was staying with a group of nice people on a craft holiday.

The coach drove out of the airport and off along wide roads. To her surprise they were on a normal dual carriageway with traffic lights and road signs. Not that Andrea was sure what she expected, but normal roads made her feel a bit less nervous. Even when the road narrowed, twisted and turned a bit through gaps in the mountains she felt relaxed and happy.

The air in the coach was fresh and she was wide awake and excited. Now and again they could see the sea and a low light was beginning to spread over everything. Gradually, as dawn began to break, the light flashed in silver beams and a pink glow showed over the sea. The road wound around the mountain passes, sometimes on the coast, more often in the bare rocky countryside. Two breath-taking bays, around another bend and then it happened.

The view was like something from a storybook. White houses rose above a mirror flat sea, and above the houses the rocks led up to the Castle of the Knights. This was Lindos. And there, on a long arm of rock that formed the bay, was the tomb of Kleoboulos, just as it was shown in the encyclopaedia. Andrea wanted to cry out loud, 'I did it, I did it, I got here.' But managed not to.

The elderly lady was crying, softly, tears on her cheeks.

SUNDAY MORNING

Kim and Beth fell into the apartment, dumped their cases and sprawled onto the beds.

'That's settled then, I have the one by the wall,' Kim announced.

'Sleep where you like as long as you shut up and sleep,' her sister replied, her head already deep into a pillow.

'I need a cup of tea first. Want one?'

'Where are you going to get tea at five in the morning?' Beth groaned.

'Here, it's all here. Tea, coffee, sugar, corn flakes with bits in, bread rolls, marmalade, all you need except egg and bacon.'

'I don't want egg and bacon. I just want to go to sleep. Well, I did just want to sleep but now I am awake I will have tea and a slice please.'

'A slice of what?' Kim asked, but as yet she had not put the kettle on to boil.

Beth got up, turned the tap on to let it run a bit, and filled the kettle.

'A slice of whatever there is in that goodie box, to have a bite of something with the tea.'

'Are you making the tea then?' Kim asked her sister, and in reply a loo roll, also from the box, went sailing through the air.

They took their tea out onto the veranda and watched the sun continue to rise, making the white buildings look a pale pink and the sky streak with orange. The air was still and warm.

'This will do us great for a few days. It was a good idea to come back to Rhodes, and we never got to see this bit before. Well, if we did I don't remember.'

'Do you mean Lindos or the sunrise?'

'Don't be smart at this time in the morning, but I expect it was both, or neither, or however you say it.'

'I say we get a couple of hours shuteye as we have to be at the house by lunch time; well, by one o'clock, if we want some food and a drink to start the week. There's no point in looking like wrecks when we get there.'

Their tea and biscuits finished, they gave each other a hug, pulled off the clothes they had been travelling in and got underneath the crisp white sheets. They were asleep in seconds.

THE CAPTAIN'S HOUSE

The group had been invited to a brunch in the courtyard of Tanya's house. Walking through the village they took a left fork past the church. It was left again and a short flight of steps later you were outside an old wooden door. The open door led into a courtyard, the ground decorated in traditional style with fish and boat designs picked out in black and white pebbles. Long tables were spread with a mixture of Greek and English buffet food, including cheese and spinach pies and bowls of salad with tomatoes, beetroot and feta cheese. The olive oil was left at the side. Mini quiches filled with onion and others with bacon looked inviting.

Ken, the chef, was unscrewing a jar of onion marmalade and explaining what was in it and had tiny wooden spoons for them to sample before adding it to their plates. Ken was everything one would wish a chef to be, expansive in height and girth, and happy to explain what each dish consisted of. His friend Tony, also from the north of England before moving to Rhodes, helped with handing out cutlery and making sure everyone had a seat to sit on.

There were no formal introductions. Tanya moved amongst the group, stopping to chat here and there, but otherwise everyone just behaved as though they had known each other back in England. Max gravitated towards Rob, being the only man there until Miles arrived. Even then they stayed by the drinks table, not that they were drinking, but they took responsibility for helping the ladies refill their glasses. Miles suggested they look inside the house, assuring Max that they would be quite welcome to do so, and Rob was so pleased to be getting a guided tour. Not that there was much space for a tour, just one large room, it seemed. But, it was a room of almost manorial proportions, Miles pointed out the decorated ceiling, with its birds and leaves still as clear as when first painted three hundred years ago.

'Pirates were the main fear at the time and there is a loose block up there where money and jewellery were kept,' Miles explained.

One half of the length of the room was taken by a wooden platform, and on that, at both ends, were raised beds. Storage was underneath, Miles pointed out. High above were gothic shaped windows that overlooked the courtyard. The floor was made of the same black and white pebbles in intricate designs, just as the courtyard had been. Once again outside, Max declined the offer to go up the steps to the Captain's Room, which looked out over the town on one side and the sea on the other. Rob was fascinated by it all and stayed there quite a while, looking over the red tiled rooftops, working out his bearings in relation to other buildings he had seen earlier in the day.

Max saw Ruth was standing alone and went to talk to her. 'How are you enjoying your first day in Lindos?' he asked politely.

'Oh, very much, thankyou. I did not think I was hungry but everything looked so good,' she smiled at him and shrugged her shoulders.

'I know exactly what you mean, and I only intended to take one glass of wine but...' they laughed about their over indulgence.

'I don't think we ought to mention this. They may label us the glutton and the alcoholic,' Ruth added, still laughing.

'I do not mind what anyone says about me, but no one would say anything unkind to you, I am sure. Not that I am alcoholic by the way, but I do enjoy the occasional drink. Do you?' Max asked.

'Very occasional, in fact I think I have had my quota for the week already,' and again they laughed at the silly banter they had established.

Mel felt rather out on her own, but she often did at these events, which was why in normal circumstances she much preferred to be an organiser than a guest. She was relieved when Heather came and sat beside her on the wooden bench.

'The food looks so tempting, but I am not fully recovered from the journey,' Heather said, and Mel agreed. But nevertheless they were both tempted and did enjoy what they chose to eat.

Andrea stayed close to Margaret and Margaret did not mind. The girl was bound to feel a bit lost to start with, and, if she lives with her grandparents, she'll feel more comfortable with me, she thought. Gradually everyone thanked Tanya and drifted off to their respective accommodation.

STEVE AND ANDREA

The group were to meet again at seven for a pre-dinner drink, and Steps Bar was the venue. At Tanya's request Steve had arranged plates of nibbles, which saved them ordering starters at the restaurant. Most were pleased to keep the costs down in this modest way.

As was the norm, the older members of the group arrived first. If the invitation was for seven, then they got there at seven, not twenty to eight. Aware that she had not really spoken to Melanie, Ruth went over to sit beside her once she had ordered a drink at the bar. She would have waited and taken her gin and tonic, but Steve insisted she be seated and he would bring it to her. She was fascinated that the younger element drank from the bottle. What next? She thought, but said nothing, just accepted that she was behind the times and, not for the first time in recent years, was glad to be so. Mel seemed to be between the two cultures. By her clothes she was used to mixing in smart circles, yet even she had her beer in a bottle. It must be a London thing, Ruth decided, not knowing that Mel last went to London on a day trip with the school, and her wardrobe was mostly from charity shops.

Busy putting a fresh supply of Amstel into the fridge, Steve did not notice Andrea when she first entered the bar. She had walked straight out onto the balcony to look at the astounding view. Rob, who had followed her in, crossed the bar also to look out onto the square with the sea beyond and the Acropolis above. She was almost hidden as he stood at her shoulder. Rob surprised himself as, usually quite shy in the company of a young woman, he asked Andrea what she would like to drink.

'A coke but no ice please, Rob,' she replied but barely turned to look at him when she spoke. For despite the panoramic view in front of her, Andrea's attention was drawn to an elegant woman getting out of a taxi. What had caught her eye was not the stylish pale mauve suit or the perfectly cut bob, but a small pink suitcase that the taxi driver had placed on the pavement. The woman seemed to ignore both the suitcase and the driver who was standing patiently waiting for his fare. Now, the lady was looking out over the orchard towards the sea. Andrea guessed she was Italian, as she had noticed they were always so smart and expensively dressed, even if only going to the beach. Then before Rob returned with her drink Andrea saw the taxi driver pick up the pink suitcase and offer the lady in the mauve suit his arm. They went off together towards the village, chatting.

'Sorry it took so long, everyone was ordering at once, and not that I know a lot about bars, but for a barman he did not seem that quick. Liked to talk to everyone at the same time as getting the drinks. I expect that is Greece in holiday mood, and we are not in a hurry are we?'

'Thank you, Mr. Thompson, I did not notice the time I was too busy being nosy watching a lady get out of a taxi,' Andrea laughed at herself. 'This is a great place to watch the people, and that is the Acropolis up there, I guess?'

Rob did not need a second invitation to regale this willing pupil with a history of the Acropolis. Andrea had a vivid imagination and could see the Knights in full regalia, riding on horseback up the steep slope. Now the path served the donkeys carrying tourists to the top of the cliff.

'Do you think there would have been donkeys in Lindos all those years ago? There were donkeys in Jerusalem, and the Knights came here a long time after Jesus, didn't they?' Andrea asked.

'Certainly,' Rob replied. He was used to talking to young people and glossed over the last part of the question. 'All the food and drink would have to be brought up to the castle on the top, to the knights who lived there and the servants who worked there, just as we have to take a bottle of water with us.' Rob was pleased to have a conversation with anyone interested in the lost world of the Knights of St. John and Andrea was brought up in such a way that she would have stayed to listen to what the man had to say even if she had not been interested. She found the information fascinating.

Only when Rob went to the bar to get himself another beer and a glass of coke for Andrea, did Steve notice the girl with copper coloured hair. 'Not that unusual, really', he said to himself. Girls colour their hair how they wish these days, he thought, and he had seen that sort of burnished red before. Not often, but often enough. Yet it never failed to take his breath away for a second or two. Never failed to bring memories of years ago flashing into his head. He was busy for the next while, getting everyone their required drink. It always took longer when you had a group of people who were not used to going into a bar. The ladies needed time to consider the choice on offer. At last everyone was happy and chatting, and he could turn his attention to four Scandinavian tourists waiting patiently at the end of the counter. Steve had a basic vocabulary of about twenty Greek words, which served him quite well. Few non-Greeks could speak the language, yet most of the world had a smattering of English. The outcome of this was many of his customers assumed he was a Greek who spoke rather good English. And many congratulated him on this achievement to the quiet amusement of 'mine host.' If the occasion merited it he told them he was English and then the conversation took a rather predictable turn as to the 'when' and 'why' of an Englishman with a bar on a Greek island, but not today, as besides wishing to concentrate on his booked party, he now had other things on his mind.

Once all his customers had been served he left his post and went towards the balcony. He needed to have a closer look at the young woman with the long copper hair. Steve had two daughters; he knew the tell-tale signs when hair had been dyed. Rob was still standing behind Andrea as she leaned onto the balcony rail, but Steve was already prepared to deal with that situation. Cloth in hand he addressed Rob,

'Just a moment, sir, I think the table may need a wipe over before you sit down.'

As he had guessed Rob immediately moved away to allow this bit of basic good housekeeping. Steve found himself staring into beautiful green eyes. Eyes exactly like those that had first captivated him more years ago than he cared to remember. Even the voice was familiar. The faint Devonian burr reached his ears as Andrea addressed him.

'Just how lucky are you, with a view like that every day?'

Steve knew how lucky he was, and looking at her

thought how lucky he might have been if things had worked out differently.

'I don't think we were introduced,' he began.

'Well, I know you must be Steve,' she replied.

There the conversation had to end for the moment. He walked quickly back to the bar as he had seen the Danish guys already waiting for a refill. The thing was, what should he do now? He knew she would be here till the end of the week, so he need do nothing at the moment. On the other hand, it was amazing how quickly the days flew past. Would saying nothing for a few days make a difference? He hated dilemmas. The bar cleared as the crafty group, as Steve always referred to Tanya's guests, left to go to the restaurant. His new Danish friends were staying up at Krana so promised to call in again the next day. Out of habit his first task was to collect all the glasses and wipe the tables. No one ever entered his establishment and found it untidy. He did the balcony, then the upper seating area and finally the low tables near the bar. He checked the seating, no drips or spills that he could see. There had been no children with ice cream for the last couple of hours.

For all its immaculate interior Steve had always made families welcome. Just the bar to wipe down now and all would be in order again. Two young Italians came in, ordered a frappe each and walked through to the balcony. He made the drinks and delivered them to their table, with the obligatory glass of water, and he finally had a moment for himself. He opened his wallet and looked at the picture that was always tucked into the corner. There was no mistake. He took his mobile phone out of his pocket. Time to phone a friend.

'*Kalispera*, my friend. I have a young lady here with green eyes, amazing red hair and a soft Devonian accent. I think we need to talk.' That was more than enough to leave on an answer phone.

HENRIETTA

Long legs and a pencil slim skirt had been Henrietta's *'mode d'appareil'* for almost half a century, and low sports cars her mode of transport, so she was well practiced in the art of exiting a taxi elegantly. Nevertheless she waited until the driver walked around the car to assist her.

'Well of all the places,' she said more to herself than to Mihalis, the taxi driver. She walked to the rail at the edge of the square and drew in a breath of amazement. So this is Lindos, she thought, suddenly aware that she was standing next to a bespectacled bronze bust, and placed her hand on the worn and shiny edifice, as so many tourists did.

'Well hello, fella, I guess we will be seeing quite a lot of each other in the next few days.' Her small pink suitcase was now on the ground beside her and the taxi driver waited anxiously for his fare. There was a queue of people and he wanted to get his next customer while he could. Oblivious of anyone's needs or intentions but her own, she continued to look at the wonderful scene before her. Directly below was an orchard with the remains of the lemon and orange crop still clinging to the branches. Then across the red tiled roofs of white washed houses lay the turquoise sea. The arms of the harbour reached out to two small rocky islands, guardians of the entrance. From where she stood you could not see the long sandy beaches, but you knew they were there. A light mist sat atop the mountains of Turkey.

'Oh my goodness, so this is Lindos?' she exclaimed to Mihalis, who was still waiting.

'Yes Madam, this is Lindos. It is just like this for over three hundred days of the year. The sun shines on white houses, orange, lemon and olive trees and a blue, blue sea.'

Mihalis loved Lindos but, like most of his fellow Lindians, he had spent some years abroad. He had appreciated the experience, as it had cured him of any wanderlust for the rest of his life. More importantly it had given him a complete command of the English language, albeit from a Detroit car factory, which the girls found fascinating. America was also a good topic of conversation as he drove passengers from the airport to their hotels.

'Where are you staying, Madam? Is anyone meeting you? 'Do you know your way?'

'Hell, no one is meeting me, that's for sure, and I have no place booked yet, but I guess you have a cousin who has just the ideal apartment for an American dame who wants a view of the sea and not too many steps to climb.'

Mihalis smiled, this lady either knew Greece or Italy or some other Mediterranean country well. 'My sister, actually, has a beautiful place. One moment while I park up and I will take you.'

The taxi queue was forgotten. This was a far more profitable situation than a ten euro trip to Kalathos, and he had had enough of Rhodes for one day. His sister did have very good apartments, overlooking the sea, and if these were full, there was, as the lady had predicted, his cousin.

Henrietta was quite pleased with herself. If she did not find Maxim Henderson this was a nice place to take a vacation anyway. She had no intention of going stateside just yet, and London was a winter city in her opinion, like New York. Theatre, shopping, lunches with friends, that sort of thing. She was pleased to leave it behind her for the moment. Yes, this would do fine. 'This would do fine,' was all she seemed to demand of anywhere she lay her head these days. How stupid could you get travelling to Greece to look up an old friend? Not even a friend really, just an acquaintance. There was no place she had really called home since Vernon had died. She had done everything wrong at that time. She had sold the house because she could not envisage staying there without him, but had yet to find anywhere as good as their rambling bungalow in Oak Harbour.

Now she was here, in Greece, for the flimsiest of reasons. It had been one of those Washington dinner parties. She was there with Vernon, Max with his wife. Vernon really liked the guy and had invited them to stay for a week or two. She had liked Max as well but found his wife a bit clingy. You know the sort, seemed to think the whole world was after her man. Yet charming as he was, there was nothing to suggest that he might roam, even given the chance. But experience had taught her that you never know. Even her dear, shy, quiet, hardly-said-a-word-in-company, Vernon, had been involved in a sordid affair once. She always shivered at the thought of the only bad time in their thirty-year marriage. How she had changed since those days. She wondered if coming here to find Max was a last attempt at finding a decent man to share her life. What a crazy thought, but it was the truth, she had to admit.

Well, Max Henderson or no Max Henderson, this was the place to be for a week or two, or even a month or two. Though having got this far she was curious to know if her informant was right and Max was here in Lindos. Well certainly her source of information was right on one score. Lindos was the sweetest little place. All the amenities of life: taxis, restaurants and sea views. It was a humdinger of a Greek village. She could hear enough English speaking voices around her to assure her she would not be struggling with the language. Anyway she could always take the taxi driver's number, he would help her at any time, she was sure. Nice man.

Mihalis picked up the small pink suitcase and offered his arm. 'First we will call on my sister. She has beautiful en-suite studios overlooking the sea. If you prefer a lounge and a separate bedroom then we will go along to my cousin Tsambika, who has apartments.'

Mihalis had seen them all come and go over the years, and guessed that here was a reasonably wealthy American widowed lady, travelling alone, wanting to experience the rural Greek life. But not too rural and the accommodation had to have an en-suite bathroom and shower, a view of the sea and a handy taverna that served Italian dishes at low prices; plus a friendly taxi driver on hand to transport her where ever she chose to go. No problem. Henrietta knew what he was thinking and knew he was right. What he did not know was that she had chosen to come here to Lindos on the very slim chance of meeting one particular man.

It had been only a few days ago when she and Deana had been lunching in Dickens and Jones. Not the most upmarket of London meeting places, but one that suited them both. Henrietta wanted to browse Liberty's to find some 'made in England' gifts to take back to friends in America and Deana just wanted an excuse to shop and lunch out in town. They had met for coffee, and wandered around the stores near the crossroads of Oxford Street and Regent Street.

How things had changed; you would not know you were in England any more. Naturally London had always been a cosmopolitan city, but now there was hardly a cut glass accent to be heard. Although there was still the cockney twang from the street traders, it seemed quite funny to turn and see a beautiful young girl in a sari selling souvenirs of London, counting out the customers change with, 'There yer ar misses,' tagged on the end.

It was when at lunch, relaxing with their purchases, that Deana mentioned Maxim.

'Honey, am I right in thinking you and Vern were in Washington when that nice English Air Force Officer gave the after dinner speech at one of Harry's charity events in the nineties? I know you were because Vern got in there first and invited him down to your place. I remember Babs Oldfield being furious about it.'

'Deana, I could hardly remember where we were from day to day at that time. Vern had his fall from grace around then and my head was such a mess over it all. But now you mention it I do recall this very tall guy and his clingy wife, very English but had a French or German name I recall.'

'Henderson, how English can you get? But you are

right on one count his first name is Max. I expect that could be French or indeed German. Anyway, do you remember him?'

'Yes, I do recall, Vernon asked them to stay for the weekend, I think he thought it would offer us a bit of diversion. He was great but she was hard work, and would not go anywhere unless he went as well. Why are you thinking of him after all these years?'

Henrietta could remember more about him than she cared to disclose to her friend. But for a change she was being discreet.

'Well I was looking through some old photos and saw one with his name on the back. I checked him out on one of those websites. It seems his wife died a couple of years ago, and he has retired of course. It gave an email address so I sent a note and had a lovely reply.'

Deana dabbed her mouth with the serviette. 'He is off on holiday, some sort of art course on a Greek island, but will be in touch when he returns. I was thinking you could always delay your trip back to the states and meet him here or, rather a long shot I know, but what is to stop you going off to this island and bumping into him? Stranger things have happened and you never know where it might lead. No need to dismiss all Englishmen just because one turned out to be a rotten egg.'

Henrietta had forgotten that Deana knew all about her love affair with Bertie. How could she have been so lonely as to walk into that situation? So lonely she had been willing to believe anything, and she certainly believed him. English upper crust she had been led to understand, just down on his luck at the moment, waiting for a business deal to materialise, but it didn't. By then she had introduced him to her friends, and said how happy she was, and how she never expected to find love again at her age. And now she knew she had not found love, just a chancer on the lookout for a meal ticket. But until her dying day she would never admit that in one small secret corner of her heart she actually did not care if he had been a fraud. Not telling her the truth was the issue. For while it lasted it had been good, and fun, and made her realise that life had to go on. Oh, what the hell, that was yesterday's news. After all these years would any of her pals even remember him, apart from Deana?

Yes, sadly she had changed, and she had changed even more after her fling with Bertie. She knew she was now what her friends would call a 'man eater'. If she fancied a guy she made it clear, and she had the wherewithal to follow her inclination. There was very little that could not be bought. It was not what she wanted out of life, but if love and tenderness were never to be hers again, then she was damned if she was going to sit in a rocking chair waiting for the Grim Reaper.

'You do think of the craziest things but you are quite right, stranger things have happened, and what is there to lose?' She smiled and raised her glass of warm wine.

So, with nothing to lose but a few spare dollars,

Henrietta rang her travel agent and booked an open ticket to Rhodes Island, Greece. Now here she was. She took Mihalis's arm, unaware that her arrival in Lindos had been the centre of attraction to those of the craft group looking down from the balcony of Steps Bar.

KALYPSO

They walked together in a rather straggly group behind Tanya and Miles from Steps Bar to Kalypso Restaurant. Having gone to the church in the centre of the village, and turned right at the corner shop, they were led along the main street. Turning right again into a side street they were surprised to be entering what seemed to be another Captain's house.

Once inside they could see the same black and white pebbled floor. The room was spacious and Rob wondered if it had previously been an open courtyard. There was a collection of china plates on the walls, and the tables were covered with snow-white linen. They were shown a long table set for twelve and soon made themselves comfortable. Tanya explained the menu to those who were uncertain what to order, but as with most British tourists on their first evening meal in Greece they all chose either lamb chops or steak, ordinary British fare. Kiki, the owner just smiled. She had been in Lindos all her life, she had seen it all before. Above them on the rooftop terrace there was a wedding party with a violinist playing and the music drifted down, lively and authentically Greek. It added to the atmosphere for Tanya's group, who seemed to be chatting away to each other as though they were old friends. Tanya breathed a sigh of relief. This week will be a particularly good one, she thought. She glanced across and caught Miles' eye, he smiled and raised his glass.

Dressing for dinner the first night always presented guests with a problem. No one wanted to appear old fashioned or stuffy, but equally no one wanted to look as though they had dressed down for what might be a smart venue. Rob and Max had chosen white long-sleeved shirts, leaving them unbuttoned at the neck. Both had a tie in their respective pockets, just in case they had misjudged the dress code. So, when they had met Miles at Steps and he was dressed in the same manner they relaxed. Problem and protocol solved. For the ladies it would normally be an age division, and, as expected, both Ruth and Margaret wore smart three-quarter length floaty dresses, with a cardigan on their shoulders, just in case. But the summer fashion of full-length dresses in multi coloured cotton meant that the young people were also elegantly attired. And very pretty they all looked, each in their own way. They did justice to the care and attention Kiki and her staff put into making an evening at Kalypso something special.

Much of the conversation was of the 'where do you come from' type, but it was obvious that most people were still tired from their journey the evening before and, once coffees had been served, Max, Ruth and Margaret made their excuses. It felt strange to him to leave the two ladies, not offering to escort either one or both of them home. But he was very tired and Max knew when he had hit his limit and dare not push himself too far. The doctor had said, 'Stay within your limits and you will be fine.' So he bid them good night and rather sadly wandered off.

At the corner by the church Margaret and Ruth assured each other that they knew their way back to their respective accommodations, wished each other a good night's rest and parted company.

MEL AND CLAIRE TALK

Mel had deliberately not gone down to the beach-side taverna for breakfast. She preferred to make a coffee in her room. That and a cigarette was all she needed in the mornings. So it really annoyed her that when she took her coffee onto the balcony someone else was already sitting on one of the white seats.

Claire turned towards Mel. 'Join me if you wish but please don't talk for a while. Sorry, but I can't cope with polite conversation this early in the morning.' It was only seven o'clock.

'Neither can I. If left alone I am fine for the rest of the day, but I must have a quiet half hour first,' replied Mel.

They smiled at each other and stopped talking. They shared the ashtray. They sat like this, in the warm morning sun, for about ten minutes; quiet and peaceful.

Then church bells clanged and they jumped at the sudden intrusion of sound. Then they laughed when the dogs barked and the donkeys brayed, and the ice was broken.

'So much for a quiet half hour, another coffee?' offered Claire.

'That would be good, especially if I don't have to move off this seat to get it.' She laid her head back onto her clasped hands and sighed. This was certainly the way to start a Monday morning. At that moment she didn't particularly care if she did not make a card or paint a piece of glass all week. She just wanted to stay in the warm sun, with no one demanding her time or energy.

'Claire Montague,' Claire introduced herself as she returned with the coffee.

'Melanie, but I usually get called Mel. Are you here for the craft course or an independent visitor?'

'Well, I have signed up for the craft week, but I will see how it goes. If it gets too overpowering I will disappear I think.' Claire was already hedging her bets.

'Sorry to hear that. I have come just for the craft really, so I will attend everything as I can't afford to waste the experience,' Mel replied.

'Oh I didn't mean to sound so negative. I had a hundred and one problems to sort out before I came here, and not sure I can cope with a "jolly hockey sticks" atmosphere just yet,' Claire said in a softer voice.

Mel took another cigarette from the packet, lit it, and

then left the open packet and the lighter on the table, turned towards Claire. The unwritten code, inviting other smokers to take one if they wished.

'I know we are all very different in how we cope with stress, but time and time again I find that doing some sort of craft work takes your mind off problems. That is not to say they have gone away by the next day, but it gives you a break from worry.'

'Oh I certainly intend to see if it interests me. But I have a low threshold at the moment.' Claire was not in the habit of confiding to strangers. In fact she was not in the habit of confiding at all. She was shocked to realize how close to tears she was. 'Get a grip, you are just tired,' she admonished herself.

'There is so much to sort out before coming away that most women need a week to calm down, let alone start to get that holiday feeling.'

If Mel had noticed Claire's moment of distress she was wise enough to keep talking as though she had not. She knew that if there was one thing to set a woman off into tears it was a friendly voice asking if everything was all right. She also guessed that Claire was not the sort of person who would like to be airing her dirty laundry in a public place. And she was right.

Despite her momentary loss of composure Claire was not unaware of the other girl's tact in dealing with the situation.

'Thanks for that, I would have dissolved if you had

asked me if I was all right. Actually, I am OK, it's just tiredness. Well, that is not very fair of me, to tell the truth, I am just getting my act together after a break up. And now and again it catches up on you. You know what it is like.'

'Oh dear, sorry you have picked the wrong person to discuss men with. You see I have one of these boring lives. Met and married my childhood sweetheart, and although I do have moments of desperation when I want something new in my life, mostly it is me and the old man against the world.'

In spite, or maybe because of this declaration of inexperience Claire felt this strange compulsion to talk and explain things to Mel. She wanted to say who she was and why she was not so enthusiastic about the craftwork. She did not want to give Mel the impression of snubbing her interest.

'Well, I expect any happily married woman would say I deserved what has happened. I was having an affair with a married man,' Claire said, dropping her voice, with some feeling of shame. Claire was amazed at Mel's reaction to this statement.

'He was the married one, so it was him that was having the affair, I would think. I don't know the guy, but if you had not come along I bet it would have been someone else. Sorry, that sounds awful, not what I meant to say at all. I am sure he was glad you came his way and that he cared a lot about you, but most men seem to be the sort that will or the sort that won't. Have an affair, I mean.'

Claire took a long drag on her cigarette. 'To tell you the truth, I have never considered it that way and, when I do think about it, you're right. We went to lots of exhibitions, which meant weekends away. There were certain men you met year after year, and were always on their own, and talked about their wife and children. There were others who were always with an employee, but not always the same one, and by 'with' you know what I mean.'

Mel was glad she had not offended Claire. She liked the girl, and was hoping they would be friends, if only for the week. They had little enough in common except being more or less the same age, and smoking, and not eating breakfast. Mel recognised the pendant Claire was wearing as the Star of David, but these days people wore what they saw in the Argos catalogue, with scant thought to the significance of the design.

'We had better make a move or we will be late on the first day. We have to make a good impression,' Claire suggested. Having to give lots of briefings at work she knew how annoying it was to have people walking in late.

'True, and I was always taught that it was bad manners to keep someone waiting,' Mel said as she took the cups inside.

'Or to eat in the street, or remove your school beret,' Claire laughed. Both young women were more relaxed and happy now they had found a buddy on the course.

MARGARET REMEMBERS

'Oh what a beautiful morning,
Oh what a beautiful day.'

Tsambikos looked at her for some time. It was not unusual for people to return to Lindos, and the Lindians were very good at remembering faces, if not always names. He moved towards the slim, elderly lady and pulled a chair away from the table for her to sit down. He knew they had met before.

'What are you doing down here in the morning?' she chided him. For it was unusual for Tsambikos to be away from his main bar in the village. He gave her the broadest of grins as memories came flooding back.

'Margaret, where is Jack?' And as the cloud passed momentarily over her face, he guessed.

'Oh, gone for that big fried breakfast in the sky,' she laughed back at him. 'We can't hang around here forever you know. Have to make space for you young ones. I saw the children playing in the street. I can spot your lads anywhere, and isn't the eldest lad like his granddad?' Like many visitors to Lindos, those who return year after year, she and Jack had known the whole family.

Margaret was the first of the craft group to arrive for breakfast at Giorgos Two, a small taverna on Pallas beach.

'You are right, it is unusual for me to be here, but my brother and his wife are in Athens until tomorrow. What will you have this morning Margaret? Are you still on the croissants and jam?'

No, he did not remember what his clients ordered year after year but Margaret always placed a 'special' with him, it was a source of friendly contention between the couple, Margaret and Jack, every morning.

'I will, just for old times sake. I am here with the craft group and also for Tracy's wedding on Saturday.'

'I did not connect young Tracy and Tassos with you and Jack. Sorry, I had forgotten that she is your granddaughter. They all grow up so quickly. His family are Australian Greeks, from northern Greece originally, somewhere near where Socrates comes from I think. Now will you wait for the group and have juice or tea while you wait?'

'I will not wait an instant,' Margaret replied. 'Full

English, please, I am close to starving and I want to go for a walk before we settle down for the classes this morning. But you can wet a drop of tea and then tell me all the news while it is still quiet.'

He disappeared into the kitchen to place the order and returned to her table. 'I am sorry Jack is not with you. He was a good man, with a great smile for everyone, you must miss him a lot.'

'Well, you knew how it was with me and Jack. I talked for England and he was happy to say yea or nay, unless it was something important. So I still talk things over with him, and when he does not reply I call him a miserable old git and go to bed and put the TV on for company. But in the morning I have the answer to whatever was bothering me. Strange but true. Like, I don't think he is missing Tracy's wedding, here in Lindos. He will be here I know,' she said with a firm nod of her head.

'Shame everyone does not have the same attitude, Margaret, but I expect it depends on the marriage in the first place. Anyway, enjoy your breakfast and your wrapped croissant will be ready for you later. Don't go without it.'

Margaret offered to pay, as it was extra but Tsambikos brushed her offer away.

'Don't upset me now, I have a long day ahead,' he told her.

Within a few minutes, others, whom she recognised from last night as being part of the group, had arrived at the taverna. They waved and said, 'Good morning,' then sat at other tables. She was glad she had that few moments alone with Tsambikos. Strange, you spent just a few weeks every year in Lindos and families here seem to be a more important part of your life than neighbours in England. She knew it was not just her and Jack. If you sit in the main bar on Sunday or Thursday morning and watch the newly arrived people. They hesitate, not wishing to presume that they are remembered, but all smiles when greeted like old friends with both a hand shake and a brotherly hug. She noticed the young girl who had sat next to her on the coach last night. Andrea was looking so crisp and fresh this morning with a lemon sundress, and her hair tied back with one of those scrunched things. Margaret was delighted when Andrea came and asked if she may join her. Andrea ordered croissants and tea and they each asked how the other had slept last night.

'I was so tired you could have hung me on a clothes line and I would have slept,' Margaret said, exposing her northern roots.

Andrea agreed. Margaret decided against her walk, not wishing to go off and leave the young girl eating alone. People were funny about such things.

Tsambikos was now quite busy. He thought the girl too young to be on a craft week, but you never know.

There was something familiar about her, but with so many people passing through each season he dismissed it as his imagination. Then two more girls arrived, about ten years older he guessed, and a lot more streetwise, he thought, but very pleasant nonetheless. He could not imagine them sticking it out doing classes when the beach and its 'talent' became obvious. Then he was too busy taking orders to give the subject more thought.

Margaret poured herself another cup of tea. The morning craft session would not start till nine o'clock. She was glad she was up and about early as it had been lovely to sit and eat a leisurely breakfast. The sea was its usual azure blue and the waves lapped softly onto the sand. Fishing boats were pulled up out of the sea.

'Shrimp boats is a coming, way out on the sea,
Shrimp boats is a coming; they're coming to me.
Da de da de da de da de de da de da de de.'

For a moment Margaret was oblivious to the present hustle and bustle that was going on around her. Her mind was back in the past again. She was thinking of the first time she and Jack had come to Lindos. They were celebrating their silver wedding anniversary and taking the honeymoon they could not afford when they got married. All a bit silly really, but she had always fancied Greece. And with Lindos she was not disappointed. They had stayed in a studio called Poppy. It was supposed to be for four, but the girl had said they could have it, as it had not been let out that week. Rather more spacious than the one room they had booked. And you could see the sea from the top bedroom window. They had a perfect week. It was not long after all the palaver of Judith's wedding, so they both needed a break. From then on they were hooked. They had caught the Lindos bug and as years went on they progressed to two weeks in May and one in September, or occasionally two in September. Many people they knew at that time talked of moving over, but few actually did it. Jack had not bought their council house when they could have done, so had nothing to sell and move with. But Margaret knew they would not have done it anyway. She could not see how people upped sticks and left, hardly seeing their grandchildren, and not being on hand to help when their daughter wanted to go back to work.

It was some years before they got to know Tsambikos and his family. She and Jack were not ones for sitting in the bars. Then when there was television put on for the big football matches things changed. She did not mind watching the football on some evenings, and it was a jolly crowd that gathered there. No bad language, but she had enjoyed the early days best. With a jolt she came back to the present. Andrea was talking to her.

'Can we get to the big beach from here, is that path safe?' she asked.

'Oh quite safe, and we have time before our class

starts. I will show you how to come back up to Electra from that beach. A bit of a steep climb, but I am sure I can still make it,' Margaret told her. They waved to Tsambikos who was now busier than ever. Then Margaret remembered her wrapped croissant and went to the kitchen to get it. Armed with her customary mid-morning snack they set off.

The path between the two beaches was often quite tricky, and if you fell it was just a tumble into the shallow sea. But not what one would describe as dangerous. They soon stepped down on to the main beach and crossed the sand to the sea.

'Not exactly Morecombe, is it, love?' she said to Andrea but as Andrea had never been to Morecombe the irony was rather wasted.

'This is the most beautiful place I have ever seen. Ever, ever, seen.' Andrea was just standing and staring out over the bay, out over the blue sea to the rocks that stand guard at the harbour entrance. She was so enchanted by the scene in front of her she had yet to take in the Acropolis. 'How far does the tide go out,' she asked.

'I can't remember,' said Margaret, 'but you come and tell me when it happens.' By teasing Andrea she was only repeating the same joke that was played on her on her first visit. Andrea stopped every now and again to pick up a piece of pottery or polished glass that shone in the morning sun. Margaret suggested that it was time they turned back. As Andrea turned she saw the Acropolis above her and again was completely amazed by the beautiful fairy tale setting of the medieval battlements. Margaret showed Andrea the path past the little church in the field near the beach. It was many years since she and Jack had looked in the hidden churches scattered around the village. She made a mental note to take her new young friend on an exploratory trip. They climbed the steep steps to the Electra studios. Not for the first time that morning Andrea stood and looked in amazement. The spacious paved veranda looked over an enormous palm tree that grew from the garden below. Beyond the gardens a wide valley led down to the sea. Margaret had stayed in Electra some years before.

'*Kalimera, ti kanete?*' was Chrisanthi's warm greeting as she showed them the way down to a shaded lower patio where the class would be held.

Here the white garden tables were laden with jars and boxes containing almost every kind and type of pens, pencils, glue and glitter you could imagine. There was even a school protractor set waiting at each place, which reminded Margaret of Judith, then Tracy, doing their homework on the kitchen table. And now here she was in Lindos for Tracy's wedding.

'Oh Jack, If you could see me now,' she smiled, for she knew he could. There was no doubt in her mind about that.

'I am sitting here, but choose for yourself, dear,' she said aloud to Andrea. But Andrea was at her side in a flash.

'I'd rather sit near you if you don't mind?' she asked Margaret.

'Of course, dear, you will help me if I don't hear everything first time.' Margaret knew the importance of being needed. So, card-making it was.

MONDAY
FIRST LESSON

Mel and Claire did not have far to go from their studio rooms to the workshop venue. Some of the other people were also staying in the studios around the courtyard, but had been out for breakfast and were now wandering up the hill from the beachside taverna. Most had met on Sunday at the buffet lunch at Tanya's house, but Claire had not arrived until two in the morning and had slept in, and had been so tired that she had opted out of the evening meal at Kalypso. So when they arrived at the lower patio Mel introduced Claire to those she had yet to meet.

There were more seats than needed, giving the opportunity to move around and not to feel they were invading someone else's space if they changed tables. In true British fashion everyone was at the patio on time and ready to begin the day.

Tanya welcomed the group, '*Kalimera*, good morning, I hope you all slept well and found your way to Giorgios or Giorgios Two for breakfast?' There were mutterings of 'Yes, thankyou,' and 'Very well, thankyou,' from around the patio.

'The first thing is to acquire a folder. There are plenty on each table. And the next thing to do is to put your name on it and, if you wish, choose one of the small embellishment stickers as well. Into this folder please put anything you may need to see a project through. This includes any paper or embellishments for your chosen design. My stock is not limitless, and here, in Lindos, I cannot go off to Hobbycraft or Colemans in the high street and stock up again.' They laughed at the thought.

'So, once you have planned what you are going to do, take enough paper, card, whatever you need to finish. Then put back the surplus, even quite small scraps can have a use. Nothing is wasted. Save another tree and all that.'

She then spent a short time going through the basics of folding and scoring card, and using standard sizes, unless you intended to make envelopes as well. Tanya showed them the bone used for scoring. Having said all that, she told the group that they were adults, and if they had a favourite item at hand which they preferred, then that was their choice.

'I am glad you said that,' Mel piped up, 'I was beginning to feel guilty at using the remote control to press in the folds on my cards.' They all laughed and the formality was broken.

Tanya had long ago deduced that by far the best way for adults to learn was to have various examples at hand. If people knew what they were aiming to achieve, most of the time they could work out how to get there. The first card was fairly simple. Nothing succeeds like success, her aunt had explained.

'For what we are going to do now you will need to have a piece of plain A5 card but for other times do not feel you have to re-invent the wheel. There are plenty of ready-made card blanks available. This morning I want you to first experiment with borders, starting with a simple strip down the left side.' She held up a card for all to see, then another with two borders on it.

'You can see how this immediately changes the way the card looks. You may be happy with one border, but try two or three. This is your sample card so fold it so each section looks like the front. Then start on a new page and try a gold or silver line diagonally across a corner, repeat this at various levels. Experiment. See which you prefer. And finally, using another face of the card, put a border all round, or make a picture frame or window. There are plain borders or chains or some that look like waves, but it is better to keep it simple to start with, then, after coffee, we will move on to using your choice of

From Lindos With Love

border to make a presentable card.'

The chairs and a table were set aside for coffee, so that spills did not happen where it mattered, and it was up to people to help themselves. Tanya interrupted briefly with a short explanation of embellishments, and showed them the sheets of lettering. Some were surprised and pleased to find 'happy birthday' and 'best wishes' in one strip.

'So to put "from" and "with love" will not be a problem,' Tanya explained, 'but to say "from Lindos with love" will take a little skill.'

Those that were getting on quite quickly were given an instruction sheet and a straight A4 card. This is an easy but very effective variation, Tanya told them. Divide the card in three, then cut off a piece of cheese, any size you like from two thirds of the card. You can see how effective it is particularly with this card that has one side darker than the other, showing the two tone effect. Now all you need to do is to decorate. But first find an envelope to make sure it will fit into one available, she reminded them. By the end of the morning everyone had chosen the border styles they preferred and added embellishments and in no time at all at least two presentable cards were completed.

At lunch time people left when they were ready as Tanya thought nothing was more infuriating than needing another few minutes to finish a project and being asked to pack away. This was Lindos, not an evening class at the local tech. Lunch was not provided, except for the welcome buffet on Sunday. This gave a longer mid-day break and more scope for the guests to go to the beach, look around the shops, or take a siesta before returning for the late afternoon session. After all it was a holiday.

By now, having had most of Sunday at leisure to explore, her group had grasped the general layout of Lindos and could find their way from one focal point to another. As Kim had told Beth, 'It's quite simple really. Go downhill to the beach and uphill to the village.' The fact that you had to go 'up' to leave the main square before going down to the long beach was totally lost on Kim and the small beach was through a maze of narrow lanes and up a few steps before descending. Only St. Paul's Bay was a straight, well almost straight, road down to the sea and yet many tourists came and went from Lindos never having explored the bay and its tiny church. And even fewer discovered Dimitris' kantina on the smaller St. Paul's beach.

Tanya used the five o'clock sessions for snippets of information rather than demonstrate a new project. She did not want any guests rushing from the beach in case they missed some major part of the course. She had plenty of printed sheets to hand out, knowing that some might not make that evening session at all. So it was in this five 'til six-thirty time slot that she spoke about stamping and decoupage. Other card samples used paper tole, quilling strips and embroidery stitches. It also gave her time to help anyone who had not really grasped that morning's session. And they were all welcome to photograph or print copies of anything they wished from her impressive collection. Tanya found it interesting to see who would actually take advantage of all the instruction on offer. Not always whom she thought from the information on the booking forms. After all it was a holiday and, as long as everyone went home happy at the end of the week, Tanya was happy. Well, satisfied with her efforts at least.

Although it was too early to make judgements, the dedicated crafters seemed to be Mel, Heather, Beth, but not her sister, Kim, and Margaret, who Tanya guessed could teach them all a thing or two but was too polite to say so. Ruth had very little skill considering she had been a school teacher! And Andrea seemed to think she was still at school. Tanya had been a bit concerned when Rob had offered to take her up to the Acropolis but Miles had said she had no need to be. Rob was just a decent single guy, hardly interested in picking up an eighteen-year-old. Anyway, Miles had taken Andrea and Heather to the 404 Bar last night, hardly a den of intrigue and iniquity.

After freshening up, Mel and Claire wandered along the centre of the village looking for a place to eat. As neither had had breakfast they were starving. They were caught by the charming smile of the doorman outside Delight. Up a flight of rather narrow stairs and they were on an open roof space and within a few minutes were enjoying a generous portion of quiche with a Greek salad, followed by the obligatory coffee and cigarette.

'You are so right, Mel, about how doing craft work takes your mind away from other things. I have not thought of Sam or work or anything much all morning,' Claire told Mel, who was turning out to be great company.

'Good for you,' Mel replied. 'I wish I could say the same, but I am here to learn as much as I can in a week. So I am afraid I am concentrating rather more than I should, in case I miss any vital bit of information.'

'You have no need to worry, your cards are beautiful,' Claire told her. 'Amazing how we all set out with the same instructions, yet end up with so many variations.'

Now that she was not fully occupied Claire suddenly found a sadness return that welled up in her throat and threatened to spill over into her eyes. Maybe it was the beautiful scenery, maybe the compassion shown by her new friend this morning. Whatever the reason for this drop in spirit, Claire felt the need to be on her own. So much had happened in the past month. Their coffees finished, they wandered back down towards the church.

'I am going to stop here and choose some postcards,' Mel said when she reached the corner shop, 'in the hope they might get to their destination before I return home.' So they separated, and Claire returned to her studio.

She did not sleep immediately but lay thinking about her life and how quickly it had all changed.

CLAIRE

The alarm clock rang and the radio came on with the seven o'clock news just as though it was any other normal working day. This was how Claire wanted her last week at Clear Elevations to be. As far as the rest of the world was concerned, everything was normal.

No one would ever guess that her life would never be normal again. Claire was always amazed at the power of a shower; amazed at how it washed the ache from her shoulders that a day of tension had produced, and now it washed away the discomfort caused by yet another restless night. Not that Claire was used to restless nights or accustomed to tension at work, but now everything had changed. On the surface it had been a day spent as usual, with her boss, Samuel Goldberg, at her elbow, poring over the drawings and pricing for a new project.

Only nothing was as usual with Sam any more. Nothing would ever be 'as usual' again. It seemed as though the whole ten years she had been with him had swept through her mind again last night.

'Ten years of your life wasted,' her mother had said when Claire had told her she was no longer with him. 'And what did I say to you when all this started.'

'Yes I know mother, you told me. Often.'

Her mother would have said a lot more, but the look on her child's face told her it was not the time to point out the obvious. Claire was taking more time than usual getting ready for work this morning. She put on the Jane Seymour underwear that had been a birthday present to herself only a month ago. 'If you need to feel extra good then start with a good foundation,' her mother had always told her. She took extra care with her make-up. The bright carmine lipstick suited her dark looks and she always swept her black curls high on her head for the office. She chose her apricot cotton blouse and navy suit. She occasionally wore grey but never went in for the new stripe that had become fashionable last year. Too masculine, she had thought. Look smart but not try too hard with the gender bending. Not when you were the only woman at that level of management, and certainly not if you expected the door to be held open for you and other little old-fashioned courtesies. A modern woman in a man's world she may be, but respect costs nothing and such behaviour from her colleagues meant it was easier to command the room when she gave presentations. And she was to give one today. Everything clear, questions answered. No one would know that it was over between her and Sam. She liked being tall in a man's world. It gave her that sense of being one of them, whilst a good perfume and what her mother always referred to as a good foundation, made sure she never became one of the boys. The petit 'little girl lost' look was not her style, not Claire. It never had been.

As she left the apartment this morning, try as she could, she was unable to lift her spirits. 'How long will it take?' she asked herself. 'How long before I can get this sinking feeling out of my stomach. To get where I no longer care?'

Strap-hanging on the Victoria line, her thoughts went racing back to her first years at Clear Elevations.

'Who is the new man?' her mother had asked when she first started.

'There is no new man, not anyone special,' she had replied. Her mother told her not to tell lies. Tell her to mind her own business if she liked, but no lies.

'Mum, it's not lies, it's just at this new job everyone dresses up more than at the other place. And you forget I am now a junior manager.' Her mother shrugged her shoulders.

'Claire, I'm a Jewish mother, for God's sake. If my daughter is seeing someone, I know. Believe me, I know. But you don't have to tell me. I just like to know what is happening in my own house before my neighbours do.'

'I do like this man at work, but he is married, with two children. So there is nothing in it, Mum. It's just he treats me like I know what I'm doing, asks my opinion about pricing the jobs, and plans for the new contracts. That's all, Mum.' Her mother was still not convinced, but hoped for Claire's sake, and the sake of his poor unfortunate wife, that things stayed that way.

Hard to imagine that that was ten years ago. She knew she had got the job with this company before she got the letter. She had wanted to move to where her degree in technical building studies was valued. Only this time, which would be her third job since leaving university, she had been confident enough at the interview to say so.

'I need to be involved with new research and to see a project through all the planning stages. If I spend any more time as a glorified typist my knowledge base will be out of date.' Brave words as she had already quit her last job, and the payment on her car was overdue. 'I saw your stand at the Earls Court trade fair last year. I really would like to work for your company if you will have me.'

Claire had done her degree thesis on stone cleaning. Not every girl's cup of tea, but Claire found it fascinating. The cleaning of the old London buildings had gone on around her for years. She loved the old places, and had watched as so many architectural features came alive from behind the dirt and grime of the city. She had been surprised to find that more harm than good had been done by the use of hard chemicals, and that now it was mostly plain water sprayed on to the facades. But even here the angles and intensity were a major issue and Clear Elevations specialized in that. She wanted both to continue to learn and to be able to use what she knew. Samuel Goldberg had suggested they consider Claire for a more senior post which would be becoming vacant the next month.

'If you accept our offer there will be no need to interview you again. I am sure everyone agrees we are happy with the impression you have made today.' he had said, and the interview panel nodded in approval.

Although Claire was still very wet behind the ears where men were concerned, she knew she would be working with Sam. There was this sort of conspiratorial feeling he gave her as he showed her out of the building. Later she was surprised other people did not seem to see his sincerity, just saw him as a demanding senior partner. And they did work well together. He was quietly spoken, with only a trace of his East End background showing in his voice. And perfect teeth. He did not smoke, not even the occasional cigar, so as he leaned over her shoulder looking at plans laid out on the table, there was no staleness that one came to expect from most of the men by the late afternoon. Although in his late forties he was slim and fit as any of the other men more than twenty years younger. Claire had only just started to smoke at the time and immediately stopped. She never quite understood why it was so easy then, and let her mother think it was her continual nagging on the subject that led her to totally quit.

It was about two years after joining the company that Sam mentioned the trade fair in Cologne. Not as big as Earls Court, but an important venue to be exhibiting in if you wished to stay up there as a force in the E.U. market. Germany had been cleaning and repairing the stonework of Cologne Cathedral for eight hundred years, and had an extensive research programme so knew quite a bit about the business. Also, so many different types of stone had been used in its construction almost all buildings were represented in this one magnificent project. Claire remembered reading about this when at university, but had never been there. And Sam had asked Claire to go. At first she thought she would be representing the company instead of him, so she was quite surprised to find him with an overnight bag when he met her at the airport with the tickets.

'Business is different in different countries,' Sam had explained to her on the flight over. 'You take a long lunch hour and go to a bar for a drink or two if in London or Dublin. But here you have short meetings, and dress for a formal dinner. But this first evening is informal and leaves everyone free to move around and renew acquaintances.'

Claire was pleased she had splashed out on the cocktail dress as well as a new suit and two new blouses.

The hotel room was spacious, rather better, she thought, than the rooms the company usually booked for their employees. Her boss had an adjoining room, but he had shown her how to lock the door on her side to ensure her privacy. For some reason she felt all this was unnecessary as they had worked together for two years. He was her boss, but also her friend. It would not embarrass her if he came into her room to talk. She was up extra early, not for breakfast, which was continental anyway, but to shower and dress at her leisure and be ready for the day ahead. Claire was surprised at the number of women in the building trade in Germany. So many people had come to talk to her, some in the same line of business and therefore part of the competition, but all friendly and making sure she felt welcome on the exhibition circuit. By the end of the first day she could go to the restaurant for a coffee and find new friends calling her to join their table. They all spoke impeccable English and laughed good-naturedly at her school German. She was so pleased with the compliments Sam gave her, how she handled the questions others put to her about the projects they had in hand and how she tactfully avoided some more probing visitors to the stand.

The day flew by and that evening she planned to wear a new long black velvet skirt with an emerald off-the-shoulder top she had bought at the hotel boutique.

'Get your hair done at the hotel,' Sam had suggested. Put it all on the account. That's what it's for.' She did not think there was anything wrong with her hair, but obviously he thought it could be improved on, so that evening she allowed the hotel stylist to clip up the back into a pleat and put spray onto the tendrils which fell in front of her ears. She felt good and knew she looked good. She was relaxed and happy and really enjoyed the champagne reception, a delicious meal, a few glasses of wine and some after dinner dancing in a softly lit ballroom. Claire had only seen settings like this in films, she never imagined herself being part of this world. If there was any reservation between her employer friend, laughing and dancing together seemed to dissipate this. Her slightly giggly head broke down any reserve she had felt but, if she was honest, thoughts about his married status never entered her head. Softly spoken, immaculately dressed, the hint of aftershave. What a wonderful escort he was. Tall, commanding, and in charge of the situation, just her and Sam. Her and Sam.

There had been a couple of romantic moments at university, more intimate than she would care to admit, so it was not as though she were a naive teenager. But nothing had prepared her for the passion she felt that night. What it is that drives you from being a rational, sensible human being into a passionate lover is difficult to define. Certainly Claire did not know or care that first night she spent with Sam. And the next morning, almost more so. They had showered quickly and, thankful for her ability to tie her hair up and look business like in double quick time, they were greeting people at the stand as the third day opened. At lunchtime he put a notice up to say 'back at 2:30' and with coffee in one hand and his other hand firmly under her elbow, he guided her to the lift and their room. He kissed her, and kissed her, but it was she who hastily undid buttons to make herself available to him. Who needed champagne? Their passion was sealed. If they could behave like this in the cold light of day then it must be love. Yes, certainly it was love, and Sam obviously felt the same way. Although they had plane tickets for that evening he cancelled them and rebooked for the next afternoon. So began what Claire later understood to be the classic mistress scenario.

As a Jewess she understood his need to be with his family on Friday nights, and would rarely see him at all until Monday evening. She went with him to the overseas trade shows, but never on a normal holiday. If her birthday was at the weekend he did not attend her party. If there was a parent evening at his children's school, any plans she had made went out of the window.

'Sorry Babe, you use the show tickets and go with someone else.'

That was fine for a while as she had plenty of single friends who had stayed around the north London area since university, but gradually they married or moved away. There were still the trade fairs, even adding New York and Paris to the list of places they travelled to. The business had grown and the contracts become more complex. They spent more time ensuring all the fine print was in place before final agreements were offered. So when they were away the evening was often spent looking at ways to add sweeteners or cut corners rather than any romantic liaison. It was the same when he came around to the flat he had bought. More work than romance. That did not mean she felt any less passionate about him, or him about her. It was just the way life was. Just as if they were married. Well almost.

Claire had seen some beautiful tapestries when in Paris and Sam had bought her a picture to embroider, never really expecting her to complete it. But she found it quite relaxing and rewarding and you could pick it up and put it away with the minimum of fuss. There were useful things you could do as well. She re-covered all the dining chairs with tapestry, and although the cat had ruined one, she had started to make a replacement. And there were those little pictures she loved to do and put into window cards (apertures they called it in the magazines) so slowly but surely she stopped planning to go out. She no longer expected him to take her anywhere. She had her embroidery to fill her evenings, and Sam and her work to fill her days.

Occasionally they found a reason to escape back to the flat in the afternoon, which was fun. But it invariably ended in discussing some point of business. What else had they in common? Did Sylvia, his wife, know about her? For some time she thought she might and half hoped there would be a reason for him to leave his family home and live with her. But if Sylvia knew there was never any scene about it. Certainly from the occasional verbal slip everyone at the company knew about her and Sam. But nothing was said. And then came the bombshell. It was Chloe's wedding, and Chloe had given her doting father an ultimatum.

'Alvin's uncle is Chief Rabbi, and I will not have any scandal coming from our side of the family.' She had informed her surprised father. 'You give up your tart or I'll tell mother.'

After ten years Claire had expected more consideration. She had expected him to at least fight for his right to make his own choices. Then she had to face the truth. He had made his choice, and it had not been her he had chosen. Of course, Claire's mother had known the score all those years ago, especially when she had moved out into her own flat.

'My girl, no good ever come from this sort of thing; going against what is right, betraying another woman, just to sleep with a man that's already taken. And what if he leaves her for you, could you trust him?'

The flat was another question. 'When do you want me to move out, I need to know? She had asked him, determined to be businesslike about it all.

'Never, Babe, it is the least I can do,' Sam told her. 'This flat was a good investment I would never have made without you. It is worth three times what I paid for it, even counting the cost of the new bathroom and kitchen we put in last year.' The shadow of surprise swept across his face when she had asked for the spare key, and suggested a lease agreement. But he handed it over muttering about workmen needing access.

'No, Sam, any repairs or alterations will be my responsibility. That will be only fair, as me staying on here is fair. But I will be looking for another job, you understand that.' Quite honestly she was not bothered whether he understood her reasons or not. It was no longer his business what she did with her life.

A card and craft break? She really could not say why she chose Greece, and even less why she had chosen a craft holiday! Something to do in the daytime and you would not have to go into a restaurant on your own in the evenings? That is what the website said. Her mother would look after the cat. In fact, her mother would stay in the flat until she got back. She'll enjoy the change of scenery, and the shops. Would her mother have agreed to look after Oscar if she knew it was Sam's flat, not hers? Well, you have to smile when you can, and Claire was now almost devoid of times when she could smile. What surprised Claire was that she had plans. Big plans. She would take her laptop with her and get a few thoughts down on paper. One door closes … Would another open?

This morning she had chosen her words with care. No way would anyone at Goldberg's ever know it was Sam that had finished the relationship. No way would anyone at Goldberg's ever know that she was going on a card-making holiday.

'I fly out to Rhodes first, just for a few days, then a cruise around the Greek Islands. The Greek guy who owns EasyJet has a sideline in luxury cruises. Should be interesting and fun.' Well, that is what she had told everyone.

MAX AND STEVE

Using the old service ploy 'it must be six o'clock somewhere in the world', Max took a leisurely stroll up to Steps Bar in the early evening. In the two days that Max had been exploring around Lindos he had visited quite a few tavernas.

It was not that he was a drinking man but where else could you wander in to a comfortable venue and sit at your leisure in an air-conditioned lounge? He also enjoyed observing the pleasantries that passed between the Greek 'mine host' and the customer. It seemed to be the same whether towards a local Greek or the tourist. You did not need to speak the language to know that the greeting was as warm as the climate. No surprise then that Steve was sometimes taken for a Greek bar owner with a good command of English rather than an

Englishman in Greece, as he had this quality down to a fine art. There was no doubt that Steve loved what he was doing. He was relaxed and happy, sitting at the end of his bar, with a cigarette, and a bottle of Amstel. There was always a book in his hand, but he was ready to abandon this the moment someone came in the door. For Steve they never were punters or customers but guests in his lounge.

The decor reflected this. An area to sit on bar stools if that is what you preferred, but also comfortable, but not lavish, settees. There were board games, including family things like Contact, and an area further away if you wanted a quiet conversation with a companion. The balcony was small but held two circular tables. From there you looked over the square directly out to sea. Here was a view that may be equalled, but not surpassed, on any of the Greek islands. On the wall between the optics and the coffee machine were cartoons drawn by his friend Miles, and at the far end of the bar was a small stand for Tanya's handmade cards. South American prints on the far walls did not seem out of place in this Greek bar run by an Englishman. Maybe it was the gay abandon of the dancers, the heat apparent from their dress, and the jazz musicians depicted in the background. For some strange reason it seemed to blend in with the ethos of the place. The music was always playing, either traditional jazz or country, but this would be moderated if someone came in for a chat.

Max had a lot to think about at the moment. An idea had been spinning in his head all night. Could he really give up his life in England for a new one on a Greek island? He knew he could financially, that was not a problem. The truth was; what life in England? Did he have one? Not really, since Joan had died he had just existed. What did he look forward to? Nothing. He ordered a gin and tonic and asked Steve to join him for a drink. Max was always able to make a quick assessment of character and was rarely proved wrong. He saw Steve as honest and considerate, with his quiet quick sense of humour, but there lacked that 'eye for the main chance' that publicans often had, and indeed needed to have. No, in Max's eyes here was a good guy. If he did decide to come to Greece, having an acquaintance like Steve would be a great asset.

'Tell me, if it is not too much of a personal question, what was it that brought you here to Lindos, and more importantly, what keeps you here?'

Steve poured another Amstel for himself and took his customary stool at the end of the bar.

'May I answer that like an Irishman, with another question? Have you read the Celestine Prophecy?' Max shook his head. 'Well, until I read that book I thought I had just chosen to come, of my own volition. But the Celestine Prophecy tells you that options and opportunities are put in your way. You choose to take them or not, but it is not merely by chance. There are too many strange coincidences in life to look on everything as chance. So, to answer your first question, what brought me here many years ago was the knowledge that Pink Floyd's David Gilmour had a place here. Anyway it was an excuse for a bit of an adventure. A few of the gang from that era are still around. But I went off to pastures new and only returned for my daughter's wedding. We had spent many family holidays in the Greek islands, but had never been to Rhodes. However, she chose to get married at the chapel in St. Paul's Bay. I just looked around and thought this place would do me very well one day, and sooner than I expected my circumstances changed and I was able to come out here, and acquire the bar. My youngest daughter came with me, so that made the venture more exciting. She is in England at the moment but will be back before the season gets busy. Now what keeps me here?

Look out on the balcony and there is the answer. Where else could you look out on a scene like that every day? Absolutely beautifully perfect. And the friends I have made. Good young people who are prepared to work hard, and play hard, I might add. It makes you feel one of them, even though you know that you were around when the first hippy scene started. I am getting cards from people who were here last summer, or the summer before. Either to say they will be back soon or to say they are on holiday elsewhere but will be in Lindos in September.'

'You certainly seem content and confident and happy. Good luck, my friend.'

'Thank you, sir and *"yia mas",*' he replied with the traditional Greek toast.

It was not Steve's way to say anything more personal. After all, people were on holiday and, apart from the occasional grumble about Greek bureaucracy, he kept his own counsel. It was one thing to wax lyrical on some vague philosophical point but it was another to blurt out personal problems all the time. Certainly he was lucky, he knew that. But despite his best efforts there were things that would not go away. Thoughts that he could not blank out, no matter how good the company and the conversation. As one of his friends had said before he came out to Greece. 'Remember that wherever you go you have to take yourself with you.' And at times when the past or the future seemed to be catching up with him he looked at the card which was always in his wallet. On it were just a few words that summed up his personal mantra. Words his friend Tanya had taught him.

Yesterday is history.
Tomorrow is a mystery.
Today is a gift, called the present.

And, as gifts should be accepted graciously, he was exceedingly grateful.

'I have been seriously considering moving out myself,'

From Lindos With Love

Max confided in Steve. 'Do you think it is a bit of an old man's foolish pipe dream?'

'Why should it be only a pipe dream? Get a sheet of paper and do a 'for and against' test. It works very well. After a few minutes you screw up the paper and throw it away. You just don't want to know about anything on the negative side. If you are honest, you know you have made your mind up already.'

'You are quite right. I have decided to give it a try. I think I was just looking for a bit of reassurance. You do get used to people thinking you are a bit of an old duffer and if not careful you lose confidence in your own powers of deduction. I have a comfortable, "middle England" home,' he continued, 'and a good pension. But the main excitement of the day is fetching the morning paper and the thought of sitting there for the rest of my life quite scares me,' Max admitted.

'I am sure that it does, and the suburbs of England are full of those who thought 'if only' and did nothing about it. You have the advantage, being a military man. You have often moved home I expect. So count it as just another posting,' Steve suggested.

Like many of his holiday guests, Max reminded Steve of a past generation where correct English and a good interesting conversation went hand in hand. Just like members of the Conservative Club along the road from his home when he was young. Not that Steve was a party member or anything that grand but they had a full sized billiards table there, and Steve was a good player and enjoyed the game. And the old boys in the club encouraged him. It was here that he received his introduction to cricket, being taken by them to matches at the county ground. Considered the gentleman's game, or it used to be!

Being a good pool or snooker player is often the sign of a misspent youth but for Steve it had been an education second to none. Now he was experiencing one of those strange moments in time. Here he was in his own Greek bar sitting chatting on equal terms with a retired Wing Commander about the merits of life on Rhodes Island. It was what everyone called those Lindos moments, like last year when he was watching a test match, in his bar, with the core of the 'barmy army' in Lindos for their friend's wedding.

He silently raised his glass to those old chaps from the Con' Club and thanked them for his introduction to the finer things in life.

NEFELI

As near to seven as could be expected from a group of people on holiday, 'the crafty lot' were once again assembled in Steps Bar.

'We are going to eat at a very different venue tonight,' Tanya announced. 'I know you all enjoyed the traditional atmosphere of Kalypso last night. All our restaurants are special in one way or another, but Nefeli has more of a Hawaiian feel than of a Greek taverna. Not sure if Nikolas, the owner, will think that's a compliment, but you will understand what I mean when we get there. It is a bit of a stroll but Miles has his car to drive Margaret, Ruth and Max down the long road to the beach. Perhaps more importantly, he will be able to take any of you back up to the village at the end of the evening.'

Neither Ruth nor Margaret thought they needed transport but were far too polite to say so and got into the car graciously. Within a few minutes they were at the beachside taverna and when they saw the straw umbrellas they understood what Tanya was referring to. The restaurant was set among lush greenery. The large red flowers of the hibiscus added to the exotic setting. The chairs were rattan. The lighting was subtle, and they were the only group there. Nikolas did not open in the evening unless there was a group booking, which was usually a wedding party. And, although there was plenty of space, he always liked to give his weddings exclusivity. But on this evening his exclusive guests were the craft group.

Miles was suggesting to everyone that they order fish, as although the menu was as extensive as any, fish was the speciality.

Kim and Beth were not sure. They liked ordinary fish, chip shop style but were uncertain about other fish.

'Try the swordfish then,' Miles suggested, as he thought that would be more like cod than any other. 'Have the pepper sauce on the side in case it is too strong.'

'Yes, I would like that,' said Ruth.

'We'll have kalamari,' Mel ordered for herself and Claire.

'Sea bass with tomato and wild mushroom stuffing sounds tasty,' and Rob agreed with Max, as he was uncertain what else to order.

Miles explained about potatoes in the oven to Heather

and Andrea and ordered snapper for the three of them. Eventually everyone was happy and with carafes of house wine they munched on cheese-topped garlic bread and chatted until the meal was served.

By the time they had finished eating the moon was shining on the sea before them. No one could manage any dessert, but the waiter brought mint wafers with their coffee. Then Nikolas came around the table with shots of Limoncello for everyone.

'I think we will all need a lift up the hill please, Miles,' Kim asked.

'Definitely not,' he teased, 'you have to walk off your supper. 'The offer is only for the over thirty-fives.'

'Well you're right there, I would not be in the right age bracket,' she lied. And everyone joined in the fun.

'Actually, although I am a little over thirty five,' Ruth began, 'It is such a lovely evening I would enjoy the walk back.'

'Then may I wait with you and escort you up the hill?' Max asked, and everyone started to wolf whistle.

'Thank you, Max, that is most kind of you.'

Eventually Miles drove off with Margaret, Kim and Beth as everyone else started on the steep walk to the village. Nikolas came speak to Ruth and Max.

'I hope you have enjoyed your evening.'

'What an exciting venue this must be for a wedding,' Ruth said. 'Tanya was telling us that the bridal party arrive by boat, how romantic.'

'Yes, we are very popular, and, as you can see, the guests can have transport from here directly back to their hotel afterwards. I must leave you now but please sit here as long as you wish. Just put the glasses somewhere safe, out of the wind, when you leave.'

'What a charming man,' Ruth remarked. And they sat on silently listening to the waves.

'This place is so beautiful I just had to stay a little longer. How kind of you to stay with me, dear Max,' Ruth said quietly.

MAX AND THE PAST

Max smiled, and sighed. He had lived for so long with his thoughts of what might have been, of what life should have been for him and Joan, that he no longer realized when he got lost in his other world.

'A penny for them,' Ruth teased.

'This must be the worst of all crimes, sitting with a lovely lady and letting your thoughts dwell elsewhere.'

'Possibly, or it could be a compliment, that you feel comfortable and relaxed enough to mentally roam.'

'That would certainly be true as my thoughts are ones I would share with you if I may. Thoughts that come to me from the past, particularly so when I am at peace, as I am now.'

Max sighed again and drew his hands over his face as if to clear his head. Then in a voice no more than a whisper he told Ruth the reason for his low spirits on this most beautiful evening.

'You see, I lost my son in an accident when he was just four, and it is always in these quieter moments that the overwhelming sadness engulfs me again. I know I should have moved on but I expect that part of me does not want to, in case I lose him forever.'

It was that wonderful velvet darkness that you can only find away from neon signs and glaring streetlights. The only light came from the moon casting a glow over the sea. The air was still warm and as what breeze there was had come off the land, the deserted patio was sheltered. Even so, Max removed his jacket and placed it around her shoulders. Ruth sat patiently waiting for Max to continue the conversation he had started.

'Tell me more about your son,' Ruth quietly suggested. Eventually he spoke.

'We rarely argued, my wife, Joan and I, but that morning we did. I left the house in a mood and let the door slam behind me, or so I thought. But it did not close and the little lad came running out. I expect he was calling me as I had not kissed him goodbye. If he was I did not hear as I noisily revved the engine. I reversed the car in the driveway.

'He died in my arms, almost instantly. Before his mother could hold him or kiss him to say goodbye. In that one stupid moment, Jack, our little boy, our dear happy child, was gone. The silence was awful, Joan did not cry or say anything, just held Jack to her and whispered into his lovely dark curls. I had rung the ambulance the second I knew I had injured him. Within minutes they were there, though it seemed like a lifetime. But nothing could be done.'

They sat in silence looking into the sea. It was some time before Max spoke again but Ruth waited until he was ready to do so.

'It is in those rare moments when I find myself totally happy that I get this overwhelming wave of sadness, I think I have dealt with the guilt by now. It is as though I want to tell Jack, this grown man that Jack should be, to tell him I had a lovely evening, to share it with him. A bit of male bonding, if you like, as in my mind's eye he is now a good-looking six foot lad about town. But then reality hits and I realise that is not the truth, and it can never be. Where Jack is there is no conversation, only this unending silence. All these years later, he is still a small child, never the tall laughing man of my imagination. Then I retreat from whatever function I am at and go home to lick my wounds.'

There was silence again except for the waves gently lapping the beach below them. In the distance was the murmur of voices from Palestra, but nothing discernable or intrusive. Ruth asked, gently, had such a devastating event taken a lasting toll on their marriage or had it been strong enough to survive? Did they have any other children?

'No. No more children. Joan said she could not risk ever facing that pain again, to lose a child. In fact, in many ways our marriage was over. She tried not to blame me, but she could not love me in the same way again. I know she wanted to but she could not get past what happened that day. We gradually learned to live together, as somehow one does. And we had good times. We were always friends and we had good friends around us who made it impossible to keep refusing invitations. She always supported me in my career, so there were many occasions when regimental functions saw us dancing and dining together. But sadly it had become a facade, even to ourselves. Then cancer came into our lives. And we clung together in fear and forgiveness. Forgiveness for the pain we had inflicted on each other over the years. That time was sadly quite short. Just a year and two months.' Max's voice was barely a whisper now.

'But forgiving another is not the same as forgiving yourself. I understand that what happened was an accident, but it is living with the consequences. If I had truly come to terms with the past I would not always feel so sad when I am happy. I have tried to compartmentalize my life now from my life then but it doesn't work.'

With a long sigh that seemed to draw a line under the previous conversation Max turned and took both of Ruth's hands in his own. 'My dear Ruth, you have been a compassionate and generous listener. And now I can only apologize for my selfishness in inflicting this on you. I have spoilt a beautiful evening by my self-indulgence. I promise this will not happen again. You came here for a holiday and I am stealing some of your precious time.'

'The man who made time made plenty of it,' she smiled to break the tension. She saw that the Palestra was still open, she could see the lights and hear the voices.

'I think we could both do with a brandy or ouzo or whatever one has in Greece for a nightcap. My shout I think.'

Max assured her he would have none of this liberated woman business and that whenever he escorted a lady to a Greek taverna at well past midnight he always bought the drinks. And giggling like teenagers in an effort to bring closure to the past hour, they strolled hand in hand towards the twinkling lights and the softly playing Greek music.

ANOTHER DAY

All were assembled bright and early for another card making session. Everyone was chatting away at the tables, no one seemed to be on their own. Max had asked Ruth if he may join her and she had hastily put her bag down onto the patio to make room for him; a point which did not go unnoticed by Kim and gave her the first smile of the day.

'Crafty old beggar,' she said to herself, and nudged her sister Beth to see if she had noticed. Beth responded to a second dig in the ribs.

'Leave them alone. He probably only wants her to stick his bits on for him. He has one hand that's not very good.' She would have helped him if he was at their table. Nice old boy, she thought.

Tanya's emphasis was more on design than decoration, so she preferred to introduce variations on the basic oblong greetings card at this early stage.

'*Kalimera, ti kanete*, how are you all?' There were lots of giggles but mostly they returned the greeting as Tanya had taught them.

'*Kala, poli kala, kai esi?*'

'*Kala.*'

'This morning we are going to look at the shape of the basic card. Yesterday I said that you need not reinvent the wheel but I want you to be aware that every card does not have to be a rectangle. And, having said that, the first card shape is a rectangle, but with a difference.' She held up a card with a flat back but doors on either side. 'This gets the name of gatefold, which I prefer, but is also called a wardrobe card, for obvious reasons. Into this you can cut apertures, or bevel off the top corners and make a gothic window. This line marker is a gift if you want to make extending or overlapping doors, but junior school maths and a ruler will do equally well. Always check your card against a standard size envelope before you start to add to your design.' As usual Tanya had about twenty different cards showing variations on the theme. The sentiments on the cards she'd made covered a wide range from the usual birthday and thankyou to get well, christenings and anniversaries. But at this stage she left out weddings.

Mel was most interested in the use of acetate. On one

demo card that took her eye, the doors of the gatefold were cut-out apertures. She picked this card and the instruction sheet that went with it.

'Wow,' said Claire when she saw the work Mel proposed to do.

'I don't think it will be a problem,' Mel told her. 'That is just thick plastic, marked off with a marker pen. The effect is amazing, makes it look like French doors onto a garden,' she explained.

Claire raised her eyebrows and gave her friend a smile.

'I am playing safe with this little gem. Borders all around the doors and two punch holes to put a ribbon through, with the message inside.'

'Whatever turns you on,' Mel replied and they giggled as they searched for the pieces needed to make their chosen card.

For Heather, the addition of a butterfly perched on the gatefold edge fascinated her. She picked it up wistfully and Tanya saw her hesitate.

'That is a very good choice, Heather. Can you see the butterflies are three embellishments put back-to-back. First find some other smaller butterflies to put inside and maybe some borders for the gates, not too much. Don't forget your message, and then I will help you with the difficult bit,' Tanya assured her. Tanya was pleased at the progress, as by coffee time everyone had at least one presentable card completed.

Mel had the gatefold and a trifold, beautifully made and in her folder. Yesterday she had spoken to Tanya about this. 'You see I am here to learn as much as I can, but I do not want to appear greedy, using more than my fair share of card and bits,' she had explained, offering to pay a supplement for any extra she might have taken.

'No problem, it is all swings and roundabouts. I doubt if Kim will use her allocated share or even Ruth may not get many cards completed, so please don't worry on that account. And though you are very quick I notice you are finding time to help Heather and Claire, so it should be me thanking you,' Tanya laughed.

So Mel was happy to beaver away. They had chatted for some time about Mel's ambitions for her wedding stationery business and Tanya suggested that Mel take a copy of all her print outs.

'Teaching a group once a week is not only a handy bread winner, but is a way of spreading the news about the wedding offers,' she told her, confident that Mel would have the ability to do this by the end of the week.

Tanya was happy that there would be more than enough for people to do at five o'clock when they returned for the late afternoon session and as they had overrun a bit and coffee was next on the agenda for those who had not yet taken a break. That was not a problem, as they could drink their coffee whilst she introduced the Chinese painting.

'Bring your coffee with you and gather round so that

you can see the table,' she told them.

'There are four elements in Chinese art, the brush, the ink, the ink stone and the paper. To the artist or calligrapher they are known as the "treasures" or the "four friends". It is universally agreed that the first painting brush was invented by a Chinese man. As this happened at least 3000 years before Christ, unsurprisingly no one remembers his name. At that time there was already a form of signwriting so that people could send messages to each other. The story goes that an army general was dipping a stick into a puddle of mud and making signs onto a piece of dried bark so that he could send a message to one of his officers. He had quite a long beard and as he wrote his beard also dipped into the mud. When he looked at the marks his beard had made he thought how much easier it would be to write with hair rather than use a stick. He cut off the end of his beard and tied it onto a piece of bamboo, and in that way the first brush was invented.' The group giggled at the story as they sat listening.

Tanya knew she had their full, but relaxed, attention. She enjoyed telling the legend of the brush, there was enough truth in it to make it both possible and even probable. If some of her students were taking it too literally, at least they would remember whenever they picked up a paintbrush in the future.

Andrea raised her hand as though still in school. 'I did read a book about Chinese painting but it did not mention the information about the brush.'

'Well, there you are. What you don't find out here is just not worth knowing.' There was laughter in her voice and all, including Andrea, joined in the fun.

Tanya held up a brush. 'Over a period of 5000 years the Chinese brush has changed little. It is known as "pi" which is the sign for bamboo, as the handle was always made from bamboo shoots. The brush has two layers, the inner core made of short hairs that hold water or ink and the outer long-haired ring that comes to a fine point. With this one brush you can make wide or narrow strokes. You can make a brush stroke that starts narrow, widens in the middle and ends in a fine line again. You should hold the brush in such a way that you can use it vertically or horizontally. You can fan it out to make pine needles and best of all you can load it with two or even three colours at one time.'

Tanya explained that in China an artist was apprenticed for seven years and spent the first five of them just grinding the ink, but as they were only on a short holiday with cards to make and other crafts to try, they had better grasp things more quickly. She continued: 'The ink is made of soot. It can be soot from pine needles, from pig fat and these days even petroleum soot. This is mixed with glue and sometimes herbs or ground pearls are added, each ink giving a slightly different quality. The mixture is then set into sticks and these ink sticks themselves are carefully decorated. In this way the ink is portable.' Tanya held up several ink sticks, each with its own distinctive pattern, and passed them to Mel to look at and pass around the group. Tanya continued, having given everyone a few moments to break their concentration. 'The third object is the ink stone, for the ink must be ground back to a liquid form for you to be able write or paint. The stone can be made of slate or be semi-precious like jade. She dropped a little water onto the stone and rubbed the ink stick onto it in circular movements. Slowly and carefully, round and round until the water and ink were mixed smoothly together. They sat in silence and watched her. 'And while you do this you can think about the picture you are going to paint.' Tanya carefully laid the ink and stone to one side and picked up the roll of rice paper. 'And last but not least is the paper. We are going to use rice paper because it is most absorbent and not too expensive. To take a piece from the roll for your picture you simply dip your brush into the clean water and run it quickly down the paper, and then tear it off.' It worked like a conjurer's trick, the paper coming away neatly down the wet mark. Tanya picked up the ink stone and started to grind the ink again. She explained briefly the relationship between calligraphy and art, a relationship often hidden from western eyes.

'You will see if I make the old Chinese word for baby.' She held up a card that had thick black signs on it. With a bit of imagination it looked like a child's cradle. 'At first all written words were in picture language. As you see, this is a baby. Gradually the extra bits were lost and this,' she held up a different card, 'is now the accepted word for baby. A Chinese person looking at a Chinese painting would see many brush strokes and hidden messages in every picture which you and I will never be able to understand. So, we accept the artwork on a more superficial level. Now you know that, you need never refer to it again, as no matter how hard you try you will not achieve the understanding of a Chinese artist.' The group were very quiet and suitably impressed. Now sure she had enough ink for her purpose she took the brush and showed how to hold it the correct way.

'Holding the brush correctly is the key and far better to get it right at the start. When you come to make more complex strokes you will not be able to do them unless you have mastered the brush.' Whilst talking, Tanya had placed a sheet of newspaper on the desk in front of her and a piece of rice paper on this. She put small carved jade stones on the four corners to keep the paper in place. She dipped the brush into the ink, flattened the brush and with a few stubby strokes produced bamboo stems onto the rice paper in front of her. Then she proceeded with the stalks and leaves. 'Start with a narrow tip, use a slight pressure to give the leaf width and finish with a narrow line that vanishes into the distance.' As Tanya held up the picture she had created so quickly they all clapped her efforts, partly to release the nervous tension they were all feeling. How were they going to achieve that kind of perfection? As the brushes, rolls of paper, ink sticks and stones were already on each table it did not take long for everyone to be organised and, apart from a few whispers and the occasional giggle, only the sound of ink grinding could be heard; though in the distance a donkey braying and children playing echoed from the beach below.

They were soon surprised by the success they achieved. Grinding the ink stick slowly, until the right degree of viscosity was reached, was a calming occupation. Tanya again demonstrated a simple bamboo shoot, explaining that to learn to paint with a Chinese brush was a bit like learning to play the piano, you copied first and only invented your own composition when more confident. Concentration was needed to make the brush strokes. The joy experienced when a picture emerged was one of quiet satisfaction.

'You will never be able to walk down a garden path again without pausing to look at the shape of a leaf. Then you will think about the brush strokes needed to put the image onto paper,' she had told them. Landscapes and the Chinese perspective were other issues not mentioned unless one of the guests was an experienced Chinese brush painter and raised the subject.

The group was hushed and, even when told that it was time to break for lunch, there was a reluctance to leave the work in hand. Naturally some were more able than others and Tanya was amused to see that Ruth had not really grasped the concept of holding the brush. Often the way, she thought. Teachers! So used to giving orders they often have difficulty following them. She knew that from her short but enjoyable time as a driving instructor. And nurses never know their left from their right, so used as they are to thinking of the patient's left side and not their own.

Funny the things your brain recalls, she mused as she wandered round quietly encouraging her group. She had enjoyed being a driving instructor. She wondered what Chiswick High Street was like now on a Friday afternoon.

TANYA FALLS

Captain Takis blew his whistle once again but there was so much confusion in the square that few could hear him, and those that did were not sure what was required of them. The tourists in their hired cars should have seen that the square was choc-a-block and not driven down there in the first place. But that was another matter. The Mayor had done what he could to alleviate congestion, but everyone tried to avoid parking where the meters had been placed, on a side road leading to the beach. The taxis had a designated area with bollards, and there were "disabled" parking bays. Assisting Captain Takis were two young tourist police. So it was not an unusual situation that greeted Tanya that afternoon.

Organized chaos, Steve called it. A shuttle bus ran continually to bring tourists down the hill into the village centre. Local people knew better and came into the Lindos from the south, leaving their cars on cliff top car parks or vacant spaces on the far side of the town. Yet despite all this there was nothing that could prevent cars and motorbikes, driven and ridden by every known nationality, from insisting there was space, somewhere, for them.

Tanya was on her way to pick up wedding favours from a shop in Archangelos. She was to borrow a friend's motorbike, as her scooter was in for repair. Not a problem. The bike was parked under the steps of Steps Bar. She just had time to skip up the steps for a quick beer and say hello to Steve. The small bar was full of cricket enthusiasts, glued to the large screen watching a three-day match. Not everyone liked to loll around on the beach all day. If cricket was your thing, then Steps Bar was your holiday retreat and Steve a knowledgeable host to add commentary and discussion.

Not wishing to disrupt the events taking place, albeit by proxy, she grabbed a beer from the fridge behind the bar and found a stool. When Steve joined her they quietly exchanged a few words of local news and resumed watching the match. Her beer finished, she waved at a few people she recognized from the previous evening and rejoined the busy square. She made an attempt to fix her helmet, but it was her old one and she had forgotten the buckle was broken. Not that the law about crash helmets was enforced outside Rhodes town, but as far as

Tanya was concerned a crash helmet was essential. The bike started straight away. Then with a wave Captain Takis flagged her down. The cars came to a halt whilst they passed the time of day, for after all what was the point of being Traffic Controller if you could not chat for a few moments to a friend.

'My new boat is ready and is being chartered for day trips,' he told her. 'It is called the Lindos, you must come on a trip as soon as you are free to do so.'

She thanked him as he then held up the traffic to let her out from the square. She laughed as the song about the Mountains of Mourne came into her head, and how good it was to have friends in high places, and looked forward to going out for the day on Captain Takis' boat. As she left the square she saw Rob walking briskly up the hill. She felt sad that Rob had booked in to the craft break but taken no part in the activities. Even in the evenings he remained quietly on the edge of the group. Margaret had made an effort to include him, but as he was not really interested in the events of the day, the conversation soon lulled. Max had done the 'we men must stick together' bit but they had little in common. As a token of good will, Tanya had booked him a coach trip to Prassonisi, but that was not till Friday. She thought he would enjoy the drive through the countryside and the views from the other side of the island.

'Go to the Light House for lunch and tell Asimeni I sent you,' she suggested. So she had done her best for him.

Leaving the square was the same chaos as usual, but with a bit of patience she was off up the hill and past the village cemetery. She started to gather a bit of speed and then it happened.

Goats roam freely over the hills that surround Lindos. They were a particular problem early in the year, often trotting across the road in straggly groups. But everyone knew this, so drivers were cautious. Now, with lots of people around they usually kept away from the roads, but not today. Just as Tanya took her hand off the handlebar to wave to Rob, a goat stepped into her path. As she braked hard the back wheel skidded from under her and within seconds she could feel her shoulder hitting the ground and the gravel scraping her leg. A jolt as the front wheel hit the wall and at last everything came to a halt.

A strange wave of peace came over her as she lay there with the bike on her leg. It seemed as though the world stood still. Then Rob was by her side, talking to her with his soft Wiltshire accent, assuring her that everything was going to be fine. No one else had been injured, even the goat had scampered away. Rob told her he was going to go through the initial checks to ascertain injuries, she only had to answer yes or no to his questions. He was shocked to realise that even someone as sensible as Tanya was not wearing a safety helmet. There certainly seemed to be no major problem apart from her right ankle and which was giving her a lot of pain, but she was able to move it. Rob took a cotton bandage out of his small back pack, dowsed it in water from his bottle and strapped it around Tanya's ankle. However, he knew that such checks were only what they claimed to be: first aid; and a hospital visit was needed to check his findings and take the right action to treat the injury. He had the hospital number in his phone. There was also a clinic somewhere in the next village. Then to his relief, Mihalis, the taxi driver was at his side.

'I don't think we need an ambulance as Tanya is not unconscious and doesn't have any major pain apart from her ankle, I have strapped that with a cold water bandage, but I do think a hospital visit is needed to x-ray the injury.'

'I was in the square and came to help. I have called the doctor but he is in Kalathos.' He addressed Tanya who was now sitting up and doing her own body check.

'I will take you. Not a problem, and bring you home again. Tell your friend you safe with me.'

That made Tanya laugh and the small crowd of onlookers that had gathered gave a collective sigh of relief and began to disperse. They did not know that Mihalis had often chatted to Tanya and offered a trip to a deserted beach in his taxi. It was a long-standing joke between them, but Tanya knew she was in good hands with the lovely Mihalis. The men helped Tanya to her feet and into the taxi. The bike had been rescued and returned to its parking place by a cousin of its owner and a full account of the accident relayed via the mobile phone.

'Rob, would you be good enough to tell everyone that I will not be at the bar this evening? We are eating at the Medeast tonight, everything has been arranged. Some of the girls have made other arrangements, going into Faliraki, I think. Manolis will look after you. He speaks very good English, so there's no problem. I am sure I will be OK. And it is only a sprain or something. I will see you all tomorrow morning.'

'If you are sure you don't need me I'll go and tell Steve what has happened. Take care, hopefully we will see you tomorrow. You have my number if I can help.' With that Rob went back down into the village only to find that Steps Bar was closed for the afternoon. Steve was probably by the pool at Krana, his favourite afternoon retreat. But Rob would not go and disturb him there. Although serious enough, it was not an emergency situation, thank God. Later would do. Then he saw Miles talking to Heather in the square and joined them. News of the accident had already spread.

'I will be at Electra patio at five o'clock,' Miles assured them. 'I'll bring some mosaic designs with me and talk about making hand-cut tile portraits and outdoor mosaics.' he told them.

'Tanya might be OK in the morning, so no point in worrying about that 'til we know otherwise.'

He would see everyone in Steps at seven thirty as

usual.

Rob thought it was much too hot now to walk out to Kleoboulos' tomb or even part of the way. He would go this evening. He bought a crepe and took it back to his room, made a cup of tea, sat on the bed when he had finished both and fell asleep.

After all, he was on holiday.

FALIRAKI, OR NOT

Heather told herself that she would go to the late afternoon class not to let Miles down when he was making the effort to keep things running. Other afternoons she had stayed on the beach. She need not have worried as the rest of the group were busy practicing their Chinese painting when she arrived, that is all except Max who was using the guillotine to make another gatefold card. The talk about mosaics that Miles had planned was not needed. She had been invited to go out for the evening with Kim and Beth and her cries of having nothing to wear had landed on deaf ears.

By now everyone knew about Tanya's accident and there was to be a meeting in Steps Bar to make plans for the following morning. So Kim, Beth and Heather left early and went to sort out their outfits for a session of bar crawling in Faliraki.

'Do you think we should ask Andrea?' Heather suggested when she arrived at Poppy apartments where Kim and Beth were staying.

'Well it's like this, Heather, you can invite her to go out with you but I am on holiday. I have two kids at home and I do enough babysitting all year round, thankyou very much. I am not looking after someone else's kid on our only night out.'

'Sorry, Heather, Kim might sound a bit hard when she puts it like that, but it is the truth. We can all look after ourselves if we got separated but I would not relax if Andrea was there.'

'I take the point. It is just that she seems quite alone.'

'Yes, well, she is alone, but you know that if you come on a holiday on your own. You are in the same boat but it hasn't made you sit around and mope on about your father coming from Greece and all that crap,' Kim shouted out from the shower.

'Do you not think it's true then?'

Kim came back to the lounge wrapped in a towel. 'Well, it could be. But I used to say my dad came from Italy and Beth had a dad from Scandinavia, which was a bit daft really as I was blonde and she was dark. We didn't understand what we were saying about our mum at the time.' Both Kim and Beth broke into a fit of laughter. 'But all we really knew was that our dad or dads had disappeared by the time we got to school age.

So, yes, I feel sorry for the kid, but I think she would be better to go home and forget this Greek thing.'

'Anyway, let's get some gear sorted. I am more your size than Beth so I have put what I'm not wearing out on the bed, just go and have a look.'

Heather was not a hundred per cent sure she wanted to go to Faliraki, but felt pleased that the sisters had invited her. The feeble excuse she gave about having nothing to wear for a night out in the bars was soon squashed by the offer to share their holiday wardrobe. She did not drink much these days, never had really, and certainly did not intend to spend part of her precious week with a hangover. They were not going until around nine o'clock. Maybe there would be time to have something to eat before they went. And that was another thing, her place had been booked for the evening meal, should she pay something for that? Hopefully they would get a bite to eat before going off out.

'What do you think of this, girls?' Heather asked them when she returned to the lounge wearing a vivid green sparkly top.

'The colour is good but it does nothing for your tits,' Kim replied.

'Ignore her, she only thinks in one direction. It looks lovely, but if you put the straps down off the shoulder it would be more suitable for clubbing than Sunday school,' Beth suggested.

By this time Kim was standing naked in the middle of

the room pulling on a pair of knickers so small she need not have bothered with them at all. Next came a skirt that just covered the knickers. The bra was maroon and added inches to her natural shape. Over the maroon bra she put an orange, almost see through, Indian cotton top with a sparkly stripe through it, and this Kim tied in a knot at the waist.

'Will this do for some lucky guy tonight, girls?' she asked them as she gave a twirl.

'You'll pass in a crowd,' replied her sister, who by now was wearing a black lace shirt tucked into red tailored knee length shorts, set off with a gold belt and gold leather sandals. She looked immaculate and stunning.

'All we need now is a bit of bling and we are set for the fray. We had better go to Steve's first as there's a meeting about tomorrow's classes. If it doesn't go on too long we might still get a bite to eat before getting the taxi.'

Well that was one thing sorted, thought Heather, still unsure about going on this pub crawl.

CONFERENCE

That evening in Steps there was a conference about the next day's programme. Without thinking, Ruth automatically took over the chair. And no one was more relieved than Miles to see her do so.

'I am sure we all agree that it would be better for Tanya to rest in the morning and get her ankle strong again. Well, we need to make some plans now to enable her to do that without worrying about us. Would you agree?' Murmurs of consent went round the group so Ruth carried on. 'As leader for the early morning card making session I nominate Mel as I think you will agree she has more card making expertise than any of us.'

There were supporting noises of approval and everyone looked towards Mel for her response.

'Thank you for your confidence in me. Yes, if I can

help in any way at all I will do my best, certainly I will organize the start of the session. I know Tanya has everything that is needed in a box at the studio, and each box is labelled with the day of the week. I will go later this evening and check what is planned so we can make an early start, just as if Tanya were there.'

'Then I'll come with you,' Claire added, partly because it would save her being allocated another job that she would not feel confident in doing. Oh dear, where had this London businesswoman disappeared to? Claire did not know or care at the moment. She just did not want any complications.

Ruth called the chatter to order once again. 'We may have a problem with the Chinese painting, which is after the card session. Any ideas anyone?'

Margaret, who had added little to any conversation up until now, put her hand up and waited for permission to speak from the chairperson.

'Yes, Margaret dear, how can we help,' Ruth said encouragingly and a little patronising, Margaret thought.

'I can do the flower demonstration for you. The W.I. committee gave me a set of Chinese paints and brushes and a booklet that went with it as a gift for organizing our quilt show last year. So I practiced and am quite good at doing the tree branch and the blue flowers, or you can have red flowers if you like.' Margaret added, in case anyone did not like blue flowers but was too shy to say so.

'Oh, how wonderful, Margaret, thankyou so much for

offering to help. This is working out splendidly. Perhaps Andrea could help you set it out.' Seeing her embarrassment Ruth was sorry she had rushed into asking Andrea.

'I know,' Andrea added quickly, 'I'll get the things out for coffee first thing and wash up while Margaret is doing the painting.'

'May I help, Margaret?' Heather added, 'If Margaret tells me what to do. I know nothing about Chinese painting.'

'Oh it's mainly giving out the paper, ink, brushes and ink stones when the card makers have finished, just as Tanya did today,' said Margaret.

'Then I think that's all settled, and Steve can tell Tanya to rest in the morning as we have everything sorted. Thank you all for being so helpful.' Then remembering that she was one of the guests, and not a very talented one at that, she added, 'I hope you didn't mind me ordering everyone about, I certainly did not intend to, but old habits of being in charge are hard to break.'

Max was there immediately with a few words of appreciation for Ruth using her teaching skills to organise the group into positive action. Without needing to call for a vote of thanks, the group applauded Ruth and words of appreciation rang around the bar. Max placed another drink into Ruth's hand before she had time to recover and she smiled her thanks. She was already asking Margaret about the Chinese painting and expressing her concern over her lack of ability with the Chinese brush.

Heather was chatting to Miles at the bar. They seemed to be having a friendly but animated argument about music and anyone could see that they really enjoyed each other's company. How Heather had changed in just a few days of sea and sun. Oh what it is to be young Ruth thought, with the whole world in front of you. Then she remembered her own problems at that age. She was unaware of Heather's situation. Unaware that Heather was trying to make a life for herself as a single mum. Unaware that in a different way, and in a very different age, both had a similar crisis to face. Just as Heather had no idea that this confident, well-dressed, posh, retired teacher had once been a single mother.

MEDEAST

They all knew where Medeast was, as you had to pass the restaurant on the way in and out of the village. But the entrance from the road was not that welcoming, just a half-open wooden door that led down into a passageway. The group was already later than usual. Steve had rung Manolis, explaining that the delay was because they were making arrangements for the morning now that Tanya was injured. So it was a rather subdued group that finished their pre-dinner drinks and wandered up the hill to the restaurant.

Steve had decided to come with them. 'It is not that you might lose your way,' he joked, referring to the one hundred metres they had to walk, 'but I never miss the chance to visit my friend Manolis, drink his beer, eat his wonderful food and listen to his music.'

Ruth and Margaret looked sideways at each other, but did not say a word. If there was one thing that sent shivers up an older person's spine it was the thought of loud music when you were a captive audience, as they both would be in a few moments time. Rob, on the other hand, had often stopped on the back road below the restaurant to listen to the mellow sound of Manolis' acoustic guitar and, a fellow instrumentalist himself, was looking forward to meeting such an accomplished musician.

The gentlemen waited to allow the ladies to go in first and could hear, 'Ooh,' 'Aah,' 'How wonderful,' and wondered what the excitement was about. But as Rob and Max came into the dining room they could see for themselves and in turn exclaimed at the view before them. The dining room was spacious and the tables dressed in the white linen they were getting accustomed to. Everything was immaculate. And beyond this was a spectacular view of Lindos: the beach and the village. White walled houses, surrounded by the dark green leaves of the lemon trees, stretched down to the golden beach. Past the golden sand was the sea, now a dark blue in the fading evening light. From the open dining room they could see a good hundred and eighty degrees around the bay. Starting with Palestra, near the arm of the cliffs that held the war memorial and Kleoboulos' tomb, past the Dolphin Taverna and the paddle boats, across the whole of Lindos' main beach. Near the beach stood the church with its white bell tower and a surrounding field of greenery; a perfect, uninterrupted view.

Manolis stood back and let them settle into their surroundings, only moving forward to reposition a chair as his customers eventually sat down. He was tall, sturdy, and bronzed. A wide smile reached intelligent eyes. His jet black hair was long and tied in a ponytail.

'*Kalispera*, ladies and gentlemen, welcome to Medeast. I am Manolis and am here to make this evening the most memorable of your stay in Lindos.'

There were mutterings of 'good evening,' and '*kalispera*, Manolis,' and 'thankyou.'

'Now, Tanya sends her good wishes and has asked me to provide you all with complimentary drinks by way of her apology. So, we will start with carafes of house wine; we have a very good full red and a sweet white, if the ladies prefer. But the choice is yours, we have a well-stocked bar. Steve, would you like an Amstel to start with?'

'Have you known me ever refuse?' he replied.

'Then I will fetch menus for you and the speciality tonight is pork fillet with plumbs.' This dish was Steve's favourite and he wasted no time extolling its delights to all and sundry.

The selection was wide. Kleftico, a lamb shank with oven potatoes was a favourite and Ruth and Mel wanted to try chicken mango with cashew nuts. But they mostly followed Steve's example and went for the pork with plumbs. The chatter flowed back and forth as though they had all known each other for years instead of only days. Outside the dusk had turned to night and the view was now lit by the sparkle of street lamps and the lights from the bars. The floodlit Acropolis crowned it all.

An hour later coffees were ordered and the smokers amongst the group moved their chairs away from the table. Steve was with them.

'Steve, is Manolis from Lindos?' Claire asked.

'From Athens.' Manolis had heard the question and replied before Steve could answer.

'Like most who establish a business here, I chanced on Lindos in the most unusual way. Have you met Socrates yet? Well that is another treat in store for you then. To continue, I was in India and I met this fellow Greek, Socrates. He was not from Lindos but had been living here for some time. He first came to Lindos with the police but had since left the force and opened a bar. He said I should visit when I returned to Athens. Well it was two years later when I finally came, and just like you I was astounded by the beauty of the place. You see I had travelled extensively after the army. From India, up into Nepal, and across Iraq and Iran at the most dangerous of times. Then suddenly, you want to go home. But when you get there, except for family, things do not seem the same anymore because you are no longer the same person that went away. Rhodes, and particularly Lindos, was like a link between home and travelling, exotically beautiful but definitely Greek. And here I have been every summer since. Twenty four years.'

Manolis had said 'every summer', so naturally someone would ask the question about the winter. It was Heather. He smiled, 'In the winter I go to Athens to be with my family. Unless you are from Lindos or out working, Lindos is not the ideal place for a young woman with small children. Your husband is busy seven days a week. So my family stays in Athens, where there are more education opportunities for the children and family and friends around. Not ideal, you might say, but it is the way of life for many of us who depend on the tourists for a living. Now it is music time. I would like to play for you.'

This was what Rob had been looking forward to all evening. Although the CDs, Manolis had played softly whilst they enjoyed their meal, had been lovely, nothing could compare to live music. And the acoustic guitar was his favourite instrument. And Manolis could play. Really play. As time went on most made their excuses and left. Only Ruth, Max and Rob remained. Several times they suggested that they should let Manolis close for the night, but there was always one more song. But eventually the lovely evening came to an end. Rob was still a bit shaken by the events of the day and said he would go off for a short walk. They wished each other goodnight, wondering how they were going to get up in time for the class in the morning. For Manolis it was not a peaceful evening. He had noticed the young girl with the copper coloured hair as soon as she had walked in. But it was the low voice with a funny accent and the piercing green eyes that seemed to follow him around the room. As soon as he had a moment to spare he opened his mobile phone.

'*Kalispera*, my friend, I think your daughter is here.' Nothing else he could do. It was up to his friend to decide. Oh how sad, he thought, already missing his own children, and it was only the start of the season. Imagine not seeing them for years, imagine not seeing them grow up. He could not. And how would you start to put things right? he mused to himself. Could it ever be put right? He did not envy his friend, but hoped he would try to do the right thing now. He collected the last glasses and turned out the lights.

Ruth and Max sat on a bench in the square, enjoying the warm night air, and the view over the orange grove to the sea. The whitewashed houses shone in the light from the street lamps. It had been a wonderful evening, and the soft sound of Manolis' electric guitar had been their kind of music. They fell silent. It was a long while since Max had been in the company of a lady who was happy to sit in companionable silence. Even through all their troubled years this was one thing he and Joan had not lost.

And now he felt a great peace surrounding him.

FALIRAKI

RED GREEN ORANGE BLUE RED GREEN ORANGE BLUE. The strobe light flashed around the bar in time to the beat of the music.

'Are you goin' out tonight; if you do you be alright. If you don't well I don't care; there are bad girls everywhere.' This was the third bar they had been in and they could tell that they would not last long here either.

It took ten minutes just to get within spitting distance of the counter, mouth their order to the lip-reading barman, and watch their money as it travelled towards the till. Miraculously, their drinks were passed to them over the mass of heaving bodies.

'No ice,' Kim had shouted, she begrudged paying for a drink half full of water, but that bit had not reached its destination. The vibrations travelled from the floor, spun into their guts and met the ones coming down from their ears.

They looked at each other to mouth the words 'What are we doing here?' But the look was enough. Did they feel old or what? As in the previous venues, the music was too loud, the boys, no way could you call them men, too young. The girls looked as though they should be in school, junior school. They drained the rest of their drinks, no point in wasting what had been paid for, and went outside.

'I thought with a few bevvies I could deal with this, but I can't cope,' wailed Beth.

'I'm sorry, I know how much you were looking forward to a night out, but I can't hear myself think. And those lights are making my head spin, I am beginning to feel sick.' She looked green, but maybe it was the neon lighting.

'We always had a good time when we came before, I know we did. Remember those Italians from Milan?'

Kim said nothing. She slumped down onto the wall and sat on the cool tiles. Beth was right but Kim was reluctant to admit this even to herself.

What a disaster the evening was. They had tried some of the old haunts but they were all much the same. They were pleased that Heather had changed her mind. What idiots they would have looked in promising her a hot night out.

'What about Kelly's? They can't have ruined that surely.' They stayed where they were for the moment, just sitting on the wall and sharing a fag.

'Well even if we met anything fanciable, it would be a brave man who'd have a go chatting us up, you look like death warmed up and I feel like it,' Kim finally admitted.

'Well you are not soddin' well getting it tonight, even if you do feel like it,' Beth came back at her sister. They started to laugh. That uncontrollable, totally unreasonable sort of laughing that happens when things go wrong beyond all expectation and there is no way to put it right. And they were too drunk to even start rationalising.

'Hello girls, why you outside tonight. You want I buy you f...... drink?'

'No, darling, you are alright, and it must be past your bedtime. Go home to Mama. Ciao. Thanks for the offer but no thanks.' And again they started to laugh. Eventually they managed to stop laughing long enough to stand up and help each other along the road towards Kelly's Irish Bar. You could not miss the green 'Kelly's' sign, the green, white and gold above the door and shamrocks everywhere.

'This is more like it,' Kim said as she took in the long lounge with tables and chairs down each side. Proper chairs, not the plastic sort. There was a good crowd but not overbearing. The youngsters were standing around the bar area. The karaoke was going, the atmosphere was happy and they were not the only ones over eighteen, Kim saw with some relief.

'Are these seats free?' Always a daft question, Beth thought, but that's what you ask and everyone understands what you mean.

'Help yourself. We are going up the chipper any road, when we have finished this one. Yous missed a good night, the karaoke 'as been brilliant. Yous should have come in earlier.'

They ordered. Beth had a coffee this time and Kim red vodka, no ice. A guy was making a great job with the Star Trekkin' song. Kim and Beth joined in the chorus.

Star Trekkin' across the universe,
On the Starship Enterprise under Captain Kirk.
Star Trekkin' across the universe,
Only going forward cause we can't find reverse.

They laughed as they did the actions, saluting and waving their arms, but were too out of breath to keep up with the words. The karaoke finished and was replaced by a mix of Irish ballads. They were feeling better and the hour in Kelly's had revived their flagging spirits. It was time to head back to Lindos, older and much wiser than when they left. They asked the barman, Liam, to ring them a taxi.

'Beffy,' Kim whispered to her sister, well she thought she was whispering. 'Beffy, you know I would never have cheated on Gerry don't yer? Yer know that, yer do know that, Beffy.'

'Yes, I know that. I know you wanted me to hook up with some fella, but I am alright as I am, Kiddo, I really am, but thanks for trying. Thanks, Kid and I am having a good time, I am. Well, until tonight, what a washout.'

They started to laugh again until the tears ran down their faces.

'In a way it's better than a good night, because we would forget a good night by the time we got home. But we won't forget being the oldest old slags in Faliraki, never, ever.' And that started them off again until Kim started to panic, bursting to go to the loo.

'Turn left here, yes just here,' she instructed the taxi driver as he neared Lindos square.

'This will do.' She jumped out of the car leaving Beth to settle the bill, as she rushed for the nearest bit of cover to pee.

'Where are you going, you daft twit,' Beth called to Kim, who had taken off in the wrong direction, walking down the path away from the village.

'I want to see Kleoboulos, I want to go up here and see Kleoboulos,' was the slurred reply. It was dark except for the stars and the street lights shining below.

'In the morning, we can go in the morning, not in the dark.' But Kim was not listening and continued until the path widened at the war memorial. She sat on a lump of rock. The moon had appeared again and they were able to look along the cliff to Kleoboulos' tomb. The music came across the bay from Amphitheatre nightclub, the beat echoing around the cliffs and bouncing back from the long arm of the bay. Suddenly Kim had a new lease of life and was dancing away on the plateau of grass surrounding the memorial, dancing by herself, oblivious to anything but the loud beat.

'C'mon, Beffy, this is great, c'mon,' Kim called to her sister.

Beth had often thought how wonderful it would be to dance under the stars, but the scene of her imagination was romantic and seductive with a man who ticked all her boxes. Now here she was under a starry sky on a Greek island, dancing to the disco music with her half p..sed sister.

Not much in Beth's life had lived up to her imaginative anticipation. Regardless, she was making the most of the moment, as she always did, and joined in, laughing and singing. Unnoticed, the stars disappeared under a cloud but the lights of the village provided their own twinkling display across the bay. Kim had sat down again and was rather put out when a cursory search of her handbag did not produce another packet of cigarettes.

'We ought to go home now and get a few hours' sleep or we'll be good for nothing in the morning,' Beth suggested.

'I want to go home, Beffy. I want to go home to my kids and my Gerry and my wallpaper. I want my kids and my Gerry,' Kim wailed quietly, before she started to cry. Yes, it was the drink talking, but sometimes it brought out the truth. Beth put her arms around the shaking shoulders of her younger sister. After a moment when her sobs had subsided she linked her arm and started back along the path down to the village. They stopped for a moment while Kim lit a cigarette from the packet she had discovered in her pocket. She took one long pull and handed it to her sister.

Rob had thought the voices he had heard were getting nearer. He was sure people were walking along the cliff. He stopped calling out, but listened for them to negotiate the semicircle of a large cove, sure that it was only a matter of minutes before he heard their chattering again. It did not happen. The only sound he could hear was the beat of the music and the lapping of the sea on the rocks below.

Nothing daunted, he called out again.

Sharing the cigarette they stood in silence, taking one last look at the moonlit sea and twinkling lights.

Beth whispered, 'It is beautiful up here, and so quiet now the music has stopped.'

'There're voices, the place is bloody haunted. Can't you hear it, Beffy? Must be those knights all buried out here somewhere. They would haunt the place alright.'

'Shush, let me listen. There are voices, or at least one voice, and it's English.'

'Were there English knights, Beffy, or were they all foreign, French or something.'

'Shush let me listen. It's along the cliff, shouting for help, listen.'

'What would a Frenchy ghost be shouting in English for, he'd say 'ello, 'ello, not help.'

Beth was now very concerned but still smiled at her sister's understanding of French. This was serious and she needed to clear her head and think what best to do. She cupped her hands around her mouth and shouted. 'Hello, we can hear you, are you in trouble or only messing about?'

'Fell on the cliff, need help,' came the reply, stronger and clearer. There was something vaguely familiar about the voice, but Beth could not think clearly enough to put an answer to her own thoughts.

'We need to get help, there is not much we can do on our own and in the dark', Beth said calmly, more to herself than to her sister. Putting her hands around her mouth she called out again.

'OK, we will bring someone with a torch. Keep still, won't be long.'

Beth persuaded Kim of the urgency of the situation and they hurried as best they could along the narrow stony path back to the main square. In any other place you would look for the police station, but in Lindos, although there was one, it was so far towards the opposite end of the village, the girls had never seen it. But as ever there were taxis waiting in the square to take tourists, enjoying a night in the Lindos nightclubs, back to their hotels. And the taxi drivers spoke English.

'Good evening, ladies, where do you want to go?' asked George.

'Sorry but we don't want to go anywhere, thankyou' Beth replied. 'Someone has fallen on the cliff out towards Kleoboulos' tomb and we need help and a torch to see what has happened.' For some reason Beth started to cry. She felt awful that she had been so useless and was worried about the person they had left on the cliff.

George threw his cigarette butt over the railings near where the taxis were parked and started talking quickly and rather loudly to his fellow drivers. He motioned Beth and Kim to get into the car. One of the other drivers got into the front seat, holding a large halogen lamp.

'If we take the car we will be able to bring them back or drive to the hospital, whatever is best,' George explained. They could only drive to where Kim and Beth had left their taxi earlier. There was no road beyond that point. The men got out and, taking a rope from the boot, walked quickly ahead. Once past the war memorial they turned on the lamp and started to shout.

'Hello, where are you? You must talk to us. *Yiassou*,

hello.'

'Hello, down the cliff. I can see the light. I am OK, just winded.'

It was only a few minutes more before the men had located Rob. He was lucky as he had landed in a gully, only about twelve feet below the path. Saplings growing on the outcrop had held his fall, without them he would have tumbled to the rocks below. George looped his rope over a rocky stump and Kostas took the other end. In no time at all Kostas was standing over Rob where he lay.

'Thank you, thankyou. I dare not move as I had no idea where I was. I can see now what happened. I am on a ledge. Nothing broken, I think. Give me a hand up please and we'll find out.' In his heart Rob knew that was not what he should be doing, but he also knew no one would think to give him a first aid check before he was moved. Rob was more than grateful that they had come for him at this hour of the night. Once Rob was on his feet he flexed his arms and shoulders, back and ankles and was pleased to find no harm done. He had just a few scratches to his face and a rip in the knee of his trousers. Kostas tied the rope around Rob, just to make sure he was safe, and with a few deft steps they were both back on the path.

A few moments more saw them sitting in the car. It took him a while to adjust to the light, then Rob saw Beth and Kim who had been told by George to wait in the safety of the taxi.

The Beer and Bier was still open and that is where they all went for a coffee. Rob thanked the drivers and went to open his wallet. They shook their heads and protested. Kostas extended his hand and Rob accepted the handshake.

'Ohi! No, you help Tanya today and the German tourist who fell getting out of my taxi, and man collapsing going up steps to the Acropolis. You are a good man.'

Rob put his cash away, not wishing to offend and Greg had already refused his offer to pay for the coffees. After wishing everyone a goodnight he walked with Beth and Kim back to their apartment, where he thanked them again for coming to rescue him.

'No real harm done, just lucky we were there. It was Kim who wanted to see Kleoboulos,' said Beth as she gave him the Greek style peck on both cheeks.

Rob soon covered the few streets to his own space. There was no bath but a good hot shower, and he let the water pound onto his shoulders. He did have witchhazel and he thought about how nice it would be to have someone to dress his scratched back, someone good and kind and sensible. Someone like Beth, and with that thought, he fell into a sound sleep.

WEDNESDAY MORNING

Mel and Claire were up, showered, dressed and out on the patio with their coffee and cigarettes a little earlier than usual. Although Mel knew that the card making equipment was ready in a box marked for that day, she wanted to get the tables set out neat and tidy, just as Tanya always had them each morning. Nevertheless she knew she would handle the whole morning better if she allowed herself that essential quiet cup of coffee and cigarette before starting anything. Claire felt the same and had automatically woken with time for that early morning relaxation. They sat there quietly in the morning breeze that drifted down the valley to the sea.

Mel was not daunted by the task ahead, not in the least worried. Only last month she had given a demo to the

Mothers' Union and they had asked if she would start a card making group in the autumn. But for some inexplicable reason there were slight butterflies in her tummy at the thought of standing in front of the craft group. Maybe it was using someone else's materials and another person's ideas as to how things were done that caused the slight flutter. But a few mouthfuls of the coffee that Claire had made and a long draw on her cigarette seemed to restore her equilibrium. Apart from saying thankyou for the coffee they sat in silence as they usually did first thing in the morning.

Mel glanced at her companion and was again struck by the dark beauty that was Claire. Even at this time in the morning she looked like a model in Mel's eyes. The blue-black curls tumbled in a halo like the hair portrayed in medieval paintings. A rather strong nose and a wide mouth seemed to be just right for Claire, yet might have been overpowering on someone else. Her shoulders were sloping from a long neck and the rest of her was in proportion and elegant right down to the scarlet polish of her pedicure. She wore a plain black sleeveless top and red shorts completed the picture. Mel did not feel dowdy or second rate beside Claire. She had enough sense of her own identity to be comfortable in anyone's company. In a way, that is what modern village life did for you. No longer did country life revolve around the master in the big house and the servant at the gate. Certainly respect was shown to those in positions, such as the vicar and old

Dr. Pearson. But everyone understood that whilst all were not financially or educationally equal, each was dependant on the other to create a harmonious way of living. Nevertheless she was glad she had a new cotton dressing gown from Marks and Spencer and not the old seersucker one she nearly packed.

'Do you mind if we go down now, I would rather be there five minutes before anyone arrives than five minutes after the others troup in. I would rather not be searching in Tanya's boxes with an audience.'

'I quite agree and was only waiting for you to say the word. I am at your command, oh great maker of cards,' Claire teased Mel as she took both cups to wash in the kitchenette at the side of the patio.

Everything was as expected. All the materials for aperture cards were there in the box. The cards were the basic pre-cut design and there were lots of variations on a theme. This presented no problems for Mel as it was a style she often used. She just needed to remember basic hints like checking that any design inside the card did not show through the window if the open, see-through style was used.

Mel had asked Claire and Ruth to each take the end seat at a table. She would sit at the third table herself. In this way Mel felt confident that if there was even the smallest problem it would be dealt with instantly. Delighted that everyone had arrived on time, she stood at one end of the patio and started the way that Tanya always did, by saying good morning.

'Kalimera, ti kanete?'

'Kalimera. Kala! Poli kala,' was the group response in Greek and Andrea added, *'Kai esi?'*

'Kala, poli kala,' Mel replied and having made a start with her first experience of teaching a craft group, she continued by explaining what the aim of the session was, i.e. to make a greetings card using the aperture method. She showed examples of the various styles, using a straight single fold or the double fold which gave your window self backing.

'Although card blanks can be bought with the window already in place, and you are welcome to use any from the selection Tanya has provided. It is a challenge to start with an A4 card and cut your own,' she explained. 'I will show you the options for using the aperture, both for the single and double fold so those who prefer the readymade version can get on, and then I will go back to the methods of cutting blank card.' The next bit was a fairly easy as there were plenty of examples only needing the briefest of explanation.

Whatever Beth did Kim usually copied, but as Beth had gone straight to the coffee pot this morning Kim was examining the samples on her own.

'Have you a favourite yet?' asked Mel, trying to encourage Kim to make a choice of her own.

'Yes, this one with lots of cut out pictures. It is just a

boat but it will remind me of Lindos. Do you think it's hard to do?'

'Not exactly easy,' Mel agreed, 'that cut out bit is called decoupage. It is more a case of having the patience rather than it being difficult, I think.'

'In the box are some pale blue cards which would go well with the boat and there are lots of shell embellishments that would make the whole scene stand out if put along the bottom of the front bit. I am sure it will look brill,' she assured Kim.

Glory of glories, no one wanted to do the cutting out bit, which let Mel off the hook, as she knew how to do it but rarely did, not achieving as professional a finish as the machine cut ones from the craft shops. This meant she could spend more time going around the tables looking at individual progress. Even that did not present a problem, as any questions arising from those on other tables had been directed to Ruth or Claire.

Claire had at first protested that she was not a card maker but Mel had assured her it was less about card making than encouragement. In no time at all they were sitting on the balcony with their mid-morning coffee, laughing and chatting.

They were surprised to see Rob as he didn't usually join the group during the day. Beth called to him and asked if he was joining them for coffee. He said he would love a coffee, and paused to look at the handiwork before taking the seat offered. Everyone listened quietly when Rob spoke, giving the latest update on Tanya. They were pleased to know that it was nothing serious and she should be OK with another day's rest. The doctor suggested that she stayed off her feet until Thursday morning, a bit of a compromise that would not cause too much disruption to the schedule. Then, once Beth was again seated, having given Rob coffee and two biscuits, he asked for a moment of their time. The chatter stopped again and most people thought it would be more instructions from Tanya about the day's arrangements.

'When Tanya had the accident I was on my way to Kleoboulos' tomb. Later in the evening, a lot later, after our meal in Medeast, I decided to continue my walk. Then, in the dark I lost my footing.'

There were gasps from the group, imagining what could have happened to anyone falling in such a dangerous place.

'That explains the cuts on your face and the nasty bruise on your elbow,' Margaret added, stating the obvious, but out of concern for Rob.

'I am not sure how long I was there for but it seemed a long time trying to stay in one position in case I caused the rocks to move or indeed fell off the edge. Then I heard voices.'

Kim took up the story, explaining how brilliant the taxi drivers had been when Beth had asked them for help.

'So I just wanted to say thankyou again and please

accept that your evening meal tonight will be my treat.'

Rob was now feeling embarrassed at being the focus of attention and wished he could just slip out of the group and back to his rooms.

'Thank you for the coffee and I will see you all at Steve's later. Bye,' and he made a hasty retreat.

Rob was more bruised than he had admitted. His ribs ached and one knee was causing him some discomfort. Physician heal thyself, he thought and decided to put a damp crepe bandage around his knee when he got into the apartment. He would then lay down for a while. 'Nothing much changes,' he muttered to no one in particular as he made his lonely way back up the path from Electra. 'Made a hash of that and I only wanted to let everyone know how great the girls were last night, not show off about buying them dinner.' He continued to mutter on as people often do who spend much of their time living alone. He wrapped the bandage around his knee and rubbed some anti-inflammatory gel onto his aching shoulder. Then having dispensed himself two Paracetamol he decided to walk up to Delight, ordered a frappe, and watched the world go by on the street below.

Margaret finished her coffee and was ready to demonstrate the blue flower. Newspaper covered the table and a rectangle of rice paper was laid horizontally, secured at the corners by four two-euro coins. She began to grind her ink whilst they gathered their chairs around the table. When everyone was comfortable she began.

'This branch and flowers is to show you another way of using your brush whilst building on what Tanya did with the bamboo.' Margaret lifted the demo picture for everyone to see. 'First we start with the flowers and add the branch later. Each flower has five petals, but they are flowers, living things, so not all petals will be exactly the same. Which is rather useful as when you first do them it is hard to judge how to space them in the circle.' Margaret spoke with confidence. She had already decided to just treat the whole thing as a W.I. meeting and not let it bother her. 'The lesson here is to use two colours on the brush, blue and black. So you load up your brush with blue paint first, then dip the tip in black ink. The point of the brush will be the centre of the flower. Keep the point still and move the heel of the brush round in an arc to make a petal.'

By now she had three petals completed and held up the paper to make sure everyone could see what she had done.

'You should have enough paint and ink to do the whole flower, but may have to add a very little black to the tip,' she continued. 'Remember the short hairs in the middle of the brush hold a well of blue paint. At first just move the brush round evenly but once you have the hang of it you can lift the heel of the brush and so flute the edges of the petals. To make the plant live, you can add a half flower at the end or above. You will see by the painting samples when they are passed round later.'

She stopped talking and glanced around the group to see if anyone needed to ask a question at this stage, but everyone was just waiting for her to continue with the next part of the demonstration.

'Now for the branch. Do not clean your brush as the little remaining blue will harmonise the picture. Load the brush into the ink, remove the excess and starting at one end, about an inch below the flowers, drag the flat brush across the paper. Make it a bit lumpy and jagged, like a branch.'

Again she stopped to show what she had done. To be honest she thought that Tanya had not stopped often enough when demonstrating the previous day.

'And as the paint runs out it will give you the shading, as it did for the bamboo. All you do then are the stamens and the stalks.'

Everyone clapped Margaret's efforts. The painting looked quite good considering she was talking all the way through. Not that talking was much of a hardship for Margaret at any time. She passed out the examples that Tanya had left ready in the Chinese box of equipment. Heather had put out the paper, ink, stone and brushes during coffee, so silence reigned while they all concentrated on their art work.

After twenty minutes Margaret walked around the tables to see how everyone was getting on. What she saw was an amazing variety of paintings, but essentially they were all reasonably true to the picture in front of them. Only Ruth was still practicing the flower petals on a small piece of spare paper, not yet happy enough to try it out on her main paper.

Margaret took the small piece and screwed it up, a bit uncertain for a second what Ruth's reaction would be.

'Well, there is a first for everything, thankyou Margaret dear. Now I have no excuse but to get on with it.' Ruth was laughing so much that she had a job to keep the brush still, which led to some interesting fluting around the edges of the petals. Within a few moments all her flowers were done and she started on the branch. Only by chance she thought to take off some of the excess ink, but as she had done this, the branch took on its shaded craggy appearance. Pleased with the results so far she was reluctant to add the stalks and stamens but, with an almost dry brush as Margaret had instructed, the picture was complete. The feeling of achievement was immense. As she looked up she saw others sitting back and chatting. Was she the last to finish? She didn't care. Ruth had found her niche in the art world at last. This was it, painting with a Chinese brush.

Ruth made a bee line for Margaret. 'Thank you for your help. Without which I might not have got started.'

'A bit drastic, but it worked, all with good intention.'

'Yes, dear, and you gave such a wonderful demonstration.'

STEVE AND MARGARET

Margaret was not used to walking into bars. Except for the football, on big screen television, nights out down the local were not part of her and Jack's life. But coming into Steps was different. You felt you were calling in on a friend for even if Steve was not there his lovely, chatty daughter was. She and Jack had come into Steps a few times to watch the cricket and one of the girls that sometimes worked there was called Tanya. Even so, Margaret was surprised to find it was the same young lady running the craft group. One thing about Steps was that you could get a decent cup of tea and there was sometimes cake, which Steve never charged for as it was left over from a party or function the night before.

'Margaret, you look very cool and charming this

afternoon. How are you enjoying the craft group? They seem a right mixture this year, though I am sure Tanya is handling it all very well.'

'Oh Steve, I can not believe what a great time I am having. I only booked in as a filler; you know, to give me company whilst my family are down the beach. I can't do that nowadays, sit on the beach all day. And there's not much fun getting the bus on your own. I don't mind in England, but I have been to all the places I want to see on Rhodes, thankyou very much. So I thought I would come here for a nice cup of Tetley's. Is there any cake today?'

'There is but I don't know what it is. Had a birthday party here last night and there is a big tin of things that need eating up, and the biscuits you brought in at the start of the week. Some of those left as well.'

You could get a toastie to eat in Steps if Steve had remembered to get the bread and a choice of filling, which he did in the middle of summer when there was more demand for such things. Otherwise there was the pizza place down below, or, if there were some friends there late at night, the Chinese takeaway was a favourite haunt. Steve was so easy going with things like that. He did not object to people bringing their supper into the bar, especially if they ordered a Chinese for him as well.

But this was the afternoon and soon Margaret was settled on the balcony with her tea and cream slice (well two actually, as Steve had insisted it would only go to waste if she did not have it). Steve had changed the music to a soft

Country and Western style, as most older people found this more relaxing to listen to. Then when he had served another couple with lattes he joined Margaret on the balcony.

'Is everything ready for the big day? Have you met all the in-laws and the out-laws? There has to be a few of those in every family,' Steve teased Margaret.

'Yes to the in-laws and - for a Greek family - there are remarkably few. And they are such lovely people. Fancy Tassos' aunt giving them that big house; they are set up for life now. They have room for a family when one comes along and room for an office to run their design business from. They are very lucky young people.'

'Yes, a good start and hopefully a fine life to come. I am pleased for them but also for you as you now have every reason to come and visit Lindos as often as you wish,' Steve suggested.

'I will come when I am invited but I am a great believer in young people finding their own way for living and getting along. Not easy if you have old people interfering and telling you what to do.'

And Steve could see that however much Margaret would want to spend time in Lindos she would never outstay her welcome. Margaret was blissfully unaware of her granddaughter's dilemma at the Atrium Palace. She had not rushed back to the hotel that morning, wishing to give her daughter and the family a chance to recover from the flight and settle in. Had she known that Tracy was in tears she would not be sitting chatting to Steve and eating cream cakes.

Tracy could not find her wedding tiara.

'Mum, I am sure you had it when we left the hairdressers on Monday. I never even thought about packing it.'

'Well that says it all,' her mother retorted. 'You never even thought. Arguing will not solve anything, so go and have another look through your cases, then we will sort something out. It is not the end of the world is it?'

'It is to me,' Tracy wailed. Having checked her bags again, Tracy rang her Nan.

'Sweetheart, please don't be so upset, we will go and find Cici at her new shop and she will know what to do. If need be she will make you another one.'

'May I come now Nan, please?'

'Yes of course you can, I'm in Steps Bar, you remember Steve. Tell your mother where you're going, no need to upset her by charging off. Get the shuttle bus.'

'Oh Nan, the bus is for old 'uns like you, I can run down the hill quicker.'

'Less cheek, young lady, I will wait here. See you soon.'

Margaret had forgotten that Steve closed the bar in the afternoon to go to Krana for a swim and to relax by the pool.

But Steve only said, 'What a good idea to go and ask Cici,' and poured Margaret another cup of tea.

AMANO

Cici started making jewellery when at university as a way to help fund her social work degree. The fashion of putting beads of every shape and colour together was in full swing, and Cici soon found she had a flair for making what her friends and fellow students wanted. Then, when she had gained her qualifications, she rented a small shop in Lindos and continued to make jewellery. Her business was a great success. And that was where Margaret had met her three years ago when looking for an eighteenth birthday gift for Tracy. Cici had helped Margaret and Jack choose the necklace, earrings and bracelet. They were put into a satin lined box and gift-wrapped, the same set that Tracy had intended to wear with her wedding dress.

Margaret was hoping she would find Cici at her new

shop, Amano, on the main street. Not only had she opened this second shop but, with Paul, her Greek-American husband, had a lovely baby boy to look after as well. Margaret was not disappointed. The young lady was serving a customer and the baby was cooing in a carry cot beside her. As soon as Cici was free Tracy explained what had happened.

'You see, I matched the tiara I bought in England with the design of the necklace Nan bought here for my birthday, now I have left the headpiece at home, and the wedding is on Saturday.'

'Oh that's not a problem! I thought it was this afternoon, and even that would not be too much of a task,' she replied in her softly spoken perfect English.

'I suggest you get the size and shape you want first, by trying some on the stand over there and then I can customize it to match the necklace.'

Tracy had only needed one kind word for her eyes to fill with tears again.

'It is a very anxious time when you are getting married. Everything has to be perfect on the day. Please don't worry, because it will be,' added Cici.

As soon as they moved away from the counter an Italian tourist, with a handful of bracelets, was waiting to pay for her purchases. Margaret was pleased about the success of the new venture. Although there were some exclusive items, on the whole most remained reasonably priced. Cici and Paul were not greedy people and realized that tourists often only wanted an inexpensive gift to take home for a friend or relative. Tracy spent half an hour trying on designs that were nothing like her original tiara. Margaret was amazed at the variety. Eventually she had decided.

'Nan, would you mind if I didn't wear your necklace? I love this one with the blue stones and there is a necklace to match and Tassos has not seen me wear it before so it will be a surprise. This is how I would like it to be, now I have time to think about it.'

You have had twelve months since you got engaged, she thought to herself, smiling at the logic, or lack of it, in her grandchild. 'Well I think that is a lovely idea and the stones show up your eyes more, and the lovely leaf shape is perfect,' her grandmother assured her. 'And I am gasping for a cup of tea.'

They stood for a moment watching the still sleeping child.

'Any ideas?' Cici asked Tracy.

'Yes, I love this tiara with the blue stones, and the matching set that goes with it. And it fits perfectly, so no need to alter anything, thankyou.'

So Cici placed each item into a satin lined box, and the boxes into a beautiful bag, and thought, not for the first time, that her social work degree had not been wasted.

FOUR FOR DINNER

They'd had such a good day. Now everyone was gathered again in Steps Bar for their pre-dinner drink. As is often the way, many of the group had decided on their favourite seats. Max, as was always his way, had stood up to greet Ruth as she entered. He thought how calm and serene she looked in a simple chiffon dress. Her only adornment was a small watch on a gold bracelet.

'Just a fruit juice, please, Steve, as I think I overdid it last night.'

'Your wish my command, Madam. By all accounts it was quite a long evening walking along the beach at the witching hour. What next, skinny-dipping?'

Ruth was taken aback. Not by Steve's teasing but by Max's indiscretion. She looked at him aghast. In a flash Steve assessed the potential trouble he had landed the guy into and hastened to put things right.

'Madam, you are in Lindos, and nobody, absolutely nobody, goes out of one door or into another without being seen. And I have it on good authority that you were taking a late drink in Palestra in the company of a certain young man. Who shall be nameless of course.'

Ruth relaxed and felt a bit foolish for thinking Max had been indiscreet. And even more foolish realizing that there was nothing to be indiscreet about. They were adults enjoying each other's company, nothing more or less. So why was she embarrassed? Obviously Steve thought there was no cause for embarrassment otherwise she was sure he would not have raised the subject, even in jest.

Max who was standing with Ruth at the bar and party to this conversation found himself blushing. He hoped that his suntan was hiding this. Now Steve had poured the drink and was taking another order.

'Oh dear, what can I say?'

'Not one thing, my dear Max. You forget it was I who asked you to walk down to the beach, also to stay longer and have a drink in the taverna. So you see I have been hoisted on my own petard, as my father was so fond of saying.'

They left the bar and sat on what was becoming their usual settee.

Tanya had not needed to organize a venue for the

Wednesday evening meal as there was a barbecue at Steps Bar, and they were all invited. As it turned out many of the guests were otherwise engaged.

As June had predicted when they met in Birmingham, Margaret was meeting up with her family, newly arrived at the Atrium Hotel.

Although Rob and the girls intended going to the Chinese, and would come back to the bar later, Miles had made sure that Heather and Andrea were coming to the barbeque. Mel and Claire had decided to go to an Italian restaurant, Gatto Bianco, near St. Stefanos' square. And everyone assumed that it was OK leaving Max and Ruth to their own devices.

On any other occasion Max would have been delighted but this was the evening he had promised to dine with Henrietta. How could being with Ruth suddenly become an issue? It was not being with Ruth but meeting up with Henrietta that was becoming a bit more than a problem. Naturally on the day they bumped into each other he had been delighted at the chance meeting with an American acquaintance. Sorry to hear of the death of her husband, and remembering how kindly he had been treated in her home so many years ago, he had met her several times for tea at Broccolino's and he enjoyed her company. But when she let slip that she had journeyed from London to Rhodes to meet him, he felt a little uncomfortable. Not that he thought he was God's gift to women, far from it. And certainly any sort of a catch he might have been years ago was a thing of the very distant past in his opinion. However, as he had found out since acquiring his status as a widower, there were many lonely and charming ladies of a certain age looking for a partner. And he was definitely not looking for a partner, or whatever fancy word they had for it these days. He certainly did not wish to leave Ruth without company for the evening, guessing that she would not really be interested in a barbecue. Then he remembered the presence of another old friend in Lindos, Rusty Rawlins. In fact, at the time of his meeting with Rusty he began to think Lindos was the same as Piccadilly Circus, and if you stood in the square long enough the whole world would pass by.

On Monday afternoon Max had taken a stroll out and around the area heading towards the small beach. He had found a route that afforded him quite a pleasant walk without going up and down too many steps, and that in itself was quite an achievement in Lindos. Then, up by the Melenos Hotel, he saw the unmistakable figure of Rusty. Yes, he had put on a few pounds since they last met at a reunion dinner, but few men in this world stood six foot five in their stocking feet and did so with a back as straight as a ram rod, and topped that with a mop of curly red hair. Well, more grey than red now, but unmistakable regardless. The Honourable Bertrum Rawlins, known to Max for almost fifty years as Rusty, was a former R.A.F. buddy, the two of them having flown together in Cyprus. Naturally he was staying at the Melenos, which was not only the only hotel actually in Lindos village, but was listed with the Boutique Hotels Around the World group. After the usual "fancy seeing you here" greeting that one makes on bumping into friends in an unusual stomping ground, they relaxed on the patio overlooking the beach with a coffee and a shot, and a bit of where and when conversation.

'Last thing I heard, you were nicely tucked up with an American widow of considerable means. What happened old boy, did you get cold feet?'

'You could say that, I expect, but it was rather the other way round.'

'Don't tell me that you finally got a dear john? Wonders never cease.'

'How long have we known each other, Max? It must be close on fifty years now, and have you ever known me to cry over a woman? Love them and leave them, that has always been my motto. But I cried over this one. Perhaps I behaved in a particularly stupid way. I did rather play the fool. No, no, not with any other woman or anything crass like that but… she was so sweet for so long, and then it kind of turned sour. Not sure why. So I am doing what I do best, travelling around on my own with no one to please but myself. So, what brings you to this neck of the woods?'

Max was lost for words now. How could you admit to an old R.A.F. pal that you were on a craft course? And how could you not? 'Actually I came on an art course, studying Chinese painting, and other art and craft things as well, otherwise I would have gone to China.'

'You sly old fox, doing the Winston bit in your dotage then. Well, well. Look, I am going up to Rhodes town for a couple of days, take the card and give me a call about Wednesday. We can do dinner and a couple of shots for old time's sake.'

And these two old friends parted company for the time being, but found their minds going back over the years that they had known each other, and the many times they nearly died together.

Max excused himself from Ruth for a moment. He left the bar and standing at the top of Steps' steps, he took the card from his pocket and dialled Rusty's number. Now he had a fourth for dinner, a good chap with plenty of bright and witty conversation.

'I would like to take you to the Ambrosia tonight, making four for dinner with some friends of mine, please come as my guest,' Max asked Ruth when he returned to his place on the sofa again to finish his drink.

'Only if you promise that I buy dinner the next evening. We are both on a pension and it is just not fair for you to shoulder such extra expense.'

'Anything, dear lady, anything. Just say yes.'

They were laughing as they left the bar, saying thankyou to Steve for his kind invitation to the barbecue, but that they would not be attending. They waved goodnight to the others and separated, Ruth claiming she needed to change into something a little smarter for such a venue, and Max going off to meet Henrietta at Giorgos Bar as they had agreed.

Max had to admit that Henrietta looked lovely in a long skirted, taupe velvet suit. On such a warm evening she wore the jacket draped on her shoulders over a cream lace vest. She was slim without being too thin, which few ladies of a certain age managed to achieve. And her make-up was perfect, though he was never sure if he liked pencilled eyebrows, but on Henrietta it didn't look out of place. He was glad there would be company for dinner as he wondered if he might say something foolish if left alone with this lovely lady and a few glasses of wine. Ruth looked charming too when she arrived and Max silently wondered how two ladies could be so different yet look perfectly right in what they had chosen to wear for the evening. Ruth also wore a full length skirt, but hers was black watch tartan, in a sort of rustling material that he thought was taffeta, but he was not sure. And she wore a black jumper in fine wool. It made her skin look peachy in the light, lovely, with hardly a trace of make-up, just a little lipstick. He stood to greet her and to introduce them to each other. He then suggested they move into the restaurant and to the table he had booked, assuring them his fourth guest would know where to find them. They were shown through to an inner table and Max asked for the wine list. The ladies complimented each other on their choice of earrings, and Henrietta explained how she had acquired her ruby pendants in Singapore. When the last member of their party arrived. Max stood to greet him.

'Henrietta, Ruth, may I introduce an old friend of mine, the Hon. Bertrum, Lord Rawlins but known to most as plain Bertie.'

The meal was superb and the wine above average and Henrietta and Bertie made a huge joke about the fact that they also knew each other. Telling Max and Ruth how they met in the States, such a long time ago. Neither mentioned the fact that they had lived together for nearly three years in the more recent past. Certainly it would have been indiscreet for Bertie to talk of that time in their lives. This did not stop him from remembering the fun times they had and, as the evening wore on and the wine flowed, he was thinking of fun both in and out of the bedroom. For Henrietta it was both exhilarating and sad at the same time, and what now? Should they just say goodnight and part company? Would she have the choice anyway? If she offered him a nightcap would he accept? And what of Max? He seemed to be paying an awful lot of attention to this dumpy grey haired English lady he only met a few days ago. Or was he just being the perfect host, not wishing Ruth to feel left out of the conversation? Did she want his attention now that Bertie was here? Bertie was a Lord or something, so maybe her friends had got it all wrong about him being just a gold digger. He was hardly on his financial uppers if he was staying at the Melenos! And it was her life anyway, but how was she going to handle this situation?

Considerate as ever, Max was aware that Henrietta and Bertie needed time to talk. As they had dined quite early there was still time for him and Ruth to walk to the beach for a nightcap. Having thanked George for his usual excellent service, he drew the evening to a close.

'We will do this again before you leave,' Rusty said, as Ruth and Max excused themselves, claiming an early start in the morning as they were catching the seven-thirty coach to Rhodes.

'Thursday we can choose as a free day,' Max had explained with a touch of humour in his voice. 'We are allowed out on a sightseeing trip. Ruth and I are going to Symi for the day. Then back to the grindstone, or should I say the ink stone, on Friday.'

Bertrum, the Honourable Lord Rawlins, had stood to kiss Ruth good night Greek fashion, a peck on both cheeks, and a firm handshake and a wink to Max.

RUTH SHARES HER PAST

Ruth asked Max if he felt able to walk to the beach again and so they found themselves strolling down towards Nefeli, and were so pleased to find it in darkness, if you can call one street lamp and a waning moon darkness. They chose their usual table. There were no other occupants under the palm trees at that time of night.

'Are you sure you are warm enough, my dear?' Max asked her. But in reply she put a finger to his lips to quash anything he might say.

'Sh, sh, please, Max, let me do the talking for the moment.'

He was curious and then surprised when she took a packet of cigarettes out of her bag and lit up. She left the packet and the lighter on the table between them.

'When you were talking about your past yesterday I could understand so much of your pain. You see, I also lost a child. A different circumstance, a different age, and my child was a little girl. That is why I wanted us to walk down to the sea again and sit in the dark. It is so calm and comforting. This is where I wanted to be when I told you about my daughter Anna.'

Ruth was shivering despite the warm evening air and was glad of the pashmina she had bought in a village shop for just an evening as this. Too warm for a jacket but needing that little extra covering. Tonight there was little light from the moon and only the warm glow of the distant street lamp. Ruth rarely smoked these days but she had bought a packet of a familiar brand and a lighter earlier in the day when she had made a conscious decision to tell Max about her life. If they were to stay friends, which seemed to be the case, she wanted no pretence.

'No one knows my story, now that my brother has died. He was the only one I trusted, and he never broke my trust. But now he has gone I feel there is no one to acknowledge that Anna ever existed. You see, our parents had married late in life and the atmosphere at home was secure, peaceful and encouraging. A home with old world standards, Catholic, of course, Daddy's brother, my uncle Frank, was a priest. Into this loving atmosphere came two children, me first and three years later, my brother, Francis. We had no reason to be other than healthy, happy and studious. We had the normal childhood spats but we were always best friends. I had this idea of being a journalist so I was sensibly encouraged to try for English at Cambridge. I could come home from there almost every weekend. I had no ambition to change the world or anything that noble. Naturally I joined the Catholic debating society and the Latin Mass group, but that was as radical as it got. I had a nice group of friends and was doing well with my studies. I looked forward to my graduation; life could not have been better.

'In our group was a boy from Dublin. We shared a lot of common ground; the same solid home background. For a long time Liam and I were friends, nothing more. But we were healthy young adults and regardless of our strict upbringings we became lovers. These were heady times, trying to balance what you knew to be right and proper with what your heart and your young body demanded. So we were forever trying to go back to our "just friends" status. But after a party or a fun day out, and a few drinks, we would wake up in the same bed.

'We worked hard in our final year, helping each other with revision at exam times and reading each other's dissertations with constructive criticism. We had become an item. We were now too tired and intense to worry about being together. We took each other for granted. Well, perhaps I took him and our relationship for granted. We never made plans or talked of the future.

One thing at a time, get a good degree first, and the rest of your life would follow. Then it was summer and he came to the conferring ceremony with his parents and his fiancée.

'And I was pregnant,' Ruth added in a voice that was barely audible, 'with a first class honours degree in classical literature.'

'You poor child, how awful for you,' Max muttered beneath his breath.

'I was no longer a child, I was twenty one and I had this responsibility. There were decisions that I had to make. No one could help me make those decisions. How grown up we think we are when we do not really know the meaning of the word, despite our first class education, or sometimes I think because of it and our sheltered home life. My brother, Francis started at Canterbury that September, I convinced the parents I needed a little time to travel around, that I could base myself with Francis and share the costs of a flat by doing some freelance work. It all fitted in. Have the baby adopted. But I never did have Anna adopted. You see, my brother had his own secret that he was desperate to keep from our parents. He was never going to want a woman to share his life.'

Max asked 'So, it did work, being a family I presume?'

'Yes it worked wonderfully well. Francis finished his degree and got work locally. The fact that my father had had a mild heart attack meant our parents never drove down to Kent. We could both visit them separately, although I longed to take Anna to see them. My father being ill convinced me I was right not risking such stress on them. We made a few friends, we never said we were brother and sister, we never said we were married. People just assumed. Our parents joked about grandchildren. We decided to home tutor to avoid the obvious questions, as we couldn't bear to tell Anna that Francis was not her real daddy. Then the situation was suddenly taken from us. Anna was diagnosed with a brain tumour. She lost her sight first, when she was seven. She bravely battled on for a year with all her senses gradually closing down. There was nothing anyone could do. We finally gave her back to the Lord two weeks after her eighth birthday.'

Max took two cigarettes from the packet and lit them both. Handing one to Ruth he looked out across the sea. The moon had come out from behind its cloud and put silver specks onto the silent water.

'Without Anna we had no reason to continue to live together and we both needed space to grieve. She was every bit as much Francis' child as she was mine. He had cared for us and protected us. Now he had a right to his own life. He moved to France, where he stayed for several years and then eventually to the Yorkshire moors. Daddy had died and I returned home to look after my mother. Initially I taught in a private school and then took a post in St. John of God, where I stayed until a few months ago, when I retired. I never wanted another child so I did not look for any other romantic attachment. I had the children at school and that sufficed. So now you know all there is to know about me and my rather quiet and ordered life, if you can call being surrounded by thirty children every day a quiet life. But you know exactly what I mean.'

They sat there in the dark, each absorbed in their own thoughts, taking some comfort in the almost forgotten experience of a cigarette. Both wondering how one moment in time can transform your whole life. Not that Ruth regretted knowing the little soul that was her daughter or Max the short happy time he had spent with Jack.

Max leaned forward and put his hand on her tear stained cheek. 'I think we could do with another brandy and it is my shout.'

'This has got to stop, I could get used to being a kept woman,' but Max was already on his feet, waiting to put his jacket around her shoulders and she was too spent to say anything but thankyou.

He held her close as they walked the few steps down to Palestra. They looked around, Steve was not there but Tanya sat at the far end of the terrace with a rather nice Scandinavian-looking man. They had begun to see what Steve had meant. You will always be seen in Lindos. But they did not care.

When settled with their brandy Max began to talk. 'Have you no regrets at the way your life has run?'

'Tell me, if you can, what having regrets would achieve. You see you cannot change the past, if you continue to live in the painful bits you create pain, both physical and mental. To what end?' She took a long slow sip of the sweet sticky drink and felt the warmth hit the back of her throat before she thoughtfully continued.

'And the greatest of these is charity. The old fashioned word for forgiveness as I am sure you know. So we forgive others, as they really know not what they do to us. And often the offence they have caused us only happens once, but we continue to play it over and over in our minds and allow ourselves to be hurt time and time again.' Her voice was no more than a whisper now. 'Of course we feel angry and hurt, but holding onto this anger and resentment does no harm to anyone but ourselves. Do people really intend to damage others for a lifetime? I am sure they do not. Yet we allow this hurt to have power over us long after the initial encounter, so we should at least try to forgive, if only for our own peace of mind,' Ruth continued, as much to herself as to Max. 'But it is just as important that we forgive ourselves. Truly forgive. To do otherwise is to hold onto sadness, keeping us in a place we do not want to be. A place we so often blame others for, yet we hold the key to our hearts and minds. We are master of our own thoughts at all times.'

Max put his hand over Ruth's as they were shaking a

little. 'Wisdom indeed, my dear. You have certainly given me a great deal to think about, and perhaps this will help me reconcile my past and deal more positively with the future. Shall I call for another brandy?' he asked.

'I think it is time we called it a day, or a night even,' she laughed as she checked her watch and found it was past the witching hour. They linked arms as they walked up the hill from the beach. An old and fond memory for Max and he tried to hold on to that happy thought. He already had the embryo of an idea creeping into his mind. What if? What if? For Ruth the experience was a new and enchanting one. A gentleman companion to walk with, one who clasped your hand as though it was the most normal and natural thing in the world. To be out and about at a beachside taverna in the early hours of the morning! What an interesting life this could be. They stopped and looked at the view when they got to the top of the long slope. Looking out again at a moonlit sea and the few twinkling lights from the village as it spread out around the bay. Both needed to get their breath back after the long climb and looking over the sea was a way of doing this without having to acknowledge the fact.

Ruth broke the silence. 'At least we know what our programme is for tomorrow, I am so looking forward to going to Symi Island.'

'Yes indeed, though I must say I have enjoyed the classes more than I expected. Part of that is the company of the young people chatting away, but we will see them all in Rhodes Old Town later for an evening meal in Romeo.'

'You pronounce it 'RomAo's,' Ruth corrected him.

'Yes, teacher,' Max teased her.

They both started to laugh and the serious tone of the evening was dispelled.

'I was thinking,' Ruth began, but then stopped in mid-sentence as his arm moved gently round her waist.

'Not a good idea at all at this time in the morning,' Max said softly in her ear.

So they stood for a few minutes more in quiet before making their way home.

SYMI
THURSDAY MORNING

Ruth had wanted to climb the Kali Strata since she had read James Collins' book, *Jason and the Sargonauts*. Just the title made her laugh and when the novel turned out to be a lighthearted mystery using musical clues, she became fascinated with the small island of Symi, and it was the prospect of visiting Symi that had attracted her to the craft holiday on Rhodes in the first place. But when Max asked to join Ruth on the daytrip she found herself hesitating before she replied.

Ruth decided it was better to be honest, to say what she was thinking. 'Max dear, you would be very welcome except that I have plans to visit some people when I get there and it will involve quite a steep walk up three hundred steps. But if you are content to find a nice taverna near the harbour and relax for the day, it would be lovely to have your company.'

'That will suit me fine as I have a rather unusual mission of my own on Symi Island,' he replied. 'A few years ago a friend acquired a beautiful leather jacket there. In fact I am to inherit the jacket in his will, but I'm damned if the fellow has the decency to die. So I am hoping to find this particular shop and get one for myself. A bit of nonsense really, but I have not bought anything new for a number of years, and if I find what I am looking for I will treat myself. On reflection I could bequeath my jacket to Steve. I would enjoy that and Steve would appreciate the thought, I know,' said Max warming to the idea.

'Yes but I don't think he would want to inherit too soon,' Ruth laughed.

So, seven o'clock the next morning saw them waiting for the coach at Lindos Reception and in just over an hour they were on the ferry. Still rather tired from the previous evening, the conversation was sparse. They had settled with coffees on seats on the outside deck but sheltered from the strong breeze.

'I have definitely decided to have a go at living in Lindos,' Max told Ruth. 'After all, as Steve said, it would be just like another posting, as I have moved around so much in my life.'

Ruth hesitated before replying. 'It is certainly a tempting prospect. I must admit I have been thinking of the pros and cons of organizing craft holidays, not quite like Tanya does, but on similar lines. And naturally not in Lindos, that would not be fair to Tanya and her aunt. Maybe on Symi, who knows?'

'But if it were possible to do that in Lindos would you consider us throwing our lot in together, business-wise and for companionship in the winter?' Max asked. 'You know, the occasional meal out on a fairly regular basis?'

'Yes, Max, thankyou. What a lovely idea,' she replied, with no hesitation at all. 'But I would not want to sell my home in England, I am not as brave as that. I am afraid I would need my security.'

'I understand, and there would be no need to if I acquired a larger house with a separate living space. I am sure there will be lots of things we will not agree on but I think we are too long in the tooth to fall out over trivia.'

'Perhaps we could talk it over with Tanya in the morning, ask her advice,' Ruth suggested.

Their conversation was brought to an abrupt halt by John, the trip escort.

'Good morning. Are you my people?' he asked.

'Well, young man, if you mean were we on the coach with you this morning, then yes we are your people. What can we do for you?'

John, still recovering from being called a young man, which did not happen very often these days, continued to smile regardless of the reprimand and the severe tones it was delivered in. 'I came to ask if I could help you actually,' he replied. 'I like to know my customers are happy and although I am not supposed to give you direct guided information I can help with any questions regarding the timing of today's excursion, or any concerns you might have.'

'Excellent, young man.' This time the reference to his youth came from Max. 'I have a business card here. It is for a leather shop. Will it be easy to find?'

'Not a problem at all. I can't tell you how to find it until I see which side of the harbour the boat docks. But either way it is only a short walk. Ask me when we disembark.'

Max was pleased with this, his day was organised and he sat back to enjoy the breeze coming across the sea on such a glorious day. Ruth was not sure how to find the Kali Strata, but she would ask later. Her eyes were closing, and she was glad she was wearing reactor glasses, which were almost dark enough to hide her eyes. Thoughts of Lindos and tomorrow were forgotten as they sat in companionable silence. The boat pulled into the bay at Panormitis Monastery and most people got off and headed into the church to light a candle and those who wanted a religious keepsake then crowded into the gift store. Any sense of a holy place was lost in the crush. Then it was time to go on board again for the half hour trip round the island into the main Symi harbour.

'There are times when you see a picture post card and the reality does not match up to the carefully taken photo,' Ruth said in quiet awe of the view before her. 'Have you ever seen anything more charming, or so perfect?' she asked more to herself than to Max, so he knew no reply was needed. The scene before them was a horseshoe shaped bay. An assortment of pastel coloured houses climbed up the steep landscape behind the harbour and seemed to touch the cloudless blue sky. Incredibly beautiful, more ethereal than real. As with other passengers, they could only stand and stare at such perfection. They moved off the boat and onto the quay, noting the time when they must embark for the return trip. Reality returned with a bang as the shop owners displayed their goods and exhorted the tourists to buy.

They stood in the shade and waited for John. After answering questions from others in their coach party and quite a few just from the general public, he was ready to join them. The girl beside him was also tall and slim but in contrast to John's grey mane, her hair was jet black.

'Let me introduce you. This is my wife, Maria,' he explained.

'Charmed, young lady. I am Max and this lady is my friend and fellow traveller, Ruth.'

First they needed a coffee and soon found a small place to sit. Max ordered a beer for himself and frappe for Ruth, John and Maria. John and Maria explained how they came to be living on Rhodes and some of the adventures they had when they first arrived.

'And what about the winter, do you find too much

time on your hands?' Max asked.

'We do a lot of walking and I also write,' John replied.

'Is that an occupational hazard when living in Greece?' Ruth asked. 'I am hoping to meet the writer James Collins today, do you know him?'

'To answer your second question first, I have been in contact with James via email, but have never met him. And yes, it does seem that you either paint or write when you come to Rhodes, even if you've done neither of these things before.'

'And are your books crime stories, John?'

'Not intentionally,' he laughed as he replied, 'I write travel books, three to date, *Feta Compli, Moussaka to My Ears,* and *Tzatziki For You to Say.*'

'Oh, well done.'

Would Ruth ever stop talking like a teacher? Max thought, and smiled, wondering if he sounded like a wing commander trying to get on with the other ranks.

Refreshed and rested, Ruth asked Maria where the bathroom was.

'I will come with you,' Maria replied. 'Were you both going up the Kali Strata today?'

'No, Max is going to Takis' leather shop and John's going to show him the way, and I am going up the steps on my own. We will meet up later.'

'Would you like me to come with you and we can leave the boys to their shopping?' Maria asked Ruth.

'What a lovely idea, but may we find the bathroom

first?' Ruth whispered.

A few minutes later and Maria had shown Ruth the entrance to the grand stone staircase that is the Kali Strata. Although she would never admit it, Ruth was pleased to have the young woman's company. It was quite a climb. They chatted easily and stopped often to take a breather and admire the wonderful views. At last they were outside Neil's photographic shop, Symi Dream. They went in, introduced themselves and were greeted like long lost cousins. The room was full of amazing photographic work, landscapes, village life, architecture and cats. Apart from the mounted prints, his pictures also sold as postcards and calendars.

'Sorry you have had a wasted journey if you wished to talk to James. He's in Rhodes for the next couple of days. He will be sorry to have missed you,' Neil explained.

'No dear, I had no intention of intruding into your private life, I was just so enthralled with the Sargonaut story, I wanted to come and see where it was set for myself,' Ruth assured him. Ruth bought a calendar, starting in September, and some postcards to keep, to remind her of the day. Neil told them about the minibus that would take them down to the main harbour again. They soon found Max sitting on a bench waiting for them. Maria said goodbye and went off in search of John. Ruth and Max strolled along the waterfront where the shops were and turned left. The stunning view they had seen as they entered the harbour was now surrounding them. Pastel-coloured houses piled up the mountainside, and the blue sky was matched only by the calm blue water of the bay.

They found a seat and sat down to order lunch.

THURSDAY MORNING GLASS AND ENCAUSTIC

Tanya was greeted by applause and 'welcome back' on return to her rightful position as tutor to the craft group. She thanked everyone for their good wishes and their understanding. And added a special thanks to Mel and Margaret for their contribution as demonstrators.

'It's Ruth you need to thank,' Margaret piped up. 'If she had not taken charge and organised everything we would still be sitting around like headless chickens.' The rest murmured their agreement.

'Yes, a big thankyou to Ruth for shepherding the sheep, sorry that doesn't sound very complimentary, but you all know what I mean. But she and Max are not here today, they have gone to Symi Island. Now we'd better get on as we will have a problem fitting you all in to try encaustic. But first we'll get on with today's card demo. Yesterday you were shown aperture cards by Mel, and the various ways you can use this technique to produce different effects. It is not often I say do it this way, but this morning I am doing just that. By now I hope you all recognise an aperture card. This one is different as it has acetate glued into the open space. What we are going to do is use glass paints to produce a card which will allow the light to shine through it, giving a very special effect; either a sea horse, rather appropriate for Lindos, I think, or a butterfly. 'On the back of the acetate on the card you need to brush a thin spread of blue glass paint. You can make this even or paint in waves if for the sea horse or go from a slightly darker blue to a very pale blue. Remember that the lines must go across the acetate when it's in a vertical position or your waves may go skywards.'

They laughed but were secretly glad Tanya had mentioned this as everyone was sure they would be have been the one to get it wrong.

'When you've done that leave it to dry. Choose your template, sea horse or butterfly, and with silver or gold outliner draw onto the spare acetate you have on the table. When that is dry, cut it out. You don't need to go too near the lines as the acetate edge will not show.'

Tanya knew that everyone was getting a little tired now. The sun, the sea and the late nights were taking their toll, so she was rather more pedantic than usual.

'Use the glass paint to colour your cut-out and, when dry, glue onto the background.' Tanya immediately took various versions of the card round to the tables so that the different effects of gold and silver outliner could be seen. With Ruth and Max missing, giving two less to worry about, she was able to sit down again quite quickly, as the group concentrated on the project in hand, and draw breath. Tanya had thought of giving the glass painting a miss, as she could not see how she was going to fit it all in. She was always reluctant to miss out anything that was on the website in case it was the one item a guest was interested in. This way she had covered glass painting, even though very briefly. She reminded everyone that she would not be there at five o'clock as they were going to Rhodes for a look round the old town and dinner. But, to be honest, glass painting was self-explanatory once someone was shown the tools.

Kim thought it was something she could try out with the children. She never let them have scissors on their own.

After coffee she asked everyone to gather round as she explained the principles of encaustic art. Tanya began, 'Once again I'm introducing you to a very old art form, but with a very modern twist. Coloured wax has been found on the tombs of the ancient Egyptians, the wax melted onto the wood in shapes of birds and plants, coloured as it was by powdered rock or berries. Heaven knows how old this art form is. Not only the Egyptians but the Greeks also used a form of burning pictures into wood then colouring with herbal dyes held in wax, so I think it safe to guess at four thousand years. But there is no need to gather berries and render down fat to make wax as we can now buy coloured wax in slabs like this.' She paused to hold her box of waxes up for all to see.

'Certainly if you look on the web you will find quite a few artists, but for me the most interesting exponent of encaustic art must be Michael Blossom. Later I will show you a selection of his fabulous landscapes. He has been the inspiration for the revival of this strange craft and you can buy card and waxes by mail order from his studio in Wales.' She paused to gather her thoughts whilst taking a much needed drink from the jug of iced water. 'But,' Tanya continued, 'not a lot of point knowing that unless you know what to do with a household iron and some coloured waxes when you get them.'

'First, your card; it must have a slightly shiny surface, and the best source to practice on is the back of Christmas or birthday cards. If the card people are so inconsiderate as to put their logo or price list there then you can still use it, just crop the picture later and, if need be, enlarge your design on the computer. The iron can be a special iron bought for the job,' said Tanya as she lifted a small craft iron up for everyone to see. 'But I prefer to use an old household iron without the steam holes in the base, if you are lucky enough to find one. There are other tools, all available from Michael, but with practice you should be able to achieve anything with your iron,' she concluded.

As she was talking Tanya had plugged in and heated the iron, and started to melt blue and pink wax onto the base. She picked up an A5 sheet of gloss card and deftly dragged the iron across it. No more, just one stroke, and the result was impressive enough to induce a gasp of surprise from everyone.

'Bloody hell,' Kim exclaimed. 'And I have been wasting my iron on the old man's shirts.' They all shared in the joke and Kim felt part of the group at last.

With a few deft strokes of green and yellow Tanya had placed hills below the sky. She turned the iron on its side and worked into the wax, making leaves appear, cutting spear-like through the foreground and into the sky. Tanya used what she had learnt about perspective from Chinese painting for the next addition to her picture and, with black wax added, she made lava rocks by lifting the iron quickly from the card. The jet black immediately drew the rocks forward and the rest of the landscape back. Dipping the tip of the iron in red, another Chinese touch, she added a few small flowers. The picture was complete.

The group broke into a spontaneous round of applause.

'One small problem, as this is Greece, that is we cannot overload the electrical extension. So I would like three people to start the encaustic now and anyone else that is interested to wait 'til the morning please.'

Claire declined the offer to try the encaustic. Surprisingly, she had taken to card making and, perhaps because of her friendship with Mel, enjoyed doing variations on the theme they had started in the mornings. It was an interesting demo to see but, she knew without a doubt, that it was not something she was keen to practice. The sea horse was enough for one day. She also needed to opt out for a couple of hours, to recharge her batteries for reasons only Mel knew anything about.

Not for the first time, she thought how strange it was that you trusted a total stranger with secrets you would not disclose to your closest friends.

CLAIRE ON DIMITRIS' BAY

Claire had discovered the tranquillity of the small beach in St. Paul's Bay. Because it was rocky with quite a sharp dip to the sea bed there were few chattering parents with small children. Dimitris was on the beach with his dog but came back to his Kantina when he saw her. She took a cold beer from his fridge.

'You prefer this beach?' He asked her.

'I prefer less chatter. I am rather antisocial at the moment. I have had a stressful time and need some peace.'

'But you are with Tanya and her group of ladies, so how can you find peace?' He asked.

'How did you know I was with the craft group? Never mind, no need to answer that.'

'I have no need to answer certainly, but I will. I saw you at Medeast on Tuesday. Make the most of your solitude. True peace is a rare commodity.'

She thought it a strange thing to say, but guessed that there was not much peace when you were running a café, even in a secluded bay. She put her towel and bag onto a sunbed, shed her shorts and top and, stepping carefully between the rocks, immersed herself in the cool, clear water and began a strong, slow crawl. Each day seemed to take London and Samuel further away from her reality. It was as though her ten-year affair had never happened. Her busy life was fading into just a distant memory, as though much of her existence had actually happened to someone else.

'So is there another life for me somewhere, a new job, as challenging and as interesting as the last one?' she asked the cloudless blue sky. But in her heart she knew that it would be a long time before she had a secure position in a large company such as Clear Elevations and was beginning to doubt her own ability to start chasing contracts and running her own ship. And what about a man in her life? Would she find a new man, this time someone who would owe allegiance to no one but her? Was there any guarantee in any relationship these days? Was there ever? Sam's wife, Sylvia, had known this only too well for all those years. And for the first time ever she felt sad for Sylvia and her family, going along with this pretence of a happy home when knowing that the man she loved, the father of her children, was shagging some tart from the office.

Claire added her tears of salt water to the sea in which she was swimming and for one moment was tempted to just swim out until she could swim no more and then there would be no more problems to solve. Who would miss her if she did? She meant nothing to anyone, few friends would send flowers to Golders Green, even fewer would miss a few hours from work for the funeral, that is if anyone actually found her and identified her.

Her mother flashed into her mind. Her mother, that little woman who had spent most of her life giving out loving retribution in a desperate attempt to save Claire from what she was experiencing now. No way could she leave her to face the mess that Claire herself had created, never in a million years. She broke into a quick crawl parallel with the beach and expending such energy and pent up anger seemed to cleanse her.

Twenty minutes later she fell exhausted onto the sunbed and slept.

RETURN FROM SYMI

Ruth and Max retraced their steps to board the ferry again for the journey home, and saw John and Maria. They thanked them for their company and their help during the day. Ruth reminded John that she and Max were staying in Rhodes for the evening. She did not want the coach delayed waiting for them at Mandraki harbour. As they walked up the ramp Max thought that it had been a lovely day out, and now they were going home.

Ruth thought, 'Can I do this, call these Greek islands, Rhodes and Symi, my home?' On the boat they found a couple of seats in the lounge.

'G and T?' Max asked.

'If I do I will sleep all the way,' was her reply.

'That makes two of us,' and that was how they passed the time sailing back to Rhodes.

Ruth was so pleased she had not thrown cold water on Max's wish to join her for the day. The truth was she felt surprised at her own reaction to even the thought of offending him or hurting him in any way. It was not a 'very sorry, but' that one would use to a casual acquaintance. He was so kind and considerate towards her, in his quiet, gentlemanly way. She would rather have missed walking up the Kali Strata than to have offended him.

Not that she wasn't considerate to everyone she met, it was part of who she was. But Max had seemed more like an old and trusted friend than many people she had known for years. And now he was talking of plans to move to Lindos. Just up sticks and move over. And if Max could do it at his age what was to stop her from doing the same? Why should it be just a dream? She already felt she knew so many nice people. Sheila at the library; well it was a laundry really with lots of books, but it was the only library in Lindos. Then there was Billy, the wonderful blind man she had met in the Ikon Bar, and naturally Steve and Miles, Tanya and her friend Sam. How lovely it would be to have more time to know Greg and Jenny at the Beir and Beer, also Sandra and Nikos, at the corner shop, whose daughter was away at Oxford. So many kind and interesting people.

For the first time moving to Greece was becoming a distinct possibility rather than just passing thought. Then she gave in to weariness and dozed off.

AT ROMEO

A minibus had been booked to take everyone up to Rhodes on Thursday evening, but Margaret had chosen to stay in Lindos. Both sides of her family were now gathered from various parts of the U.K. to attend the wedding on Saturday. She had understood that her brother, Gordon, a Methodist minister, would not be able to come, so it was a lovely surprise when he and his wife Joyce had walked into the hotel the previous evening. Tanya said they could join the outing, but they had been to Rhodes before, so declined.

With Max and Ruth already in Rhodes following their day out in Symi it was a depleted group that gathered to wait for the minibus, until Miles and Bertie joined them. Kim and Heather were deep in conversation, laughing again about the sisters' Faliraki adventure.

'These little geeks with their shirts off - each one of them red as a London bus from sunbathing. They looked as though they had skipped school to get here,' Kim told Heather. Again she told of the chat-up lines from the Italians and they laughed about being too old for Faliraki.

When the girls made no attempt to board the bus, Rob got on and Beth indicated for him to sit beside her. He was a little embarrassed by this, but sat down anyway. He went to offer Kim the seat when she eventually stepped onto the bus, but she laughed and said she would sit with Heather for a change. Heather was a bit miffed by this as she had hoped to sit with Miles. Miles stood to allow Andrea to sit in the window seat beside him. She would be pleasant enough company, as he rather liked the kid. Claire was not the least bit concerned to find that she was sitting on her own. Then a tall elderly man, obviously English, with a mop of grey curly hair bounded onto the step, ducked his head to get into the seating area, said, *'Kalispera,'* to everyone and sat down beside her. He did not stop talking and she did not stop laughing until they were almost in Rhodes.

'Let me tell you, my young lady, and you must believe me on this one, one ruddy world monument is much the same as another,' Bertie said as they came down the hill to the coach stop near the Top 3 Bar. 'I think you and I should find a nice bar and start the evening with a decent drink, or maybe two.'

Claire could not think of a more civilised suggestion.

There were several parts of Rhodes old town that looked as though they were out of a Shakespearian film set and one of these gems was the precinct of the restaurant, aptly named, Romeo. It was here that the group were going to meet later that Thursday evening, but first they had an hour and a half to wander around the old town at their leisure. Tanya had given them little cards with a map on which Romeo Restaurant was shown with an arrow.

'If you go up the Street of the Knights, take the first turning on the left and walk straight through, eventually you will come to the right place,' she had told them. 'If you are in the centre of the old town, look for Socrates Street. Walk up past a monument and take the next turning on the left. Everyone will speak English so if you are lost, just ask any shopkeeper.' Having pointed everyone in the right direction, Tanya and Miles slipped around the corner to the Top 3 Bar for a much-needed coffee. Greeted by their friends, Spiros and Maria, they joined coach escort, Josephine, for an hour of chat before they needed to go through the town to Romeo.

Spiros was from northern Greece and had first come to Rhodes as a young police officer more than forty years ago. Maria grew up in the village of Kalathos, near Lindos. When she was young, everyone wore goatskin boots to avoid being bitten by snakes, and the people of

Kalathos had a reputation for making the best boots on Rhodes. They had opened the Top 3 more years ago than they cared to remember and, with the boom in tourism, Spiros left his police career to run the bar full-time. Maria shared the bar duties as well as raising their family. The coach escorts were always made welcome, as were the tourists who gathered at Top 3 to await their return transport.

Beth had accepted Rob's offer of a guide to the main points of historical interest. This was his third trip to the old town and he was confident he knew his way around. The other girls went looking in the clothes and gift shops as though there were not enough treasures to be found in Lindos in the past week. But, after all, they were on holiday and indulging in spending the evening doing absolutely nothing was what holidays were for.

As for Ruth and Max, they were very tired after a day spent on the boat trip to Symi Island. They sat in the Square of the Jewish Martyrs with a glass of wine, watching the world go by. It had been an extraordinary day. Not just the trip itself, but the mind blowing plans they had made to find somewhere on Rhodes or Symi to run craft holidays together.

'I wish we had not agreed to go to the restaurant this evening, though I do look forward to seeing Bertie again,' Max said as they finished their drinks.

'Me too, but I could quite easily curl up and sleep the evening away,' Ruth replied, stifling a yawn.

But that evening the members of the craft group were not the only ones to make their way to Romeo.

The phone calls Penny had taken during the week from Steve and Manolis had left her in no doubt that Andrea was her daughter. After much soul-searching, she had contacted Adonis. Now they hoped to see for themselves the young woman that their child had become.

Both of them came to the restaurant regularly, but it was many years since they had been here together. George, the owner came towards them with a welcoming smile. *'Kalispera, Penny. Ti kaneis?'* It was impossible for her to answer as he hugged her with one arm whilst kissing her on both cheeks and shaking her hand at the same time.

'Kalispera, Adonis, ti kaneis? How is the baby, is she looking like her mother?' And he hugged and kissed Adonis as was the way for good friends. They made their way up to the balcony and found a table with a clear view of the seating area below. Aris had spotted them and, leaving his post as a greeter, came up to see them. There followed handshakes, hugs and kisses once again and the questions about family directed towards Adonis. Though this time mobile phones were produced and pictures of their offspring admired, a normal conversation for friends in Greece. Aris returning to his post as greeter at the front of the restaurant, asked one of

the waiters to come and take their order. Immaculately dressed in polo shirts each waiter was multilingual and between them there was not a language in common European use that they could not understand. Greek, English and their native Albanian were common to all.

Neither Penny nor Adonis were in the mood to eat but they ordered a Greek salad and garlic bread, with a carafe of red wine. They had not seen each other for about twelve months so managed to fill the first half an hour with snippets of Lindos gossip.

Dear Adonis, Penny thought. He had not changed. If anything he was rather more handsome than the boy she had known twenty years ago. The fuller face suited him. He was still well-mannered and softly spoken. 'If only' came unbidden into her mind, but she refused to go down that road tonight.

As the years had gone by she had forgiven herself for panicking when she was pregnant, not having faith in Adonis and rushing back home to Devon. But Penny never really understood why she had not defied her parent and returned to Greece sooner, bringing Andrea with her. And in those three years in England she had lost Adonis to Voula. They sipped their wine in silence.

'Adonis, you don't have to do this. You have Voula and the family to consider, I can cope on my own,' Penny told him.

'You said that nineteen years ago,' he reminded her.

'Voula knows I am here with you this evening and she

knows why,' he continued. 'We must tell Andrea now, tell her that she has family, a father and mother and brothers and a small sister.'

'I know you are right. She is a grown woman and has every right to know about her past. I doubt if she will ever forgive me but she will have you, Voula and the family, and not before time.'

'Will the trust she has in your parents be broken?' he asked.

'They made the rules. I lost my child because of the ultimatum Dad gave. I always imagined it would all blow over and I would be able to go home. It was hard to stay away forever. Now they must face up to their past as I must face up to mine, and if that means they lose Andrea now, so be it.' She took a long slow draft from her glass.

'I hope that Andrea will understand. And is mature enough to see that everyone was acting in what they thought were her best interests? That is, everyone except me.'

'Penny, we both know that I could have made more effort to find you. But for some reason I did not. Perhaps I was afraid of the responsibility, perhaps marrying Voula was too easy. I do not regret my life but I am sad that I let you both down. I hope you have forgiven me even if Andrea is unable to do so?'

'We were so young, Adonis, just kids really. It is wrong to apportion blame for what we did then. No hard feelings friend. *Yia mas,*' Penny lifted her glass again by way of reply.

Adonis did not return her toast. He could not look at Penny at that moment. His gaze was drawn to the group of chattering young women now entering Romeo. There was no mistaking which one was Andrea.

Bertie guided Claire to the opposite side of a long table where Max and Ruth were already seated. But Mel stayed with Heather and Miles. Andrea, Kim, Beth and Rob completed the group and everyone seemed satisfied with the company they were in. Carafes of house wine had been ordered and waited to be poured but Aris had already placed an ice bucket near Bertie with his usual champagne.

Ruth was surprised to see Claire joining their company and wondered why Bertie had not invited Henrietta, though secretly she was pleased not to have to listen to that Atlantic drawl all evening.

'Claire is thinking of a cruise to the islands. Where do you think she should go first?' and without waiting for a reply he added, 'I have already told her you cannot really do both. Either you cruise the Med or you visit the islands, would you agree?'

The waiter arrived with garlic bread and the first starter dishes of their mezze, sea food platters.

Ruth looked at Claire across the table and thought

how beautiful she was, with her dark curls piled high and held in place with diamante combs. The emerald green shirt, neck open and tied at the waist, complemented her olive skin. The make-up was light, except for the eyes, and her nails were immaculately manicured. She thought it unfortunate that there was such an age gap between Claire and Bertie, as they obviously enjoyed each other's company.

'Ah well,' she murmured to herself, or she thought it was to herself.

'Ah well what?' Kim piped up. 'This place is fabulous, what's the problem?'

'No problem at all, my dear. You are quite right this place is absolutely fabulous.'

'*Yia mas,*' said Ruth quietly and held her glass towards Kim to cement the toast.

Kim found herself caught in a Greek moment, that sudden flash of a reality check, when you have to pinch yourself and think 'Am I really here or is it a dream?' Kim constantly reminded herself that she was as good as anyone but she often found it difficult to maintain the confidence that such a thought was supposed to install. Yet here she was, her and Beth in fact, in a Greek restaurant, sitting with 'nobs', doing an art class. She joined Ruth in clinking her glass.

'*Yia mas,*' she said quietly and, looking directly into the gentle eyes of this elderly lady, for a moment dropped her brash exterior and let the lost, unloved child show through. For, even with Gerry and the children to love and care for, she could never quite erase the scars of a neglected childhood. Quick as a flash it was gone again as she yelled, 'Yee ha!' with an ear shattering screech. She turned to Heather, raising her glass again and starting a chain reaction down the table.

Over the past twenty years Penny had remained a beautiful woman but only when Adonis had seen his daughter did the passing of time strike hard. Not surprising I fell for her mother, he thought. Anyone would. In fact, as he recalled, everyone did. But he had been the one, the lucky one, and yet somehow it had all gone wrong between them. He decided he must not dwell on that now, he must only think about what's right for this lovely young woman who was his child.

Andrea negotiated the steps to the ladies loo to wash her hands before eating, something her grandmother had installed in her since a small child. As she went to wash her hands Penny moved away from the sink to the automated paper dispenser. They glanced at each other for an instant then Andrea fluffed about trying to turn on the taps, which were sensor activated. Penny fled in tears and was shaking when she returned to her table.

Heather was delighted that she'd sat next to Miles, as he managed to give a witty and irreverent comment on the scene around him whilst holding an in-depth conversation with Rob concerning the Knights of Rhodes and their defeat at the hands of Suleiman the Magnificent. All this washed down with a glass of red wine as the main dishes arrived.

Dishes of chops, meat balls, dolmades, cheese balls, mini spinach pies all accompanied by oven potatoes and bowls of Greek salad were placed on the table before them, an array of beautifully cooked or prepared food that made everyone's mouth water.

Above them on the balcony Penny could not hold back the tears, 'I just couldn't speak, I didn't know what to say, did not know where to begin,' she sobbed to Adonis.

'I think you were right not to say anything yet. After all, it is me she is expecting and I think I should make the first move. But wait until the meal is over, there is no rush for the moment. We cannot risk spoiling things and, after all these years, what is an hour or so more.'

Penny knew he was right but there was so little time to be with her daughter. Then, a familiar figure came up the stairs and she jumped up and, shoulders shaking with a new wave of tears, buried her head into Steve's chest.

'Hey, what's all this about. If I had known it would cause all this upset I would have kept my mouth shut.' He put his arms around her shaking shoulders but looked beyond her to Adonis, who was also on the verge of tears. At the same time Steve caught the eye of a waiter and ordered three brandies. They drew a third chair to the table.

'I could not leave my best friends to sort this out on their own, but feel free to tell me to back off. It is not really any of my business, I understand that well enough.'

'No, no,' Adonis answered quickly. 'In fact, now you are here it has occurred to me how to handle it all. That is if Penny agrees.'

'I am too emotional at the moment and can't stop crying. This is not how I wanted to be this evening, so anything you suggest I'll go along with,' she replied.

'What I suggest is that you take Penny home to Lindos with you, Steve, now. In a while I will ask George to bring Andrea up here and I will introduce myself. That will give us about three quarters of an hour to talk and then I will arrange to meet her at Steps tomorrow at eleven thirty. And Penny, you will be there then and we will stay in the bar or go to Steve's house for more privacy if you prefer.' Adonis had turned to Steve for his assent.

'Anything I can do to make it work my friends,' Steve assured them. 'I came up with Manolis, so give me ten minutes to let him know what's happening and we'll be off.'

'Thanks, Steve, once again we owe you,' he replied and Penny was nodding her agreement with the arrangements. Oh, that we were all this wise twenty years ago, Steve thought to himself, but knew it would be little consolation to his friends to say so.

Then with hugs and the Greek kiss on both cheeks, Penny and Steve left Romeo by the side entrance, making sure that they were not noticed by those in the craft group, finishing their meal.

They had done well with the main course but had not managed to clear all the platters, nevertheless dessert menu's were handed out to the ladies. Despite the wonderful dishes on offer, which included fresh strawberries and cream, they all resisted temptation.

Tanya felt very pleased with the way things had fallen into place this evening. There had been enough time for her guests to wander around the Old Town, just to soak up the atmosphere or to shop as they wished. Everyone had enjoyed the mezze and the live band with their Greek music provided a lovely background. No one seemed to be left out of the conversations and only Andrea seemed a little pensive. Tanya had noticed George lean over to talk to Andrea and Andrea leave the table to go with him, but that was some time ago. She wondered if she should go and check the bathroom, in case she was unwell. Then, seeing Kim and Beth head off in that direction, decided that she had no need to concern herself. Another hour and she would need to draw the evening to a close. They were to gather at the Top 3 Bar to meet the minibus and could not be late. After all, tomorrow was the last full craft day and then there was the evening party in Rocos' Oasis Restaurant. She was sure everyone would enjoy the Greek dance night. So far so good, she thought.

She wondered what it was Max and Ruth wanted to talk to her about in the morning. She was sure it was not a complaint. She glanced along to the end of the table. They looked a little tired but quite happy. Certainly Ruth was more relaxed than she was when she arrived a few days ago. And that was what holidays were really all about, even hobby holidays, giving yourself time to relax. Tanya took time to look around her. The large central tree with its ceiling of branches, the old wooden balcony, the coloured light bulbs; the rows of tables covered with immaculate white cloths and the waiters in casual, but coordinating, polo shirts, each one of them alert and watchful to the needs of their guests. On the far side, George moved among the customers, shaking hands with old friends and introducing himself to new clientele, always asking if everything was to their liking and how they were enjoying their stay on Rhodes, and most importantly how much he would look forward to meeting them again next year.

Then a strange thought crossed Tanya's mind. Had she enjoyed her stay on Rhodes? Yes, she had. But with a flash of insight she knew it was time for her to move on. Time to go. Time to leave Lindos. Time to leave Rhodes.

Thrown suddenly out of her private thoughts, she was aware of Andrea standing beside her and saying, with a smile that lit up her hazel eyes.

'Tanya, may I introduce my father, Adonis, Dad this is Tanya, our art teacher.'

Both Adonis and Tanya gave only a flicker of recognition, accepting the introduction with the gravity that Andrea had placed on the meeting. They drew in another chair and another glass and allowed Andrea to tell Tanya all about her Dad and her new family. By now the group had split up as the meal was over, some having left to have a last look around the Old Town.

'Please be at the Top 3 by half past midnight, Tanya repeated again to the stragglers. We can't keep the minibus waiting.'

'So, what are your plans now, Andrea?' Tanya asked, but the question was directed more to Adonis.

'We are meeting up in Lindos tomorrow morning after the class,' he replied. 'Andrea is determined not to miss any of the tuition,' he added.

'In that case we had better make a move to the Top 3 or there'll be no teacher there in the morning,' Tanya told a proud father and his loving daughter.

EARLY FRIDAY MORNING, PRASSONISSI

It was rather a last minute thing, Beth deciding to go on the trip to the south of the island. Tanya had booked Rob on the coach earlier, but after a quick phone call last night, Beth's place was reserved for the morning. She was unsure if Rob would welcome her intrusion into his day but at least she knew he would be too gentlemanly to say so. And he seemed to know something about everything without being boring, so he would make quite good company on any trip.

But what Beth wanted was a day out, away from the classes and instruction and away from the shadow of her sister. She loved Kim very much but she was rather noisy and inclined to take over any conversation that might start within the craft group. And in Beth's opinion there were times when she gave just too much information to total strangers.

'Why did you have to tell Max I worked in a corner shop?' she had asked Kim the evening before. 'It is my business where I work and what I say about it.'

'Well, don't tell me you are after the old guy,' had been Kim's instant reply.

'No, of course not. Why do you have to be so crass? It's just that I want to say what I choose about myself, not have you saying it for me.'

'But that is the point. You never say anything to anyone.'

'You know that's not true, I just don't tell them the same details you tell everybody. I like to keep some things private. Well at least 'til I know if I like them enough to spill the beans about my life, or as you would say, lack of a life,' Beth snapped back.

They were silent for a while. It was a long while since they had last fallen out. Kim knew Beth was really upset as it took a lot to get her to make an angry comment or start any sort of disagreement.

'I hope you don't mind but I am clearing off for the day tomorrow. I am tired of the chatter, not used to it, living alone most of the time.'

'No problem, I want to spend the day on the beach anyway and I know you don't like sunbathing that much. Will I see you at dinner then, as I doubt I'll be up in the morning when you leave?'

'Silly moo, I will still have time to bring you a cup of tea first thing. It's only a day out, not a trip to the Himalayas.'

'Hope not as I think they are in India or China somewhere and we're in Greece. And who's calling who a silly cow anyway?'

All was well between them. If it had not been sorted there was no way Beth could have gone out the next day. When she had told Rob she was on the trip in the morning he had suggested they meet and walk up to the coach together, so she felt more relaxed about the intrusion into what she saw as his space. Beth was not to know that, whilst Rob was often alone, it was not a situation he always enjoyed. Though, in his opinion, to be alone was preferable to being in loud or vulgar company. Rob knew he was a bit old fashioned, but it was his life and he would lead it how he chose. Now he was looking forward to the coach trip as the day dawned, bright and crisp. He packed the two small bottles of water he had placed in the fridge overnight into the rucksack that travelled everywhere with him.

'What do you find to do all day when we are busy crafting?' Beth could not think of anything more original to open the conversation, once she and Rob were seated on the coach.

'Difficult to say really, but somehow I manage to fill the day and often have to rush to get ready for the early evening at the bar. I must admit I am not rising very early.

Well, I am, but I am taking a long time over breakfast, so that accounts for some of the morning. And I love to swim before my breakfast so that's half the day gone.' He shrugged his shoulders and grinned at the thought of his own idleness.

'I have been to Rhodes Old Town a few times and will try to go again before the holiday is over. Take more photos, potter around the back streets, getting a feel of what it was like to live on Rhodes many years ago. It hasn't changed you know, not for centuries.'

'I still wanted to see more of the shops, though that was a lovely meal we had in Romeo.'

'I expect that's exactly what ladies did in olden times, look around the shops and market stalls, have a meal out. It's all part of being in another town, another country. Not all history is in the museum you know.'

'You are right, we were soaking up the culture, and we did give Marks and Sparks and McDonalds a miss,' she laughed.

The tour guide was explaining that she was not an official guide but an escort who was there for their safety and to make sure everyone was accounted for. But if there was anything they needed to know she would do her best to answer any questions. She would tell them which villages they would be going through, and explain that some of the Greek letters, though they looked the same as English, sounded different, so, for instance, the village of Gennadi was pronounced, 'Yenahdi', but there was no problem with Sianna, which was the first place they stopped at. This was just a short stop at a little gift shop where they were given a shot of the local ouzo and a plastic spoon to try the local honey. It was a pretty place with panoramic views from the nearby vantage spot. If you were under the impression that Rhodes was a barren rock, then you would be surprised at the lush farmland that lay below the village. Then it was onto the coach again and back down the narrow winding mountain roads.

In no time at all they were getting out of the bus to look at the view of Monolithos. Rob had his camera and had just taken a snap when the escort, Josephine, came over and offered to take a photo of Beth and Rob together. Rob thought that was a good idea and put his arm around Beth's shoulders. So in the spirit of things Beth moved closer to Rob. He was wearing a rather nice aftershave and as she was quite small she sort of tucked under his arm in a very comfortable way. She laughed to hide her embarrassment, but Rob seemed unaware they were standing closer than strangers usually do. Maybe he hadn't noticed, maybe there was nothing to notice. Rob fiddled with his camera and asked to take a snap of Beth standing on her own.

'How do you want me? Like this or like this?' she joked as she struck a few exaggerated poses.

Rob looked at her as one does a child who is being silly

but not naughty, waiting for her to stop playing the fool. 'Would you just smile looking at a spot over my left shoulder please? That's perfect, absolutely perfect. Now I think we'd better get on the coach or it may leave without us.' And when Beth looked around she found they were the last two left and the coach was waiting. How embarrassing. But Josephine just smiled and the coach door closed behind them, they continued on their way south.

The next stop was a small café at the base of Monolithos. From here you could walk up stone steps to the castle, within which was the small church of Agios Panteleimon, the same place they had looked down on a moment before. Carefully they climbed the stone steps and stood in wonder at the scenery. Returning to the woodland café, they ordered tea and sat on benches in the shade. A tame parrot hopped around the visitors waiting for crumbs. The guide came over to speak to them.

'Have you been to this part of the island before?'

'No, this our first visit to Rhodes and we are staying in Lindos, but it seemed a shame not to see more of the island while we had the chance,' Rob had replied for both of them.

'Oh don't rush to see it all this visit, you will be back again, everybody does come back to Lindos sooner or later. It is one of those places. Many people come year after year. And some of us stay,' she laughed. Then she moved on to talk to other couples sitting nearby.

Back on the coach again they journeyed on to Prassonissi. They fell into a comfortable silence while watching the countryside unfold. They went on through an area of burnt olive groves, which gave a strange lunar landscape to the fields. It was quite scary to see the extent of the fire which had caused such devastation.

Beth was pleased to find that, while Rob knew things, he did not keep on all day pointing out the obvious as many people do who enjoy imparting what they know. It was Beth who restarted the conversation, wondering how and when the fire had started and whether the tourist places on the coast had been affected. Rob said he did not know but would ask when they got to Prassonissi. Beth was more impressed by Rob admitting to not knowing than if he had regaled the last detail.

When she thought about it she realised that she knew no one who could talk about so many things in such an interesting way as did Rob.

REGRETS

Steve was up early and took tea and biscuits in for Penny, then left her to shower. She had slept well, aided by her emotional exhaustion and the stiff nightcap Steve insisted they have on their return to Lindos. Soon they were sitting in the courtyard drinking their second coffee.

'This was such a good idea, coming here with you. It gives us all a chance to calm down. No way could I have coped last night.'

'Last night was last night,' said Steve with his usual shrug of his shoulders. I expect Adonis has told Andrea about you, about both of you.'

'But Steve she is so beautiful.'

'And so were you, my darling, and you still are. You broke all our hearts when you left. Then I went back to

England and met my wife and all that is now history. Though my wife and I had some great times when the girls were young, so many sandcastles on so many island beaches. And now I am here and the sandcastle days are gone.'

'At least you had that relationship with your children, I just gave my child away.'

'Rubbish, you left her safe with people who loved her, and still do love her. Now we need to go down to the bar before Adonis and your daughter arrive and are knocking on the door.' He took the cups and put them by the sink, and picking up the keys they left the house.

Such a short walk, such a long journey.

THE CRAFT GROUP

Friday was a complete mish-mash, and this was not how Tanya liked to work. At least she could get some semblance of order by showing everyone how to do inserts. 'Double sided tape. In my opinion there is no substitute for it,' she told those of the group who had made it to the early morning session. 'For those of you with access to a computer there is no limit to the amount of sentimental verse you can add but unless you are making a card for a friend, less is often more.'

'What the hell does that mean,' Kim asked Heather.

'Not much, hen, I will tell you in a minute when she's finished,' was the unsatisfactory reply.

Kim missed having Beth with her but was pleased her sister was having a day out. Rob was nice enough, but a bit boring, in her opinion. Not that her opinion mattered. If Beth liked him then that was good enough. She was so busy thinking about her sister that the next bit, about cutting the paper insert a fraction smaller than the card, went right over her head.

At the same time Tanya needed to do something for the high flyers, Mel, Claire and Heather:

'For anyone who would like to try something new, there is quilling and paper weaving. Here are the samples. Just ask when you've finished putting in an insert, and I will answer your questions and get out the materials. After coffee we will look at how to use what you have learnt during the week to make all you need for wedding stationery,' Tanya told them. The advantage of it being Friday was that everyone knew the procedure and was no longer shy about helping themselves. As she looked around she could see they were all busy concentrating on their insert.

Ruth and Max had asked for a moment of Tanya's time, they needed some advice last night, but would not say what it was about. And Max had yet to appear.

Andrea looked radiant and was singing away to herself, much to the discomfort of Claire who was suffering from a hangover, but no way would anyone dampen Andrea's spirits. And as June had guessed in Birmingham, once Margaret's family had arrived, try as she may, Margaret found little time for the classes.

Tanya drew Mel, Claire and Heather to one side.

'Have you seen this before?' she asked them, wielding what looked like a small soldering iron.

"It's a Printmaster, a hot foil gun and you can use it for simple messages, or to personalise a card with a name. The easiest way to demonstrate it is to put the DVD on my laptop. My friend Brian Goodwin does tend to rabbit on a bit, so, as time is limited, use the button to get to the demo. Then have a go on this card and see how you get on. I'm sure you'll get the hang of it quite quickly. It works on almost anything. Last Christmas I made leather bookmarks with my friends' names on them and a little sketch of the crib scene using a mix of gold silver, red and blue metallic print strips, but watch the DVD and then have a try.

Tanya wondered where Max was, as now was a good time to talk.

MAX ASKS SHEILA

Max stood in the doorway and peered into the small room, which was not only the Lindos Library but also the Lindos Launderette. He raised his hat and addressed the lady, originally from Boston, who was working inside.

'Mrs. Markiou I presume?'

'Well that's what the taxman calls me but to everyone else I'm Sheila. What can I do for you?'

'Good morning, I am Maxim Henderson and I have been told that you are the person who would know where I can find a property to buy in Lindos,' he began.

'Can I presume that you have more than half a million euros to spend, and then another twenty thousand to install some modern amenities?' she asked him, without stopping from her task of taking tablecloths from a dryer.

'Oh, you might presume but it would be incorrect. At least, that is not what I would expect to pay for a modest property here.'

'There is no such thing as a modest property in Lindos. It's a uniquely picturesque village with a good return on the investment. But more than that, the people have been through times when they let their heritage slip through their fingers because of dire financial need. Everyone is more careful now and there are very few properties that come onto the market.'

'Then if I wished to live here,' Max began.

'Then I suggest a long lease, ten or maybe fifteen years, paid in one lump sum. You can bequeath the lease if you wish, and be free to make moderate alterations to suit yourself, as long as there are no structural alterations. But this is the wrong time of year to discuss such things. Come and see me again in October and I'll know what's available then. Bye.' And Sheila carried on with the task in hand.

Oh, thought Max, now I've been told.

He was not the first person to mistake Sheila's brisk manner for indifference. She was always busy, what with the library and launderette in the summer and managing property repairs for absentee owners in the winter. She had no time for time-wasters. However she always had time to help anyone who needed her. Being a fluent Greek speaker, she was an invaluable source of information and advice to the ex-pats in the community. A tireless fundraiser and charity worker, she and her car were always available in an emergency. But this was definitely not an emergency. She wondered if Max would be back later in the year, or was the idea of living in Greece just a bit of midsummer madness? Who knows, she thought, you never can tell.

Max then made his way to Electra for what was left of the morning class and his chat with Tanya.

RUTH, MAX, TANYA

At coffee time Tanya drew two chairs over to the table she used as a desk and invited Ruth and Max to join her.

Max told Tanya he was definitely selling up in England and moving to Greece. His only hesitation had been some sort of project to occupy his mind in the winter. Ruth then explained that she had decided not to sell her house but was interested in living on Rhodes or Symi and starting some sort of craft lessons and holidays as had Tanya and her aunt. She and Max would be partners in this venture.

'But I think it will have to be Symi as I would not do anything to cut across your business here, never in a million years,' Ruth assured Tanya.

'That all sounds brilliant and I can dispel some of your concerns immediately,' was Tanya's swift response. 'You see it's not really my business. I am just helping my aunt this year. Now June has other plans and is not returning to Lindos except for a holiday.'

Max and Ruth were delighted with this news, though a little concerned as to why Tanya was not keeping up the craft breaks. They did not like to ask.

'My aunt's house has only ever been on a ten-year lease and that expires next April, so if you would like to rent the studio for the moment Max, and take over the house in October when I leave for a winter break, that would be a great help to us and give you a base whilst you look around for something more suitable long term,' Tanya added.

The news was getting better and better.

'Tanya, my dear, I cannot remember the last time I had so much to look forward to, and everything is falling into place. And to think I nearly changed my mind about coming on the craft holiday,' Max told her.

'Well. Lindos seems to have that effect on people. It changes lives.' And aware of her responsibilities went off to talk to the rest of the group.

'Well I need a stiff drink both to celebrate and to steady my nerves,' Max told Ruth but added quickly that it would only be one at this time of the day.

Ruth laughed. 'And I need to finish my work and start

to collect my bits and pieces, so I'll see you this evening in Steps Bar.' She did not add that she was still exhausted from her day in Symi and the late night meal in Rhodes and planned to take a siesta.

Tanya was surprised that it had taken such a short time to decide on her own plans for the future. But in her heart she knew she was ready to leave last winter and only stayed to help her aunt with the craft holidays. Not that she had any regrets, but now June was not coming back they would both close the door on the Lindos chapter of their lives. And for Tanya that meant she could also close the chapter that had been her and Ed. Yes, she was now truly ready to move on. She would tell Steve and Miles, but not yet. Tell them on Sunday when the 'crafty group' had gone home.

Max naturally headed to Steps bar and was disappointed to find a note on the door saying, 'Back in an hour.' So he went to the Beer and Bier and ordered a sandwich and a beer. He liked sitting outside and watching the steady stream of tourist wandering by.

Jenny, Greg's wife sat by him. 'Have you enjoyed staying in Lindos?' she asked him. 'I am sure you've had a very instructive week.'

'A wonderful week and I have made the decision to move over here. It's not only the scenery and the warm weather that attracts me, but the warmth of the people here in Lindos,' he replied.

'Yes, you will never feel you are on your own here. If

you have a problem there is always someone who'll help. So never worry about coming to ask Greg or myself if you need anything.'

'Thank you, that is very reassuring.' Somehow it seemed more of a reality now he had said it out loud. And unlike many other places, the Beer and Bier was open all year round, at least for a few hours each day. He was pleased at the way things had worked out that morning. He should have stayed and finished off the lesson, but was too excited. Silly old fool, he thought to himself, yet at the same time he was proud of himself, having the courage to take on a new venture.

Andrea had managed to keep fairly calm most of the morning and had enjoyed answering questions about her dad and what her plans were, now she had family on Rhodes. But she simply replied that she had no plans yet and tried to get her inserts done. At last it was eleven thirty, the time she had asked Tanya if she could leave the class.

STEPS

Steps Bar was closed for an hour or so because Steve did not want any intrusions. He had even gone downstairs to Dimitris and bought some pizza, just in case anyone would be hungry. Adonis and Penny were on the balcony. As Andrea walked across the square she looked up to the balcony and saw her father and waved.

Standing beside him was the red-haired lady she had seen in Romeo the night before. Perhaps they are friends, she thought and he's brought her down from Rhodes for the trip out. Andrea skipped up the steps.

'Hi Steve,' Andrea greeted him as she came in the door. 'You missed the most amazing thing last night. I met my dad. Isn't that just brilliant?'

'Yes, he's told me all about it, and is here now.' Adonis

and the lady came in from the balcony.

'Good morning, Dad, hey that is the first time I have said that! May I say it again? Would you mind?'

'Say anything you like sweetheart, but first I want you to meet Penny, a lovely lady, who has been my friend for a long, long time … and Penny is a very special person in your life.'

Andrea moved forward expecting the usual kiss on both cheeks. But instead Penny opened her arms and hugged her daughter until Andrea was almost gasping for breath.

Penny held her, not daring to predict her daughter's reaction once she knew the truth. So scared of rejection from this child she had loved silently, and from a distance, for so many years.

'Andrea darling, I know this will shock you but I have to tell you, I am your mother. I am so sorry I left you in England. Please don't be angry at not knowing the truth about me. It was for the best'.

Andrea moved away, but not towards her father but to Steve. Eventually she found her voice.

'I came to find my Dad and now I have my Mum as well. And if I had not come to Greece would anyone have cared enough to come and find me?'

'I don't understand how you could both forget me. I never forgot you and I was the child, not a grownup. Did you not even care what I was like, never even having a photo of me over all these years'.

When Penny answered it was in a whisper.

'That is not true. Your Aunty Marian sent me pictures

all the time, and your school reports, and when she took you on holiday I sent the money for your summer clothes and spending money, and as much as I could at Christmas. I wanted you all the time, but it was not possible.'

'Why not? Why not'? She sounded like a small child, confused and hurt, and she felt again all the years of hurt and rejection; the legacy of growing up alone.

'We were young and foolish and did not do the right thing at the time. Nothing I can say now will ever put that right. But we have never stopped loving you. You must believe that, please?' Adonis begged his daughter.

Andrea believed because she wanted and needed to believe. She moved into her parents' arms and was enveloped in the hugs and kisses each had waited all these years to bestow.

'I think this calls for a drink,' Steve suggested, guessing that Penny was hanging on to her equilibrium for dear life.

'I have a bottle of high class plonk, or low class champagne, however you wish to describe it, in the fridge.' And they all laughed which broke the tension as Steve had intended. They moved to sit on the settees and Steve poured the drinks, and plated the pizza before he joined them.

'*Yia mas!*' he raised his glass.

'Can I call you Uncle Steve now?' Andrea asked.

'Only when we are on our own, and then very quietly,' he teased her. They looked at the pizza and were uncertain what to say next but, with an openness that shamed her elders, Andrea bounced in.

'I really must be the luckiest person alive. I have my granddad and gran at home and now I have a family here; a mum, a dad, and some brothers and a baby sister; also their mummy, Voula, who sounds very nice, and an Uncle Steve. Wow, it's just amazing,' she concluded.

And they all started laughing at her addressing Steve as 'Uncle Steve.' Again Adonis asked his daughter if she wished to stay longer in Rhodes. He could easily book her another flight. But she declined.

'I am going home to Gran, and to school to finish my exams,' she told him firmly. 'If I may, I will come back in the summer holidays to see you all again. Then we can talk properly about everything. I don't think I can cope with any more shocks at the moment. I am out with my craft group friends this evening, as it would be rude not to say goodbye to them properly, and to Tanya and Miles.'

'Well that is all settled then. I am afraid, sweetheart I have to go now, can I give you a lift up to Rhodes?' he asked Penny.

'Yes please, and we will all meet again in the summer holidays, if that is what you want, Andrea?'

'That would be just brilliant, and I will be sending Dad an email so he can organise everything,' she replied.

'But please give me one really big cuddle before you leave, 'cos I love you all so much.'

And that was it. Almost twenty years of worry and hurt brushed away in a few words.

PRASSONISSI CONTINUED

The coach was now following the main road on the west coast of the island. As they came inland they passed through the army base where signs displaying the skull and crossbones were scattered over the area. The base was used in the winter for target practice by the Greek army, mainly local youth doing their national service.

Josephine, who was not one of those tour reps who kept prattling on, even if there was nothing of interest to say, told them an amusing anecdote, 'Not long after I came to live in Rhodes, a charming Greek man offered to take me to a deserted beach, with sand dunes and palm trees. As he took the car off the main road towards the sea the tracks became bumpier and every so often there were signs with a skull and crossbones on them. But I could not read Greek at the time, so was not alarmed. We had a lovely day out, perfect. Only some years later when I came to this part of the island on the coach, and I understood Greek, did I realize we had driven across the army grenade training fields.'

Everyone laughed and enjoyed the mental picture she had conjured up, and this diverted attention from the only long stretch of the trip, so in what seemed no time at all they approached the brow of a hill and saw Prassonissi before them. Now they could see the small village and the tiny green island that was the southernmost tip of Rhodes, and where the two seas meet, the Mediterranean and the Aegean, one robust and noisy as waves crashed on to the beach and the other calm and as still as a millpond. On the waves bodyboard surfers sped through the white-topped water and on the mill pond, windsurfers with sails of many bright hues cut across the sea at speed. On both beaches there was a wide stretch of fine sand.

Beth was not sure what to do next. The coach had stopped for the passengers to get off, and they were free to explore until half past three. Would Rob welcome her company for the rest of the day? Just as important, would she welcome his?

Rob waited till there was a gap in the line and stood up. He thought it best to get off the coach first and plan the day from there. Naturally he waited at the steps giving others a helping hand and so was there to assist

Beth down to the path.

'Shall we sit for a few moments and plan our day, then we both get to see what we want, either together or on our own, and join up for lunch?'

Problem solved in one sentence, thought Beth, with a quick flick of her eyes heavenward. She wanted to explore the shops and was certain Rob would view that as a waste of their time in such a lovely place. They sat on the low wall by the Light House restaurant, just taking in the vast scene before them.

'That is what the word Prassonissi means, green island,' Rob told her. 'Sometimes it is cut off from the mainland and sometimes the sand builds up in the winter storms and it joins on to the rest of Rhodes, so not technically remaining an island.'

'There are some places like that down in Devon and Cornwall,' Beth offered.

Rob thought most of those places would be just tidal, but said nothing. For one thing it could be possible and for another he was not in the habit of putting people down.

'Well I would like to walk to the beach, just to stretch my legs,' Beth offered by way of an opening. 'Then come back and eat as I don't like to feel in a rush over my lunch. Let's go to the Light House Restaurant, especially as we were told how good the food is there. But I'm not worried about eating alone if that doesn't fit in with your plans.'

'That will suit me fine, if you're happy to have my company. But if you're hoping to meet up with a nice Greek windsurfer, I would not want to cramp your style,' he surprised himself that he was so cheeky with Beth.

'I doubt that the surfers are Greek, probably German or Italian, and I would not trust them an inch. No, I would choose your company any time rather than those all-beef-and-no-brains sort. I know, shall we walk down to the island, then we can say we've put a foot in each sea?' Rob was delighted at this as that had been his plan, but he thought it might be too far for Beth, so had not suggested it.

So their day was organized. The walk to the sea proved further than they expected and the sun sapped their energy, though both were sensibly covered with sun hats and factor forty suncream. Removing their sandals they dipped their hands and feet into the sea but even the water was warm. Stepping out from the water onto the hot sand had them squealing as they tried to get the sand from their toes without burning the soles of their feet. Beth fell onto the beach incapable of moving for laughing.

Rob took the cotton sling from his emergency kit out of his back pack. 'Now, young lady, if you will only stay still I can clean one foot at a time and you can put your shoes back on.'

'You mean you are not going to give me a fireman's lift back to the restaurant?' she asked still laughing.

'No, if that is your preferred mode of transport then I am afraid it is the Bavarian brigade of surfers you need to talk to, so behave, young lady or I will abandon you to a fate worse than death, a shoeless walk in the hot sand back to the Light House.'

Beth sat still and allowed the sand to be dusted off. She had pulled her skirt up a little to allow it to fold between her legs, but it did not afford her any modesty at all. Looking up into Rob's face as he cleaned her feet she felt a warmth that had little to do with the sun. She saw him as a guy for the first time, a guy she enjoyed being that close to. She wanted to kiss him, to kiss his large gentle hands and his quiet shy eyes.

Rob was used to touching people in all sorts of situations but wiping the sand from Beth's feet was a strangely different sort of touching. He knew he had cleaned them enough but found himself reluctant to replace her sandals, but he did so with the utmost care and resisted the urge to brush the sand from her legs and kiss her toes. That would have been an unacceptable imposition in Rob's eyes. To take advantage of anyone without their consent, and no way did he want to lose Beth's friendship with some unwanted attention. 'There you are, my lady, all ship shape and Bristol fashion.' He offered a hand to get Beth to her feet.

'Thank you, my liege, you may kiss my hand as your reward.' To Beth's surprise, he did kiss her hand. Not just on the back as she had offered but he turned her palm up

From Lindos With Love

and gently brushed her with his lips before kissing the inside of her wrist. As he raised his eyes to hers Beth felt her legs melt and she could not resist moving towards him and, putting her arms around his neck, kissed his mouth, gently, not sexily and pushing but calm and quiet. She felt such a wave of longing but it was different than anything she had experienced before. Almost as though she was scared he might break if not handled with care. And she was right. He would have shattered into pieces if she had been more demanding.

'I hope the lunch is good,' she could think of nothing else to say.

'Well one thing is for certain we won't find out if we stay here all day. Not that I would object to that,' Rob replied, and her hand linked into his arm they made their way back to the Light House where Asimeni took their order.

They had such a marvellous lunch, sea bass with oven potatoes, a Greek salad and a carafe of white wine. This was followed by baklava with peppermint ice cream. And eventually, a cappuccino, as neither of them could drink the strong Greek coffee.

The drive back to Lindos was along the main eastern road and only took half an hour. They held hands most of the way but said little, except to agree to make no remark about the day, other than the information given was interesting, the sun shone, the sea was warm and the meal was very good. In fact, all in all a great day out.

A NIGHT AT OASIS

Tanya had chosen the Oasis for the last night out because of its simple informality. The restaurant was run by two young brothers from northern Greece. No outward show of style for them: plain walls, where they existed, as the restaurant was open on three sides; square tables and wooden chairs. Immaculate white shirts and jeans were the only uniform they possessed or needed. White-clothed tables were scattered around the edge of the main space and steps led to a raised level that overlooked the dance area on one side and the bay on the other. And on a Friday evening there was a Greek Night with traditional dancing and music.

The menu was quite extensive, mostly Greek food but with plain alternatives like lamb chops and oven potatoes. And the prices were as good as anywhere in Lindos.

Tables had been reserved for the group so they could

all chat to each other during the evening. The music was soft and melodious and would only get more powerful when the dancing started. Carafes of red and white house wine were brought to the tables and poured by Rockos, who then went off to serve others before returning to take their orders. There was no rush, no deadlines, no need to do anything except sit under the stars and relax.

During the latter half of the evening girls appeared in traditional costume and, without any introduction, started to dance, Greek style, to the music.

When it seemed that meals were finished they went among the tables asking people to join them on the dance floor. Soon they had a crowd up on their feet and, with linked hands, the line began a simple slow step. Well, it began simple and slow but gradually got faster, and the leader took the dancers out onto the path and back again, everyone laughing and losing their grip, ending up in chaos. On these occasions both dancers and those who only watched from their tables had a good time. The singer took over to allow the visitors and dancers to get their second wind and another glass of wine. Then the call went out for another dance and almost everyone was on their feet to join in the fun. This time the girls picked several men and took them into the middle of the ring and stripping them of their dignity got them belly dancing and hopping around and the more ungainly they were the more the crowd enjoyed the fun.

Rob more than held his own and was an excellent

dancer, never losing his step. But at last the dancers gave up on Rob and they turned to the audience to give him a round of applause. The music changed and Rockos and his brother Yanni took to the floor. There was something about the simplicity and gracefulness of the young men that brought an immediate hush throughout the restaurant. They had danced together since childhood, and it showed. The beat of the music got faster and when the dance had climaxed Yanni left the floor to enthusiastic applause. But Rockos stayed and with the music slow and deliberate took a table and, dancing around it, raised it up, then gripped it in his teeth and to the astonishment of the guests continued to dance around the floor. Once more applause echoed around the open dining room. Then Rockos swirled a liquid onto the floor and using his lighter set fire to it. The flames were blue and green and shone in the darkness of the night. The music started up again with a very slow beat and he danced in and out over the flames. The guests were mesmerized by this unusual display, and the craft group now understood why Tanya wanted this very Greek experience to be their last night.

The girls took charge again and soon had everyone taking part in what became a Greek version of the conga, until everyone was laughing and exhausted and returned to their seats. After another traditional dance by the costumed dancers, they waved their goodbyes. The evening began to draw to a close and other diners left until it was only the group who remained. The keyboard was now playing softly and it was then that Rob, quiet, shy Rob, went over to the singer, spoke a few words to her and was handed the microphone. He held his hand up, and Max realizing Rob was trying to gain everyone's attention, tapped a spoon on his glass.

'This has been an absolutely splendid evening, one of many I should say, and I know I speak for everyone in thanking Tanya for a wonderful week.' He stopped to allow the supportive clapping to die down. 'But unaccustomed as I am to public speaking,' which brought the customary tap of cutlery on glass from Max and Miles, 'I would like to render a few words to say how I feel about Lindos and everybody I have met this week.'

There was a silence while everyone wondered what would happen next. Then in a soft tenor voice, Rob began.

'I've had a real good time as stranger in paradise.
Who knew what a week would bring,
on a flight bound for paradise.
And I can only say of my time here in paradise.
Where else would a guy like me
meet someone like you.

He had been looking directly at Beth but now turned to the singer, taking her hand.

'Hold my hand, I'm a stranger in paradise
How else can a mortal stand, a stranger in paradise.
Though I stand starry eyed, that's a danger in paradise
For a mortal who stands beside an angel like you'.

The girl took up the tune, which was just as well as Rob did not know all the words, then he joined in the repeated verse and others joined in as they ended the song together.

Everyone cheered and clapped as Rob handed the microphone back. But now the keyboard had taken up the tune. Max reached for Ruth's hand and gave it an affectionate squeeze. Heather tried not to look at Miles but he was determined to catch her eye and when he did he gave a smile, a shrug and a wink.

Rob took Beth onto the floor to dance. Max and Ruth joined them, a little hesitantly at first but soon found a mutual style. Miles was up and had Tanya dancing a jive to music that was not for jiving, but that did not seem to bother them. The music changed to disco. The moment was over, but for some would never be forgotten. Miles and Tanya separated to get more people to the dance floor, Yanni joined in, as did two German guys who had just walked into the bar for a quiet drink. Mel found tears in her eyes and gave a grin to Claire. Rockos, putting one hand out to each girl, got them up from their seats. A circle had formed, including Andrea and Kim. No one cared about the steps as the music suddenly changed to something all too familiar. Auld Lang Syne. They crossed hands, showing the German lads how it was done, and nothing could have been more incongruous than the keyboard imitating bagpipes in a Greek bar. After two repeats of the familiar refrain they all dissolved into laughing and clapping. It was a wonderful end to a lovely evening.

'I think this calls for a nightcap at Steve's. On me of course,' Max announced. And after thanking Rockos and Yanni for a brilliant evening, they trudged up the hill to Steps Bar.

RUTH AND MAX SATURDAY MORNING

You would think that Ruth had had enough wine and conversation last night to keep her from rising early. But to the contrary, she awoke before sunrise and showered and dressed as the dawn light spread from behind the Acropolis.

She took her jacket from where it had hung for most of the week. The sun had not yet sent its warm rays over this part of the earth. She crept out of the courtyard and onto the slate path, no bells ringing, no donkeys braying, everything peaceful. There was just enough light for Ruth to make her way past the Broccolino and on down the long slope towards Pallas beach. Everything was cast as a silhouette against the dark turquoise sky. There was a dawn chorus, but not as she knew it in England. Hooded crows circled above with their eerie sharp caw. Above her the rocks were pitch black and the walls of the Acropolis stood as a two dimensional cut-out in a child's picture book. The trees were as though an ancient Chinese man had painted them with his black ink, ground from a glue stick onto a stone, their outline etched in crisp black just as the oriental prints had shown them.

It could be anywhere in the world on a fine morning. The air was fresh with a gentle breeze, and as still as that moment between the night and day often is. A chill swept over her as she walked quickly and quietly, down past Giorgios Two, behind Jack's, behind Skala and up onto the rocky path. It was barely a ten minute walk to reach this sanctuary, where heaven seemed to meet the earth. Ruth found her favourite seating spot, sat comfortably in the hollow of the rock and took her rosary from her pocket.

'In the name of the Father, and of the Son and of the Holy Spirit.' Tears came into her eyes and blurred the vision of Kleoboulos tomb across the pale water.

Max had been awake for more than an hour, had made a cup of tea and taken his tablets. He put the last one out next to his electric shaver ready for the morning. He had done it, despite the distractions of this week. He had taken all medication at the appointed time. In fact he had felt incredibly fit. He felt as though the fear and restrictions of his mild stroke a year ago had finally left him. He felt like himself again, no longer young, but at least he was reasonably fit.

'Well, old son,' he addressed himself in the shaving mirror. 'They say there's no fool like an old fool, so you might as well take the bull by the horns.' He repeated his

R.A.F. motto that had stood him in good stead all these years, 'Per ardua ad astra', through struggles to the stars. Well, he was certainly reaching for the stars this morning, if the opportunity arose. No, that attitude was not good enough. He must make the opportunity happen one way or another.

'If you think so highly of the lady then you must trust her judgment, and that means starting from today.' He reprimanded himself for the moment's hesitation. He had gone so far with the life changes last night he felt he must say what was in his mind, know where he stood before Ruth left for England. A splash of cologne and he was ready for whatever the day would bring. Despite the crazy way everything had happened this week he had really enjoyed being part of the gang. He had spent his life within a group. Max had enjoyed the jokes and the ribaldry that an officers' mess can give. In later years he had been amused by the company of young people. Yes, he was a sociable creature. Running the craft centre with Ruth would see him out in a splendid way. He was also a man who enjoyed the company of an intelligent woman, a man who needed someone to love and to care for.

Back in the bathroom again, he tied his dark blue cravat. Per ardua ad astra. Maybe I am not such a silly old sod, he thought as he stood to attention and saluted himself in the mirror.

Ruth looked down at the gold cross that hung from her rosary beads. She put her fingers onto the appropriate spot and looked up as she began the Lord's Prayer. 'Our Father who art in heaven, hallowed be thy name.' Why was she crying? She could not answer, just the sheer beauty of what lay before her, the morning sun glistening on the sea and the haze over Palestra at the far end of the beach. The crows had long stopped their clatter and short bursts of song from other birds echoed over the distant trees. The church bells had not yet rung. A great stillness on the earth, in her heart and in her mind. Had Ruth finally found what had eluded her for so much of her life? Despite the strange way everything had turned out, Ruth felt more alive, yet more calm and fulfilled than she had for years.

The almost confessional talk with Max the other night had left her feeling clean and whole again. His arm gently round her shoulder had been both strong and protective, like Francis had been for her through all those years of loneliness. Those wasted years.

Max had been firm about that, 'Never wasted, I am sure, just spent differently than you might have thought,' he had kindly said. Enough.

Ruth sang softly,

'God has created a new day,
Silver and green and gold.
Live that the sunset will find you
Worthy His gifts to behold.'

And for her, that new day must mean an end to the

sorrow that had been part of her life for so many years. She had this chance to renew and she must do just that. The choice was hers, just as the paths she had chosen previously had been hers. What was the saying? Ah yes, it is not the cards you are dealt with in life, but how you play them that counts. Now she was onto a new hand, and laughed at her strange analogy, as she could not recall the last time she had played a game of cards. This week had shown her that much lay ahead, new friendships based not on her career, or her place in local society, but just on a whim to change her life.

Who would have thought at the beginning of such a relatively simple holiday that so much could happen? Had she actually managed to make any cards? She was certain she had. And she had painted the Chinese way, so simple, so effective. She did not do the other things. She had found her artistic niche.

It was unrealistic to expect everyone to keep in touch, but Rob was a dear soul. He had asked if he could correspond with her, as he so enjoyed writing and receiving letters and so few people did these days.

The young people, Mel and the little rough diamond, Kim, would return to their homes, their husbands and children, renewed, refreshed, seeing them with a new appreciation perhaps. And Margaret would be back next year to stay with Tracy and her lovely Greek husband, and maybe a great grandchild by then. Perhaps she would find a nice balance by just coming out early and late in the season, as so many older visitors did. Time alone would tell. Ruth looked down at the little black rosary still in her hands. The beads uncounted, the formal prayers unsaid. It never worried Ruth if she set time to pray and her mind was diverted to mundane things. 'Just using the time to bring your troubles to His feet at the start or end of the day,' Father Paul had assured her many years ago.

She had been reluctant to add retreat holidays to the boiling pot of ideas last night, but it was not without its possibilities.

One step at a time. Perhaps when everyone went home the magic of Lindos would drift away and grand plans would come to nothing. But she intended moving out here anyway. She needed the challenge, and the joy of her friendship with Max and the craft holidays.

She knew that Claire had been talking to Tassos and Tracy. Once she had her own stone cleaning business she could send them interesting work via the internet. That is if she ever returned from her Med cruise with Bertie. Now that was a turn up for the books!

The sun had now turned the sea and sky into a bright blue. She took her jacket off and let the warmth wash over her. Footsteps drew near, echoing on the crunchy gravel of the narrow path. Without turning around she knew it was Max. His slight limp and the cane he carried on such expeditions betrayed him.

'Tell me to leave, Ruth, my dear, if you need more time

to be alone,' he suggested as he came near.

'No, my thoughts were more earthly than heavenward I am afraid this morning, and you were part of them, so please pull up a rock and join me,' she called softly back to him, not wishing to break the spell of the dawn breaking.

'I thought I might find you here, and hoped you were by yourself. I needed to ask, do you have to leave tomorrow?'

Ruth immediately thought it might be a problem concerning the craft venture, particularly finance, which is always a sticking point in any mutual agreements. 'I am not leaving tomorrow, Max dear. I have already booked myself a few more days to do some shopping and perhaps an excursion. My flight is not 'til Wednesday. Is there a problem that we need to sort out with Tanya, something that cannot wait until I return in a few weeks time?'

Max sat on a rock as best he could, it was a little lumpy but nothing that could not be endured. He leant over and took Ruth's hand. 'I would like to say that regardless of other people's plans or how they feel about Lindos when back in England, I wish to come here and make a new life.'

'Well yes, dear, that has, I thought, been decided. I thought we sorted that out in principle on Thursday on the boat, and in more detail last night.'

She could feel that 'she who must be obeyed' tone

coming into her voice, but continued. 'I will not sell my house, but you are putting yours on the market. That is entirely up to you. You know you do not have to. We can rent any suitable premises, whether from June or the librarian, Sheila; she has long term rentals. You don't have to make any commitment to me at all. If either of us feels we have made the wrong move, well, we can work out a plan from there. I am looking forward to another few days, just to relax and have a better look around the area, without the classes to think about. I have enjoyed it all, but it has been a little tiring. I must say I have felt more peaceful and happy here than I have felt for many years. I don't see any major problems at the moment. Do you? Thank you dear for thinking about me,' Ruth added, not giving Max the chance to answer her question. 'And if there is anything more to discuss we will have the opportunity. But it will only be for a few more days. I can't expect Merle to keep calling in to feed the cat.'

Oh dear, Max had made up his mind to propose and now Ruth thought he wanted to hedge his bets a bit with the joint venture. How did that happen? What should he do now? He had planned to say, 'I would wish that our new life here would start with our marriage,' but suddenly it seemed the wrong time and place. Ruth had gone into her 'let's get organised' teacher's voice. A tone of voice you did not argue with. Not that he wanted to fall out with Ruth, never in a million years.

Ruth felt let down, yet it was only in her own silly imagination that she had read more into their friendship than there obviously was. How stupid can you get? So Max was just a good friend after all, and he probably enjoyed the company of the American, Henrietta, more than he did her rather dull homely prattle about parish and school life. What else had she to talk about?

Max was in a quandary. Should he risk all and start again to say what was on his mind? Per ardua ad astra. Remember you have nothing to lose but everything to gain, he thought.

'Ruth, please just listen for a moment, do not comment on what I have to say, just let me speak.'

She was surprised by his tone, and the sad look on his usually smiling face.

'Oh, my dear, what has happened, what is wrong?'

'Why I wish you to stay on here for at least a few extra days has nothing to do with houses or craft or anything practical,' he continued, looking into her gentle, kind eyes.

'You see, I was hoping we would have a little time together whilst you consider a rather indecent proposal. Do you think you would consider living in Lindos as my wife? Oh heck, that sounded all wrong. I mean, Ruth dear, would you marry me? I know I am not much of a catch these days and friends that share their lives may be a solution or just forget I said all this and we continue to be business partners as planned. But I would be so honoured if you said yes.' By now he was out of breath, as he hardly stopped in his speech, scared he might lose his courage.

Ruth did not move. Her eyes were cast down and tears welled up for the second time that morning.

'I could not ask you this last night. I wanted to be sure your reply would be made in the cool light of day, knowing that my proposal was sincere, not tinged with wine and soft lights. We are not children … and at this time in our lives … please stop me if I am saying too much, I would not wish to hurt or offend or...' His heart was almost at breaking point as he saw her downcast head and then she looked up at him as the tears welling in her eyes brimmed over and fell one by one down her upturned face. He did not know what else to say or do, so just sat there, holding her hand as this great well of sadness washed over him.

'Talk to me, please. Tell me if I'm wrong, if I have said too much?'

'Yes, you old duffer, you said far too much. Just 'a new life starting with our marriage' would have been quite enough. I have such great joy when with you, and a sort of inner peace. I know I could trust you with my life, I will and I do.'

They did not move, but just sat together looking out over the bay. Two people who had found love and companionship and, though knowing each other for only such a short time, were willing to risk what was left of their lives to marriage.

Was there anything to say now? Max asked himself, yet knew the answer. There would be so many things to say, to arrange, to plan. But not yet, not yet. Let's just enjoy the moment, he thought.

Ruth smiled when thinking of her plans for a restful and uneventful retirement. Well, of all considerations that had gone through her head this past year, she had to admit getting married was not one of them. But why not? She had no one to please but herself. With no obligations to family and the certainty that Merle would take her cat, she was free to do exactly as she wished. And what she wished was to be with Max, and now it was going to happen. And they would live here, in Lindos. Beautiful, beautiful Lindos.

Max started to laugh, 'Some lover I am going to be, I have to move, I have cramp in my shin.'

'At least you are honest about it. I dare not move for the same reason, I've not got cramp but thought I might if I moved the wrong way.' They both drew apart, Max laughing despite the pain he felt.

Ruth rolled forward onto the mound of scrub in front of her, onto her knees and holding onto a convenient rock pulled herself to her feet. Max was still laughing as he ran his hand down his leg. The pain subsided, he stood, tall and straight and reached out to her. They embraced in that warm cosy way you do when at ease with someone. She had always liked tall men and loved how she seemed to fit into his chest.

'We had better make our way back for breakfast, or we will be in trouble,' he joked. They stopped for a while longer just to savour the moment.

'May I announce our engagement? I have an old brass key ring somewhere that might do the job.'

'Yes do, I'm sure Tsambikos can rustle up some bucks fizz,' she giggled.

Max stopped for a moment and looked down into the lovely, gentle face of his fiancée, the smiling eyes, and the dimpled cheeks that dispelled the frown lines that so often appeared when she was sad. They held hands going down the path.

Sorry, Lord, I will say a full ten decades tomorrow morning, Ruth silently promised her Maker. She had waited so long for such a moment as this, such a long, lonely time. Now on this crazy holiday on a Greek island she had found love and a plan for the rest of her life.

ATRIUM PALACE

Margaret was up early, not just because it was the day of her granddaughter's wedding, but because it was the habit of a lifetime. She made tea in her room and took it out onto the balcony. The Atrium was a picture-book hotel, with swimming pools, fountains, palm trees and red hibiscus everywhere. Certainly the most beautiful place Margaret had ever stayed with pathways leading through exotic gardens to Kalathos Beach.

She went down to the hotel restaurant for breakfast and, sensibly, had cereal and the "Full English" with toast and marmalade to follow. She had been to too many functions that, despite the good intentions of the host, left you starving for most of the day. When she was on her second cup of tea and tucking into her toast, her daughter came to join her. Margaret was surprised to see her looking relaxed and happy. In fact, more relaxed than she had seen her for some time. And Judith was the mother of the bride!

'I went to your room, Mummy, but I should have guessed that I'd find you here. How do you feel? Not been overdoing it or anything, nothing to spoil the big day?'

'I am fine, dear, thankyou, never felt better, and you seem quite calm. I hope it's not the calm before the storm!' Margaret wanted to bite her tongue off but it was said now and no taking it back.

'That's not very positive of you. Not like you at all. Actually I wanted to have a quiet word. Let me grab some coffee.'

Oh dear, thought Margaret. Whatever she says, just say nothing. Let it wash over. Nothing must spoil today. Jack, love, she is your daughter; talk to her. But when Judith returned to the table she was still smiling. She sat down.

'Mummy, before anyone else comes down there is something I must say, something I should have said to you many times, but did not. The thing is, since Tracy was a baby you have done everything you could to care for her and help us bring her up and I don't think I have ever thanked you properly. In fact I don't think I have ever thanked you at all.'

'I felt so bad when Daddy died,' Judith continued in hushed tones, 'I never thanked him for letting me go on all those expensive school trips. Then there was my wedding and my fancy ideas. Not once did I think about the cost, or that you and Dad never had a proper holiday till you came to Rhodes for your twenty fifth. Yet you never stopped me.'

'Why would we, Juju?' calling her daughter by a childish nickname which Margaret had not used for many years. 'Everything we did was for you, that's what our life was about and…'

'But Mum…'

'Never mind the buts. We thought we would not be blessed with a family and then you came along. And as for the wedding, you have not let us down. You are still happy and together and that is all the thanks we ever wanted. As for looking after Tracy, that was our pleasure. I only worried that you might be missing out on her childhood.'

'Maybe we did, but we had the choice because of you and Dad and I just wanted to say …' she sobbed. And Judith, the smart executive, would need a whole box of tissues to stem the flow.

Margaret stayed calm. 'Well dear, from your dad and me, thankyou for what you've said. There was no need, but glad you did.'

GOING HOME

The craft group was to meet for the last time at Chrisanthi's Electra studio to say a final goodbye. Tanya already knew about the engagement of Max and Ruth, but for everyone else the spread of canapés and bottles of Champagne were a surprise. Max could not believe how quickly Ken's Kitchen had come up with his request. It just happened that Ken had been up since five that morning preparing a wedding buffet and he and Tony had brought some of the food to the craft group venue. The wedding was not until four that afternoon, so plenty of time to make replacements.

Max had taken the liberty of inviting Bertie, but as he had only seen Henrietta briefly since the Wednesday evening meal, had thought it better to leave that decision to his friend, not wishing to cause any embarrassment.

He went over to chat to Mel, Claire and his old R.A.F. comrade. 'I'm off in the morning,' Bertie told him. 'I rang a friend and arranged a Med cruise for this young lady and she thought she might be lonely and invited me along.' A blatant lie, but he winked at Claire as he said it and she just shrugged her shoulders and smiled, just as though it was the most normal thing in the world, to go cruising the Med with the elderly, but totally charming, Lord Bertram Rawlins.

Heather had already left for her flight to Manchester. To her delight Miles had told Tanya that there was no need for a taxi; he would collect her Saturday morning and drive her to the airport. Not that there was anything in it, Heather had told herself, but she did feel she had made a good friend in Miles.

Not that there is anything in it, Miles told himself, but he had enjoyed her company. And he did feel he had made a good friend in Heather. They would keep in touch on Facebook.

Rob, Beth and Kim were on an early afternoon flight to Gatwick, but they had time to drop in on the craft group to say goodbye and thank you to Tanya. Beth told her about making cards for Mr. Patel's shop, and how she had not felt confident to do this before, but now that she had the expertise, the sky was the limit. Tanya felt quite guilty at realising she had overlooked Beth all week, only seeing her as a companion to her mouthy sister. Then later she noticed that Rob had his arm around Beth's shoulder as they stood chatting to Ruth and Max. Obviously there were more important things than making cards, so she felt better about it.

Mel told Tanya how much she had appreciated the tuition and the marketing tips. She had Tanya's email, and would she mind if she contacted her about setting up a website?

'No problem, any time,' Tanya had assured her. 'But you may not need a website if you set up a Facebook page, and that's free.'

'Something my daughter will know about. Thanks, I will ask her when I get home.' Oh dear, more technology, Mel thought to herself. Her mobile phone rang and she excused herself to answer a text from Keith.

Andrea was on the same flight as Mel. Steve had kept Tanya up to date with what had transpired, and gradually the good news had spread amongst the group, as Andrea had told everyone her strange story.

'I am going home today as planned, but coming back again in July. My dad agrees I should not miss taking my A levels, and I wish to thank my gran and granddad for all they have done for me.'

Privately Steve and Tanya were appalled at what they

had done, but it was not up to them to say.

This was always a strange time, the end of the holiday. Promises were made to keep in touch and sometimes that happened but, more often than not, after a few emails the link was lost. Mel had suggested that Tanya start a blog, but as she was uncertain where her own future lay so she had brushed the idea aside.

'You never know, one day I might write a book about people who come on craft holidays,' she joked.

SAINT PAUL'S

After her early encounter with Judith, Margaret spent the rest of the morning chatting to friends and relatives who had made the trip to Rhodes for the wedding. It was quite a small family gathering as apart from Gordon and his wife, only three of Jack's nephews and their partners had come over. About twenty or so other young people were friends of Tracy and Tassos from university. Even Tassos' family were few compared with a usual Greek wedding, but two generations in Australia, and not from Rhodes in the first place, had weakened the links. All that was important to Tracy and Tassos was that the people who mattered most to them were sharing their big day. And at the centre of their big day was the wedding service in St. Paul's Church.

At twelve thirty Margaret went to her room to shower and change into her wedding outfit. She looked in the long mirror and was pleased with what she saw. 'I still scrub up well,' she said to herself. Now she was ready. Her tears for Jack had been shed in the shower, no need for more.

Tanya arrived with the minibus that was to take the senior guests down to the lower road, the nearest vehicle access to the church. She had her list, told them there was plenty of time, which there was not, but nothing would be gained by concerning the guests with that.

And timing was the reason that the young couple had asked Tanya to help things run smoothly, as they did not need a wedding organiser in the accepted sense of the word. But Chrissi, Judith's friend from Infinity Weddings, thought they might need just a little help to ensure the older people in the party were taken care of.

By one o'clock all were assembled in the courtyard in front of the tiny chapel, the sparkling turquoise sea behind them, the small jetty nearby, and the rocks towering above. Chrissi and Zoe, who were also the Lindos florists, had framed the old oak door with an archway of scrunched white net, greenery and flowers, and Tassos was there, suited and booted, as Margaret had told him, using an old northern saying, with his *koumbari*, a group of best men, quietly chatting.

Papa Yiorgos unlocked the door and entered the tiny chapel, indicating that the people were to wait outside, except for Gordon, who was invited into the church by the priest. And Gordon, who usually avoided the gilt and gold, statues and symbols of the high Anglican or Roman Church, was impressed by everything he saw. The large candles had been decorated with flowers, and a silver tray stood on a small table near them. It contained the red wine and the *koufeta*, or almonds used in the service. But it was explained that, as much as Papa Yiorgos might wish it otherwise, he could not allow Gordon to take part in the actual service, 'But stand by my side if you wish, and please give an English blessing at the reception.' Gordon was overcome by the kindness and was not sure he would have been so generous were the circumstances different, but he would be in the future.

They returned to await the bride, and at ten past one the long silver car stopped at the top of the pathway. Mark helped Tracy from the car, and they began the long walk down to the sea. Even from a distance Margaret could see the good job she had made of the wedding dress. It shimmered in the sunlight, and framed Tracy's pretty young figure to perfection. The blue stones of the necklace were matched with a ribbon at the base of the elegant cream lilies she carried as her bouquet. The tiara was just right, sparkling in the sunlight just as though it was made of real diamonds and sapphires.

The *koumbaros* had lifted the table from the church and placed it, the candles and accoutrements outside so that everyone could see the ceremony, except when the priest took the couple inside to kiss the icons. There was a hush of quiet dignity as the priest led the service in the time-honoured way, with a shawl wrapping the couple together, plus candles and chanting. Margaret shed a tear of thanksgiving for having lived to share this day with her beloved granddaughter. The bells were ringing as they emerged into the sunlight. The photographs were taken and then they had to move away from the church as another couple with their families came down the path.

At the jetty they were helped into the motorboat that would take them to Skala Restaurant for the wedding breakfast and, as the boat swung and twisted in a celebratory ride around the bay, the music rang out across the sea to the nearby beaches. 'We are family' and they were.

SKALA

The boat pulled into the main pier on Lindos' small beach, the official village gateway by sea. And as they stepped from the pier, across the sand was the Skala Restaurant. Tables and chairs ran along under the cliff edge, but the main venue was a two-tier white building reached by crossing the narrow beach. Here, a wide, shaded veranda was used for the clients, but for wedding receptions, the flat roof with ornate white railings provided a private venue.

Pink balloons were tied everywhere and the tables were dressed with pink flowers, ribbons, and napkins. Sparkling glasses and cutlery completed the picture. Margaret had never seen such an array of nibbles passed around among the guests. Then when the bride and groom were ready and, having posed for endless photos with friends and family, they took their places at the table and everyone sat down.

Gordon stood, his stole around his neck, and by that very action the table hushed. 'Today we have witnessed the marriage of Tracy and Tassos and now we are doing exactly what Christ did two thousand years ago, joining the bride and groom, family and friends, in a wedding feast. Would you please stand and join me in giving thanks for this day and the food prepared for us.'

He began, 'Dear Lord, You said where two or three are gathered together, there You would be in the midst of them. We acknowledge your presence at all times but give thanks today at the wedding feast of Tassos and Tracy, who have been joined together in your universal church. Bless those who prepared this food for our use and us for your service. Amen.'

Margaret and Judith sent a look of relief across the table, and then Margaret quietly told her brother how appropriate his few words had been, and thanked him. Even Methodist ministers need encouragement, she thought, and it was true, what he had said was just right for the occasion.

It was dusk when Max and Ruth thanked their hosts for a lovely day. They took their leave of Margaret but not before making sure they had exchanged addresses and phone numbers. They had intended to walk across the rocks to the long beach, but both were too tired do so. They saw Jacob and said good night. He asked them if they could manage to get into his small pick-up, which they did and were so grateful for the lift up to the village. They had already discussed their plans for Sunday, so it was a brief kiss and a hug good night, and they parted company.

Was this what life in Lindos will be like? They both wondered as they climbed into their respective beds and slept.

HEATHER ON THE WAY HOME

Ken was half an hour early and the plane was twenty minutes late. Just about right, he thought. With a cup of coffee and the morning paper he settled down to wait for his daughter to come through the airport. She would ring while waiting for her suitcase. There were times when a mobile phone was invaluable, and he had to admit this was one of them. He had expected Heather to ring more often during the week she had been away but, except for a call to say she had arrived safely, they had not heard a word. Ken had mixed feelings about that but kept his concerns to himself. Bad news travels fast enough, he believed, without helping it on its way. And if everything was not as it should be, then he would hear soon enough.

'No doubt a postcard will arrive next week. It usually does,' he had assured Shirley.

The phone rang. 'Morning Dad, see you in a few minutes, that is if you are at the airport and not home in bed having forgotten all about me.'

'Ready and waiting, sweetie pie. See you in a while,' he replied. He was not prepared for the bronzed young woman with a radiant smile that came towards him at the arrivals point. Heather looked wonderful. Not just the suntan but the way she walked and the grin from ear to ear just like the kid he used to meet coming out of school.

They hugged for a moment, then he took the handle of the case and she held his arm as they went in search of the car.

'How was Lucy, Dad, not too much trouble I hope?'

'Nah, a bit. We have enjoyed having her, every minute of it. We will miss her if you decide to leave Edinburgh again.'

'I guessed you would say that, but I have some great news for you. And it will be OK, you will still see Lucy and me, I promise you, Dad, I promise.'

'Hold your horses a while, let me get out of the airport traffic before you spring any surprises on me, you know I am not keen on these junctions that go everywhere.'

Heather knew she should have waited until they got home before talking about Lindos but it just blurted out.

She never kept anything from her dad.

Ken guessed that something important had happened or was about to happen and he used the excuse of the busy road to delay any conversation and to give himself time to act reasonably to whatever Heather had to say. He spotted a service station and, although he had already had one coffee whilst waiting for the plane, he thought another might be needed. Heather had a fresh orange juice, something she had taken a liking to during the week. They found a table by the window and sat down.

'So you got on all right with the craft group then. Did you find it easy or a bit of a challenge?' He asked his daughter, still bowled over by the wonderful change in her after only a few days away.

'Well the bits I went to I got on well with, but after the first few days I only went for the morning session.'

Ken felt his heart hit his boots sure that she had met some ne'er do well and, being hurt and vulnerable, had fallen for a load of codswallop. 'So has he got a job this chap you met?' He asked wanting to get the worst over with.

'What chap? Oh Dad you don't think I would pick up with some beach bum. Really, Dad, how could you say that, though there was one really nice lad who lives out there, but I don't think he was interested in me, but that is not important. Now just listen a while and stop jumping to conclusions.' Heather took a long sip of her juice, partly to tease her father and to reprimand him for jumping in at the deep end. She knew it was because he cared that he was worried. 'Each afternoon I went to the beach to swim rather than do art classes. They say that it is OK to do what you want to do and I needed to relax rather than concentrate. Well, after the first afternoon I got talking to this really nice English girl who goes to the beach after picking her children up from school. They start school early and finish just after lunch time. They used to live in Lindos when they first came to Rhodes, and still bring the children there to swim and play on the beach. They now live further down the island in a rambling old house. There is a garden with orange and lemon trees, and a short path leads down to the sea.'

Ken was not sure where the conversation was going. He began to guess, but he had been wrong once already, so he said nothing and took a drink from his lukewarm coffee.

'The thing is,' Heather continued, 'they are starting a business out there. Not sure what it all involves at the moment, but whatever they do they have to break into the day to either take the girls to school or pick them up, which involves a drive and then a walk through the village, and because the house is on its own they have no childcare for the evening. Well, they have asked me if I would like to move out there and work for them. They will get a caravan or something suitable for me and Lucy to live in, so we can have our own space and I can generally work as a Girl Friday. Dad, I know it sounds crazy but when we get home I will show you the photos of their children and you will see what a great chance it will be for Lucy.'

Ken rose from the table and put their cups onto the dirty crockery stand. He was not thinking of photos when they got back, more like his wife's reaction to Heather's news.

'But best of all, they go to England each summer. So you and Mum could come out and stay in the house for the summer and Lucy and I will come back for Christmas for a few weeks. What do you think, Dad?'

'Phew, lass, that is a bit of a story to take in all at once. And you want to do this after only knowing these people for a few days? Are you sure that makes sense, not wishing to throw cold water on your plans and all that? And do the children speak Greek or English in school and how do they get on?'

'Well, the younger they are when they start the better it is, but there are lots of non-Greek kids in the school. As well as Brits there are Italians and Albanians just as there are in our schools these days. That's where my maths comes in handy as no one wants their children to miss out on sums while they're still getting to grips with another language, so I would teach all the girls maths after school.'

Ken saw the great change in Heather and had to admit that anything would be better than how she had been the past few months. 'It's a lot to take in, but if it will make you happy then you must do what you think best. Please don't say anything straight away. Get in the door first, then when Lucy is in bed tonight we can sit down with your mother and thrash it all out. But if the idea of living and working in Greece can bring such a change in you, then I'm all for it. We can afford to come out a couple of times in the year and stay in a flat or a cheap hotel and, even if we can't afford it, we will do it anyway. Now let me get on this motorway before the traffic builds up.'

Ken swung the car out onto the exit road and tried not to think of the turmoil this news would bring to the household. His girl was happy and if it only lasted a short time he did not care. Life is too short not to take chances. He knew that better than most.

MEL GOES HOME

Mel was quite tired, even though she'd arrived home on Sunday morning and today was Tuesday. Not surprising really, with all that had happened. Her head had been buzzing with all sorts of thoughts, telling Keith snippets of information about the week, but Keith's news had not been good. Mrs. Blake had died. He knew how upset Mel would be and thought it better to wait until she got home before breaking the news. He was relieved to know that Mel was grateful for this. She had known Mrs. Blake all her life, but the elderly lady had not been in good health for some time, so the news was not entirely unexpected. But a sad event even so.

The funeral would be on Thursday and the vicar had

left a note for Mel to sort out an Order of Service sheet. Mel already had the family's favourite hymns on the computer so it was not a problem. In fact, Mel considered it a privilege, long before the chat with Mr. Blake yesterday. It was unusual for Keith's employer to come to the house, but there had been quite a lot of turmoil these past few days. Keith had poured his boss a whisky and they all sat down in the small sitting room.

Mr. Blake turned to Mel.

'You know, my dear, that Gertrude was at school with your grandmother. They were great friends. Well my wife always had it in mind to do something for you Mel and she admired you, young man, always did.' He winked at Keith.

'Now to get to the point, I came to tell you that Gertie has left this house to you, Mel.'

He smiled at the thought of Keith being his wife's tenant from now on.

'It will take a while to sort out the legalities, and I want to check that there are no outstanding repairs. It's not much of a gift if the roof needs replacing.'

Mr. Blake went on, 'Now Keith, that nasty business has been sorted out at the office, so will you accept my apologies and take on the job as manager.'

They were dumbfounded, unable to find the words to say, and trying to come to terms with their good fortune. Keith had shaken hands with Mr. Blake and accepted the apology and the job.

So that was yesterday and Mel's head was already racing with her plans. First, she would hand in her notice at the supermarket, no more filling shelves. Then, start card making classes in the conservatory, only once a week at first. She would go on a course to learn more about making fascinators and silk flower corsages, and a computer course so she could have a Facebook page for the wedding stationery business. And twice a year she would go to Greece and teach card making for Ruth and Max.

Keith never imagined when he made the booking at the Mandarin Palace ten days ago that they would have so much to celebrate. But all that really mattered to him was that Mel was home again.

ROB GOES HOME

Rob sent Beth a text, 'Missing you already.'

KIM AND BETH GO HOME

Kim and Beth were met by screams of delight from the children. Gerry put the kettle on as they searched in their hand luggage for the treats they had bought for them. The t-shirts could wait 'til later. They were in the kitchen, as the door of the living room had a big ribbon on it and a sign, 'NO ENTRY'.

Gerry had intended to wait 'til the kids were in bed to show Kim the great job he had made of the decorating but, as they had helped some of the time, mostly by being good, the children could wait no longer. They pulled their mother along the hallway and demanded that their Daddy open the door.

'I painted the door,' her daughter announced proudly, and Gerry whispered that it had taken longer to get the drips removed than to wallpaper the room.

Kim was a bit apprehensive. It was not unusual for her to choose a paint colour and go off it before it had time to dry and then ask Gerry to paint the whole lot again, never mind the cost of the paint. The door was opened and it was like walking into an exotic garden. The room was beautiful. The wallpaper they had chosen was dark green with large white flowers. There were little gold bits in the flowers that you didn't notice in the daylight, but they sparkled now the light was on them. Kim could not believe that he had looked after the children and finished the room in a week.

'I bet you are desperate for a pint, Gerry?' Beth asked him.

'Why don't you two go down to the pub for an hour, and I will put the monsters to bed?'

'Thanks, but no thanks,' Kim told her sister, 'Now I am home I want to stay home. Gerry, please will you ring up the Chippy and order us all fish and chips; proper English fish and chips?'

When Gerry left the room to make the phone call Kim and Beth gave each other a bear hug.

'Thanks for taking me, it was a great trip, and without you I would not have met Rob,' Beth told her sister.

'And without you I would never have got the front room decorated,' Kim joked back to her. They both knew the holiday had meant more than that, but there was no need to say more.

SUNDAY, SUNDAY

'I have it all arranged,' Ruth told Max on Saturday, referring to Sunday morning. 'I emailed the secretary at St. Francis Church and they have found someone to give me a lift from the square. I need to be there at a quarter to nine. I rather think I want to go alone, to have some quiet time, I hope you understand.'

'Certainly dear,' Max replied, 'and whilst you are busy I will be taking a lady friend to lunch. I hope you understand,' he teased Ruth.

'Not quite the same thing, but yes, you must do as you think best. Give my regards to Henrietta please, and wish her a safe journey, wherever she is off to next. She seems such a lonely person and no amount of dollars can compensate for that.'

Max did not reply, but thought Ruth was probably right.

Ruth was to wait in the square for a man called John who had a grey car. So that is what she did and, at exactly the pre-arranged time, a grey car came to a halt by the tree. A tall, solidly built man walked around the car to greet her.

'And you must be Ruth?' He asked with an accent that was decidedly from the north of England. His hand was outstretched. 'Pleased to meet you, I'm John, I live in Kalathos, just a few k up the road. Were you waiting long?'

'Not long at all and you were exactly on time,' Ruth replied.

He drove carefully out of the square and off up the hill to the main road.

' It is so good of you to fetch me, and you have come out of your way to do so?'

'Oh aye, but not far. Not a problem especially on a fine morning like today. Have you been up to Rhodes town during your stay?'

'Yes, but only for the evening, when returning from Symi. I have been too involved with craft classes. That was why I booked an extra few days, intending to see the old town on Tuesday. But I did not want to leave without going to church.'

'Well, Mass here is truly multi cultural', he continued to explain, 'The readings and Gospel are printed in nine languages. The Parish priest is English, his assistant Polish and the young servers Albanian. Only Michael, the elderly alter server, is Greek, and has served San Francisco all his life. You will be pleased to know that most of the Mass is in Latin, which I am sure you are familiar with. The choir is also multilingual and multiracial'. He stopped for a while concentrating on the traffic.

'Christian, the guy who phoned you, is English, except that he was born in China. He and I are the greeters and try to hand out the books and readings in the right languages as the people come in.'

Ruth was laughing at all this information, trying to take it all in whilst not wishing to miss any of the scenery during the drive.

'If you are greeting you must know most of the people on a Sunday morning?' she asked.

'I know our own regulars but, when a cruise ship comes in it tends to confuse the issue.' John replied.

Suddenly they came to a large grey building with a stone statue out front. This was San Francisco, Saint Francis Roman Catholic Church. He pulled up at the edge of the forecourt and waved to a slim bronzed lady who was perched on the steps.

'Pauline, this is Ruth. Take care of her while I park the car. See you in a mo,' and John drove off down a side street.

There was no mistaking Pauline's Irish accent. She introduced herself. 'We might as well go in and find a seat. There is a good crowd of tourists here today,' and

Pauline led the way up the steps.

The elderly man who greeted them was dressed in a smart black top and designer, white, three-quarter-length trousers. His trainers were silver. 'Hello dear, English or Mandarin?' He joked as he gave Pauline the customary Greek greeting of a kiss on both cheeks. 'And who is this? A visitor, hello dear, looking after you is she?'

Ruth found it hard to reply for laughing. 'Good morning, Christian, I'm Ruth, we spoke on the phone.'

'Yes, and you are very welcome,' he said as he kissed Ruth. 'Did John meet you in the square? Well of course he did otherwise you wouldn't be here,' he said, answering his own question. 'He's parking the car I presume? Plenty of time.' With that he turned to greet others and Ruth saw that John had slipped in and was distributing leaflets.

So this is San Francisco, she thought, as she made the sign of the cross and blessed herself with the Holy water and followed Pauline down the side isle to find a seat.

Max and Henrietta had arranged to meet in the Icon Bar and have a pre-lunch drink. Then it would only be a short walk to Delight, a small restaurant where you could look down on the people below on the main street if you chose, or sit and look at the bell tower and rooftops of the shops if you preferred. But first, in the Icon, they sat back on the comfortable settees and relaxed with a glass of wine.

'I am leaving Lindos later this afternoon,' she

informed Max. 'I am going to Symi for a while. Not sure what my plans are after that. Do you know if Bertie is returning to Rhodes and, if so, when?' she asked.

'He didn't say, he is very much a free agent,' Max replied.

'You know we were together for almost three years a while back, in the States?'

'No, I did not,' Max said truthfully. 'What a surprise it must have been to meet up again, a happy one I hope.'

'It could have been, I was very fond of him,' Henrietta admitted in regretful tones.

'Indeed,' was all Max could think of to say.

'And you are leaving on Wednesday?' she asked him as she sipped her wine.

'No, I am staying on for a while. Ruth has consented to be my wife and...'

Henrietta could not avoid spluttering into her glass and Max offered his folded handkerchief as she regained her composure. 'So you came here together, you did not say,' she accused Max.

'Not at all. Until last Saturday night at the airport we'd never met.'

'And you are getting married?'

'Well not just yet, but that is the plan. I am staying on here indefinitely, renting the art teacher's house until I find somewhere for us to live.'

Henrietta said all the right things, but her heart was not in it. She had let Max slip from under her nose just because Bertie had come on the scene. Well, she thought he had, but obviously not. Now he was off on a cruise with that dark haired young woman from the art holiday. What is it with these English? She asked herself.

'Is that the time?' she asked Max, looking at his watch upside down.

'Yes, would you like to go and eat now?' He enquired.

'Thank you, but I really do not have time, let me leave my cellphone number, and maybe we can meet up again at a later date. I have packing to attend to.'

'I am sorry. We should have eaten first and chatted later, I am so sorry you'll miss lunch now,' Max said very apologetically.

'No problem, It has been an interesting week. I don't think I will forget Lindos in a hurry. Keep in touch.' And her high heels clattered away on the slate pavements. Max ordered a pizza and another glass of wine.

Henrietta was ready with her pink suitcase packed when Mihalis knocked the door. He took the case in one hand and Henrietta's arm in the other. Yes, she had enjoyed her stay, and yes, she would come to Lindos again, but not for a while.

'I have a cousin with some good apartments on Symi,' he began.

SAN FRANCISCO

The church was spacious and surprisingly stark. Behind the altar was a large wall painting depicting St. Francis gazing up to the crucified Christ. The picture extended around the curved side of the apse, showing the saint with his simple monastic buildings and several birds in the air and at his feet. Ruth wondered if this was to emphasise the simplicity of a Franciscan monastery. It was most unusual and rather strange at first, with a stark charm of its own.

Regardless of the diverse languages the service was very simple and Ruth had no problem recalling the Latin Mass and its sung responses, as did Pauline. Both guessed that they shared the common background of a convent education. The music was particularly beautiful, a complete mix of Latin, English and an enchanting, haunting air which Pauline told her was Polish.

As the last blessing was being given, Pauline nudged Ruth to leave their pew. They walked quickly to the back of the church, where Christian was waiting holding two small plastic pots.

'Hold this, dear,' he said to Ruth, 'Pauline will tell you what to do. Give her a card Pauline.'

'I will if you just give me a chance,' she replied.

'I'm sorry but I have just retired and I don't wish to volunteer for anything,' Ruth began.

'Oh no, dear, we don't have volunteers. There are not enough of us to bother with volunteers. When there is a job to be done you just do it,' he informed her.

'Hold the card up. It is for the restoration of the cemetery. Quick, they are coming out now, that's right, stand at the bottom of the steps.

'Well now you know,' Pauline said, still laughing at the shocked look on Ruth's face.

Most of those leaving the church did not quite comprehend what the collection was for, but contributed just the same, good Catholics that they were.

'That will do,' declared Christian after most of the congregation had left. 'Now come and get a coffee and a piece of cake, John will be waiting there to take you home again.'

They helped themselves to coffee, went into the garden, and Ruth was introduced all round. They sat chatting for a while, a mix of nationalities but thankfully everyone was speaking English. They wished her a safe journey back on Wednesday.

The drive to Lindos seemed to race by with comfortable silences as well as times when they chatted easily.

'A rare mix, wouldn't you say?' John asked her. 'And Christian is right, there are too few parishioners and there is always something that needs doing.'

Oh dear, what have I let myself in for, thought Ruth. Thank God I will be far enough away in Lindos not to get too involved. She invited John into Steps Bar for coffee or a beer if he preferred.

'That's very good of you, but no thanks. I am off to Castello's Bar in Kalathos to see Sunderland play against Spurs and it starts in half an hour. Thanks all the same.'

She had wondered where his accent was from, now she knew. She went into the bar, thinking Max would still be entertaining. She fancied a glass of chilled white wine before going back to the flat to make some lunch. The bar was empty so Ruth sat on a stool, which would make it easier to talk to Steve.

'Exciting times,' Steve remarked, and she was not sure if it was a statement or a question.

'So it seems,' Ruth replied, in pensive mood.

Steve knew better than to say any more, and as soon as he had poured her drink returned to reading his book.

Suddenly the full implication of moving to Greece hit her. The Mass was lovely but she missed the usual conversations that took place every Sunday morning outside St. John of God, her own parish. Was beautiful scenery and a warm climate enough? Was her affection for Max enough for them to make daily decisions together, instead of just having to think about herself? Was that it? She had thought - affection, not love?

'Did you have lunch?' Steve asked. 'I will get a three cheese pizza and make a cup of tea,' he announced without waiting for a reply and was down the steps to buy it fresh from Dimitris.

Perhaps I am just tired, Ruth told herself and I've had nothing to eat since early this morning.

Within minutes they were sitting on the balcony, sharing the pizza.

'Is that the American lady, Henrietta? Look, down there with the pink suitcase. I am sure it is,' Steve said answering his own question. 'They come, they go, and everyone takes what they need from Lindos. I don't think she will be back,' he added philosophically.

Aware that Max must now be on his own, Ruth expected him to come to Steps but she and Steve had finished their pizza lunch and he had still not arrived. Ruth found Max where she guessed he might be, asleep on his bed in the studio. The door had been left unlocked so she crept in. Slipping out of her frock and sandals she lay down beside him. He murmured something as he turned towards her, laid his arm around her and dosed off again.

This is a lovely place to be, she thought, and closed her eyes.

EPILOGUE

Tanya and Miles arrived at Steps at the same time and before they had entered the bar their drinks were being poured.

'*Yia mas*,' Steve called the toast, raising his glass of Amstel. 'Another successful week, Tanya?'

'*Yia mas*. Yes thankyou, Steve, and thankyou for your contribution. It does make a difference.'

'And what about my contribution?' Miles asked, 'Am I not to be congratulated for keeping your young lady safe and sound? Not that it was a chore I assure you.'

'*Yia mas*, Miles. Thank you for your help. Just knowing there was someone on hand to take charge, even though, as it happened, they managed themselves.'

'Delegation,' he began, paused and smiled, '…is the key to good management.'

'And thankyou for taking Heather to the airport. Was that good management?' Tanya could not resist teasing him.

They were still laughing and Tanya wanted to tell them she was leaving Lindos but didn't want to spoil a lovely afternoon. Maybe some other time. There was still the whole summer ahead. And if so much could happen in a week, well, who knows.

'*Yia mas.*'

P.S. MARGARET IS HOME

Margaret let herself into the flat, hung up her mac, pulled her small case on wheels into the bedroom and turned on the electric blanket. She made a cup of tea and took a packet of Jaffa Cakes out of the cupboard. It was lovely to go away, she thought, but good to get back inside your own front door. She took the photo of Jack from the sideboard and sat in her favourite armchair.

'We had a lovely time, but no need to tell you that,' she said aloud and to herself, but she firmly believed that her dear Jack was with her, as he had been all the years of their marriage. 'Our Tracy is off to a great start with her lovely young man and lots of nice people in Lindos,' she rattled on as she took another Jaffa Cake from the packet.

The phone rang on the small table next to her chair.

'Just a quick call, Mummy, to check you got home

safely. Was it a good flight and everything?' Judith asked.

'Yes, thankyou, dear,' Margaret replied. 'I was back home and had the kettle on in no time.'

'Thank you for everything Mummy. The dress looked fantastic, as I knew it would. I can't wait till the photos are printed and I can take them into the office.'

'And I will take some to the W.I., but not 'til we have the official ones,' Margaret added.

There seemed to be a different tone in Judith's voice, softer and more caring.

'Goodnight, Mum, speak to you tomorrow.'

'Goodnight dear,' Margaret replied. She washed her face, cleaned her teeth, and was soon snuggled under the duvet. Closing her eyes, glad to be back in her own bed, she sang, very softly.

'At the end of the day, just kneel and pray,
Thank you God for my work and play,
I've tried to be good, for I know that I should,
That's my prayer at the end of the day.'

Yes, there are some words you never forget.

Special thanks to...
Steve Wakelin and Miles Davis for fun and friendship at Steps Bar.
John and Maria for whitewashing and book formatting.
To my friend John Camphuis and surgeon Dr. Vasileios Karydakis for
   keeping body and soul together.

'Encouragement is a gift of the spirit'
My sister Marian and sister-in-law Patricia for listening to the first
chapters, Patrick and Stephanie in Wigan, James and Julie on Vancouver
Island, Lauren and Jamie in Northampton, Ian, John and Samantha in
Ireland, for lifts from the airport and computer know-how.
Desmond for the Christmas 'gift' of Liz at EJL editorial services.
The final accolade to my daughter, cruise and coach escort Josephine, for
inviting me to share this special time in Greece.

A picture paints a thousand words...

Ambrosia - www.lindostreasures.com/ambrosia

Atrium Palace Hotel - www.atrium.gr

Brian Goodwin - The National Gold Card Company

Delight - www.exclusivelylindos.com/index.php/pages/delight-restaurant

Dorothy Alexander (Blaze Writing Course, Strathclyde University - www.strath.ac.uk/cll/alp/blaze

Electra - www.electra-studios.gr

Giorgos Bar - www.exclusivelylindos.com/index.php/pages/giorgos-bar

Infinity Weddings (Chrissi) - www.infinityweddingslindos.co.uk/

Kalypso Bar - www.kalypsolindos.gr

Kelly's Bar, Faliraki - www.youtube.com/watch?v=R9sawrz0sLU

Lindos Hair Studio - www.exclusivelylindos.com

Liz Lockwood - www.elizabethlockwood.co.uk

Light House - www.prasonisilighthouse.com

Medeast Restaurant - medeastrestaurant@yahoo.gr

Melenos Hotel - www.melenoslindos.com

Michael Blossom - www.michaelbossom.com

Nefeli Restaurant - www.lindosrestaurant.gr

Palestra Restaurant - www.facebook.com/pages/PALESTRA-DI-LINDOS

Romeo - www.romeo.gr

Symi Dream - symidream.com

Takis Leather, Symi - www.symivisitor.com/takis.htm

Pat & Robert - www.rhodesluxuryvilla.com/Villa-Rhodos-Poppy

Josephine Kelly, June 2012.
www.lindosrhodesholidaybook.com

Printed in Great Britain
by Amazon.co.uk, Ltd.,
Marston Gate.